Art, Society, Revolution
Russia 1917–1921

Editor:
Nils Åke Nilsson

Almqvist & Wiksell International
Stockholm / Sweden

Printed with the aid of a grant from
Humanistisk-samhällsvetenskapliga forskningsrådet

Cover illustration by Olle Kåks ©

Columbia FLL Partnership
PK 265. 9 . A7 A77

Printed in Sweden by

Almqvist & Wiksell, Uppsala 1979

Table of Contents

Foreword

In 1974 the Ford Foundation announced an international research competition in Soviet/Russian and East European studies. Professor Nils Åke Nilsson, representing the Department of Slavic and Baltic Languages at Stockholm University, submitted a project tentatively entitled "Language, Literature, and Society in Russia, 1917–1921". More than 240 projects from a number of different countries were entered. 17 of these, among them the Department's proposal, were chosen to receive research grants.

The aim of the project has been to study developments in literature, art, film and the theater as reflected primarily in the Russian press immediately after the Bolsheviks' assumption of power in October 1917. One of the most important bodies of source materials consisted of a thus far little explored collection of newspapers and leaflets of the revolutionary period deposited at the University library in Uppsala. These materials were collected by Torsten Lundell, son of Sweden's first professor of Slavic languages in Uppsala.

Lundell first served with the Swedish legation in Petrograd and later represented the Swedish Red Cross in Siberia. He was keenly aware of the significance of the contemporary press as an historical source, and through personal contacts he was able to enlist the co-operation of the Commissar of Enlightenment Anatolij Lunačarskij in collecting the materials on behalf of the Uppsala University library. The collection eventually comprised over 8 000 newspaper issues and several hundred leaflets and posters. (See further L. Kjellberg, "The Collection of Prints from the Russian Revolution in the Uppsala University Library", *Otium et negotium. Studies in Onomatology and Library Sciences presented to Olof von Feilitzen.* Stockholm 1973.) It is of course by no means complete, and the project has therefore also drawn upon the holdings of various European and American libraries.

Whereas historians have analyzed post-October political developments in Russia almost day by day, changes in the cultural sphere have attracted much less attention. One reason for this relative neglect is probably that cultural development during this period has been

7

considered to be less important than politics. These changes, however, were quite dramatic, and they raised questions and illustrated political strategies that have continued to shape Soviet cultural life. In the last ten years some important books have tried to fill in this lacuna. A special interest in Anatolij Lunačarskij, who as the first Folk Commissar of Enlightenment was responsible for the reorganization of the cultural field, has resulted in several books published in the Soviet Union and in Sheila Fitzpatrick's excellent *The Commissariat of Enlightenment* (1970). The decoration of the cities in connection with the first anniversary of the October revolution has also attracted attention, and certain new materials have been published (Speranskaja 1971, Drengenberg 1972).

The project has attempted to use the newspaper materials to uncover new facts, clarify events and processes that have thus far been treated only in general terms, and present a more vivid account of developments than that provided by official decrees or reports. The often subjective nature of these materials has naturally been taken into account. It has not been possible, of course, to provide any exhaustive view or strictly chronological survey of developments between 1917 and 1921. Rather, the project was obliged to limit itself to a series of more specific studies determined by the interests and specializations of the participants. This explains, for example, why there are certain obvious gaps while the volume includes two articles on film; on the other hand it can also be maintained that the cinema was more important than other branches of art during this particular period and that it paved the way for an evolution that was to become even more significant. It is at the same time natural that the project should concentrate on the period when the newspaper materials were richest in information, that is, to the summer of 1918, when the rather outspoken non-Bolshevik press (which included Menshevik, Socialist-Revolutionary, Anarchist and other non-Bolshevik publications) was closed down.

The following persons have participated in the project: Bengt Jangfeldt, Halina Jelinski, Lars Kleberg, Anna Lenczyc, Henryk Lenczyc, Nils Åke Nilsson and Charles Rougle, from the Department of Slavic and Baltic Languages; Kate Betz, from the Institute of Theater and Film at Stockholm University; Stefani Hoffman, Jerusalem, and Richard Taylor, University College of Swansea.

8

Nils Åke Nilsson

Spring 1918. The Arts and the Commissars

On March 15, 1918 the Russian futurists published the one and only issue of their *The Futurists' Newspaper* (*Gazeta futuristov*). The purpose was apparently to remind those interested and, perhaps above all, those not interested in avantgarde art that the futurists were still around and should be taken into consideration now that the time had come for a more radical settlement of accounts with bourgeois literature and art.

In an "open letter to the workers" Majakovskij noted that four months after the October revolution art, literature and the theatre continued as if nothing had happened, following in more or less the same tracks as before the revolution. Not only the bourgeois public but also the proletariat were apparently quite satisfied with this state of affairs. Majakovskij addressed "the workers" (highly fictitious readers of the paper, to be sure) with reproachful pathos:

> С удивлением смотрю я, как с подмостков взятых театров звучат "Аиды" и "Травиаты" со всякими испанцами и графами, как в стихах, приемлемые вами, те же розы барских оранжерей и как разбегаются глаза ваши перед картинками, изображающими великолепие прошлого.
>
> (Majakovskij 1959: 8)

This impression was confirmed from a different point of view a few weeks later by the journalists in a daily newspaper: everything, so it seemed, was back to normal again. On April 4 the Menshevik evening paper, *The Evening Lights* (*Večernie ogni*), published a review of the newly opened Spring art exhibition. The art critic (N. Kravčenko) began by pointing out that this was the first time in five or six months that he had sat down to write about art. The long pause seemed quite natural. How could there have been any interest or need for art during these past months?

9

Казалось, что в этом хаосе, в бесконечной серии расстрелов, арестов и всяких иных насилий — обычных спутников "бескровных" революций — нет места интересам духовным, не может быть увлечения творчеством высшим. Проснулось и развернулось во всю чувство животное, заговорило чувство мести. Люди более мирные прятались в свои норы и чутко прислушивались к тому, как по всей земле великой, бесконечной России бушевала толпа ...

Только иногда, когда жертвой разгула делалась какая-нибудь редкая коллекция, когда громились дворцы, исчезали или портились редчайшие произведения искусства, точно дуновением тихого ветерка проносился слабый ропот и ... опять затихал. Грохот революции прикрывал все, все замирало и думалось, что никому искусство не нужно, никого оно не интересует.

The critic now admitted that like most other people he had been wrong. Even during this chaotic and turbulent period a group of people had cared about art, regarding it as something essential that should survive. Under the guidance of persons like Gor'kij, Lunačarskij and Aleksandr Benois they had done everything possible to protect museums and palaces from plundering and vandalism. And what was equally important—in spite of all difficulties theatres continued to play for an even growing audience, art exhibitions opened as usual and people seemed to be interested in buying and collecting pictures as before.

Another critic writing in the same issue vividly described a Petrograd theatre audience settling down minutes before the raising of the curtain to enjoy an entertaining comedy:

Светло, тепло и уютно ... В фойе недурной оркестр весело наигрывает поппури из опер и разухабистые шансонетки ... Много женщин с черезчур рыжими волосами, черезчур черными глазами и черезчур открытыми платьями ... Бриллианты, которые слишком велики, чтобы быть настоящими, дорогие меха, концы которых небрежно волочатся по полу ... Пряный и острый запах раздражающих духов ... Вокруг каждой женщины, точно каштаны вокруг жареной индейки, сытые, гладкие, кругленькие "представители банковских сфер", безукоризненно выбритые, напудренные и напомаженные молодые люди без определенных занятий, но с утомленно наглыми физиономиями и крупными жемчужинами в галстуках ... Прекрасно скроенные "френчи" ... и изящные лакированные кавалерийские ботфорты ... без шпор ... Резко перехваченные в талии визитки и панталоны в полоску, вроде шлагбаума ...

(VO 1918: 9.4)

Nothing, it seemed, had changed. Everything was as before: the atmosphere, the audience, the repertory. The only thing which suggested that something had happened were the discussions during intermission, which concerned less the play and the performance than the now rather delicate question of where one could still get a decent meal afterwards, "comme dans le bon vieux temps".

It also happened that a reporter from the same newspaper dropped in to one of the former private theatres in the suburbs, now taken over and subsidized by the local soviet. "It is nice sometimes", he began his ironic review, "to seek recreation for the soul and attend a performance on a socialized stage, which follows exclusively cultural and educational purposes". And what did he get? A repertory of great current interest addressed to a new audience? Nothing of the sort. The repertory still consisted of farces with titles like "Lucky cuckolds", "Secret marriages" or "Favors from Carskoe selo" which became popular after the February revolution. In other words, the critic concluded, "plays treating very ethical subjects, indispensible to the education of the proletariat" (VO 1918: 16.6).

The journalists and the futurists agreed on one point: cultural life had changed very little after the Bolshevik take-over. The journalists saw this as a joyful sign: theatres played as before, the traditional Spring art exhibition had opened, museums and private collections had been saved from pillage. To Majakovskij and his fellow futurists this was no cause for joy, however. On the contrary—it was exactly this cultural stagnation and inertia in the public's taste which should be opposed. True, said Majakovskij, one should refrain from using "physical violence against the remains of old art". They could be handed over to schools or universities as study objects for those interested in the history of the past (some six months later, however, he sharpened his tone and demanded in the poem "It's Too Early to Rejoice"—more rhetorically than concretely, to be sure—that museums and libraries be set on fire and Puškin and other classics put

11

against the wall instead of the generals). New times required a new art, a living art. No stones and fossils for the people, but "the bread of living beauty"!

The futurist reaction was no unique phenomenon. Impatience with the pace of change—in political, economic or cultural matters—is a well-known general feature of revolutionary psychology. Just a few months after the February revolution, in fact, the newspapers began to complain that nothing had really changed in art and literature. In March 1917, for instance, they expressed their astonishment that "the greatest upheaval in the world had not yet manifested itself in the repertory" and that the theatres still showed the same trivial plays, intended for "the after-dinner digestion of all kinds of wheeler-dealers and their wives" (Rafalovič 1933: 23). A few months later a newspaper recalled the French revolution and concluded sadly that the revolutionary enthusiasm in Russia had not yet produced any comparably brilliant poetry:

> Почему же у нас нет гения, нет песен, нет даже своего Беранже, который украсил песнями вторую революцию во Франции? Отчего у нас до сих пор нет своего революционного гимна? Отчего у нас не нашлось Руже-де-Лилля?
>
> (ОТ 1917: 7.7)

Art is Silent

These comments in an evening paper and a futurist pamphlet allow us to distinguish some different attitudes toward the question of the immediate impact of the October revolution on Russian cultural life.

The first one is the well-known view that in times of war or revolution there is no room for art. People have other and more important matters to think about. One of the critics pointed to some obvious consequences of the revolution—arrests, executions and pillaging. To this could easily be added others, often mentioned in the press, such as searches, the break-down of the urban transport system, the shortage of food and fuel, the risk of epidemics, a general insecurity on the streets at night. Times like these, the critic concluded, do not excite any desire to produce art, to write about art, to care about art. Art is silent.

Art is silent. This idea appeared in the press already a few months after the February revolution. In an article entitled "The Silence of

Talent" a newspaper asked why "not a single talent had spoken in the language of freedom in this time of freedom":

Молчит театр. Молчит беллетристика. Молчит поэзия. Живопись тоже молчит. То, что появляется нового в печати, на сцене, в живописи — недостойно ни переживаемого времени, ни своих титулов.

(OT 1917: 7.7)

After the October revolution the question was raised again and again, becoming more importunate with every year. It finally culminated on November 14, 1921 in a general discussion in The House of the Press (Dom pečati) devoted to the question "Why are the writers silent?" ("Počemu molčat pisateli?").

Such a question seems to bespeak a certain bewilderment and surprise. The situation was unusual. Russian literature had never been silent before. Even in times of war and oppression literature had always had something to offer the Russian people, in accordance with its traditional role as a public and social factor. Now expectations were higher than ever before: at last, freedom had come to the Russian people and to literature. The disappointment when literature did not seem to live up to expectations was obvious:

До какой высоты парения духовного, до каких подлинно художественных ценностей доходили народы в периоды безправия и угнетенности. Казалось бы — кончился гнет, и еще пышнее распустится цвет народного творчества! Но не так на деле.

(ZT 1918: 4.1)

During the four years of revolution and civil war there were many and different explanations of this situation which confused and alarmed the intelligentsia. The newspaper which in July 1917 spoke of "the silence of talent" pointed to political unrest, lack of national unity, discord between "songs of beauty and clarity" (i.e. a traditional concept of art) and actual reality:

Мыслимо ли запеть песни красоты и света перед зрелищем той постыдной борьбы против родины, каковая сделалась почти лозунгом дня. Можно кричать от боли перед этим зрелищем, можно проклинать, можно рвать на себе волосы — но нельзя творить песни, нельзя писать вдохновенные произведения искусства!

(ОТ 1917: 7.7)

After the October revolution similar interpretations soon appeared. In late January 1918 a charity concert for the benefit of the political prisoners was held in the Teniševskij hall. Zinaida Gippius, Anna Axmatova and Fedor Sologub read their poetry and Dmitrij Merežkovskij pointed out in a short speech that "the Word had always been with the Russian intelligentsia, but now at this most vital moment it was not there. You have to be silent, to keep your mouth shut, like a person held by force under water. And we are all now under a red, a blood-red wave" (VZ 1918: 23.1).

Such political interpretations of the writers' (by which was usually meant the writers of the old generation) silence were characteristic of the first period after the October revolution. Later more practical reasons were pointed out, for instance, the difficult material conditions under which writers and publishers were forced to work: "No doubt somewhere in the quiet of studies great works are being created, but ... there is no paper for printing, no time to do the kind of work masterpieces demand—one is forced to interrupt creative work in order to earn something to live on" (*Znamja* 1920: 3/4, col. 31).

This was written in 1920, and although it could be argued that Russian writers had always known hardship, even starvation, and nevertheless written great things, the years 1919–20 were certainly one of the most difficult periods they had ever experienced. An inquiry made by the Union of writers showed that only 10 % of its members could exist on their professional earnings (*Krasnaja Moskva* 1920: 622). The closing of private publishing houses, the shortage of paper and the limited number of literary journals were some obvious reasons for a general exodus to a safer existence in departments, committees, institutes. At best, the poet became a teacher or lecturer on his own profession, at worst he assumed the role of his traditional enemy and he became a bureaucrat, a *činovnik* with a portfolio and fixed working hours.

The well-known writer and stage director V. I. Nemirovič-Dančenko later painted (VL 1921: 3, p. 9 f.) a grim picture of what a Russian writer's life could be like in the winter of 1919/20:

14

Никогда не забуду зиму 1919–1920 г. Было тяжело: голодно, холодно, жутко. Чернила, случалось, замерзали, приходилось работать карандашом. Назябнешься, продрогнешь в хвостах, а дома от 4–5 градусов выше 0. Не отогреться и все таки тянет к столу, к привычному и любимому делу. Пишешь в шубе, в теплых (не принимайте буквально!) перчатках, обернув ноги в плед, заменяющий ночью одеяло. Дрова еще удавалось хоть изредка доставать, но печи несколько лет не чищены, некоторые развалились, мастеров не оказывалось. Дым густился в кабинете, оставляя на всем густой слой сажи. Водопроводы лопались от мороза. Я заболел воспалением легких.

Another immediate explanation was the lack of perspective and distance. Writers and artists were still in the midst of gigantic changes, and it would be asking too much to expect masterpieces from them right now:

Нельзя ждать монументальных произведений в дни, подобно нашим. Их некогда писать, их тесно писать. Дай бог явиться им лет через пятьдесят–семьдесят. Если бы они возникли сейчас и очаровали — мы не вправе были бы поверить этому очарованию.

(*Znamja* 1920: 2 col. 51)

Life itself had become art, and in a way which the symbolists or the futurists, dreaming of a fusion of art and life, had never imagined. Life had even surpassed art, leaving it behind, puzzled, not knowing what to do:

Сама жизнь стала искусством. В лихорадочном темпе своем она развертывает картины, так недавно недоступные самой пламенной фантазии ... Искусство отстало. Оно растерялось. Оно пытается поставить перед собой задачу быть действительно "лишь отражением". И эта-то струя и принижает роль искусства и, видимо, она порождает настойчивые толки о "буднях искусства", о падении его.

(*Znamja* 1920: 3/4 col. 37)

It is interesting to note that besides such obvious explanations, some critics regarded the problem as above all a philological one— after Symbolism, Futurism and Opojaz it was natural to discuss the relationship between literature and society also in linguistic terms. From such a point of view the silence of the writers could be seen as a lack of agreement between language and reality. Too many words were missing right now, as one critic put it. Since "language is thought" (a direct reference to Potebnja) and the existing language reflected a way of thinking and a view of the world which was lagging behind actual life ("mysl' i rassuždenie daleko otstali ot živogo opyta") the latter could not be expressed in words:

Действительность нам во многом представляется безумной, но это не потому, конечно, что природа сошла с ума, а вследствие несоответствия наших понятий новому, нам открывающемуся опыту. Мы его рассказать не можем, он невыразим.

(ZTV 1918: 1, p. 30)

The question of language and society could also be approached from a different angle: as a collision between poetic language and language as used for practical and political purposes. In the present situation, one critic argued, poetic language was in imminent danger of loosing its identity by yielding to the impact of purely utilitarian demands. He pointed out, for instance, the new fashion of abbreviations, and saw them as a threat to the "obraznost'" of the Russian language (again a reference to Potebnja):

Особенная опасность грозит художественному слову. Слово по существу своему, текучее и обреченное на служение общению людей друг с другом; остается во власти времени, — и тяжелы его удары! Тускнет образность русской речи, и слово, лишенное своего художественного значения, низводится до степени простого условного знака.

Недаром русская современность вводит в употребление условные названия, вроде "Центробалта" и "Главковерха", идя в этом по стопам американцев, уже утративших сознание самобытности своего языка.

Стоит только вчитаться в современные брошюры и прокламации, проще того, заглянуть в любой из газетных столбцов, чтобы с горестной очевидностью убедиться в неуклонной гибели русского художественного слова. И это именно теперь когда все печатное читается на расхват, когда газетные строки забираются в самые отдаленные, медвежьи уголки и звучат там, как пророческие откровения.

Что будет с народным творчеством?

Что будет с образным языком деревенским?

(ZT 1918: 4.1.)

These lines appeared in *The Banner of Labor*. They reflected an interest in folk poetry and folk language typical of critics connected with this Left Socialist Revolutionary paper. One notes that the article "blamed" the Americans for the current Russian predilection for abbreviations. The important point was apparently to connect the Bolsheviks with something foreign, modern and ahistoric. In contrast the Socialist Revolutionaries were linked to history, folk tradition, the Russian soil.

The opposition "poetic"—"utilitarian" language goes back to Potebnja and Belyj, but after the revolution it assumed a new meaning and importance. In *The Nature of the Word* (*O prirode slova*, 1922) Osip Mandel'štam stated that "any kind of utilitarianism is a mortal sin against the Hellenistic character, against the Russian language" and pointed also to abbreviations, to "this tendency of telegraphic and simplified expediency" (Mandel'štam 1971: 246). "Silence" is a recurrent theme in his poetry of this period (it would become even more important later on) and expressions in the article like "opasnost' grozit xudožestvennomu slovu", "slovo ... tekučee", "vo vlasti vremeni", "obraznost' russkoj reči" recall Mandel'štam's concern for "the blessed, meaningless word".[1]

In 1921 a new literary journal in Moscow *The Life of Art* (*Žizn' iskusstva*; not to be confused with the theatre journal of the same name, founded by the Petrograd TEO in 1918) pointed to the threat posed by the political language which had invaded literature with its clichés and hollow pathos after the February revolution:

Подобно "керенщине" революции 1917-го года, утопавшей в словах, громких, давно истрепанных, лживых и эффектных, есть теперь "керенщина" послереволюционной литературы, искусства и журналистики.

Это не литература, не мысль, а какие-то эклеры, мозолящие вам глаза на всех перекрестках, приторно-слащавые, дутые и пустые ...

Где же жизнь искусства? ...

Где же искусство жизни? ...

Где то, недостающее нам, искусство жить, творческая сила, столь нужная нам теперь, когда старое, если не погибло, то должно погибнуть, уступить подлинно новому и здоровому? ...

The answers to the question why Russian writers kept silent, were, as we have seen, partly political, partly practical, referring to the lack of paper and material conditions, partly linguistic, referring to a discordance between language, specifically poetic language, and the new reality. There was one more answer, however, which increased in importance with every year, dominating the discussion to a large extent around 1920. The explanation was found in the new repressive bureaucratic apparatus that had replaced the old one.

An article in the journal *The Banner* (*Znamja*) by Leonid Sabaneev, later known as a scholar in musicology, took up the question of what he called "the crying silence of art" ("vopijuščee bezmolvie"). The reason was, in his opinion, the fact that beginning with the February revolution "our artistic circles have been, as it were, crushed by a public spirit" ("zadavlenny obščestvennost'ju"). The deeply personal and anarchistic nature of art and creation was suddenly forgotten. Everybody was seized by a desire "to organize something externally and to organize himself". And so it happened that "our social and public efforts of the first days of the revolution in a fatal way found their outlet in the form of 'bureaucracy'" (*Znamja* 1920: 1, col. 48).

The result was that "art became Soviet art". And a question arose: "State art ... Is such art possible? Is such art alive?" The state possesses only one kind of pathos—"the pathos of state and public spirit" ("patos gosudarstvennosti i obščestvennosti"). In the new society the artist has both an obligation to create something of social importance and the right to be paid for it. But art is also and above all a personal and subjective matter. The artist is a "priest in an inscrutable domain" ("svjaščennodejstvovatel' v nepostigaemoj oblasti") and here the state has no right to lay any claims on him. Here he is a "worshipper of beauty and ideas" and since art could be considered as the religion of the future (the old religion being abolished) it should, as any cult in a socialist society, be separated from the state.

The article thus ends on a highly idealistic note: the romantic

18

credo of the artist as a worshipper of beauty is combined with topical slogans of the separation of art from society and of art as a substitution for the old religion. The first part of the article is the most interesting. Sabaneev pointed here to a tendency towards bureaucracy in art and literature as a consequence of the revolution. Such things run contrary to what he considered the deeply "anarchistic" spirit of art.

Better known than Sabaneev's contribution to this topical discussion is an essay which appeared shortly after his article: Evgenij Zamjatin's famous "I am afraid" ("Ja bojus'"). It was published in a collection edited by the House of Arts (Dom iskusstva) in 1921. It was also one of the last contributions—the extent to which it reflects a "burning question" of the years 1918–21 has not been fully recognized. Its interest lies, however, not simply in the fact that it sums up the earlier discussion in some striking formulas but rather in the way in which Zamjatin placed the discussion into a more general, philosophical context, that of "the eternal revolution".[2]

The beginning of the article seems to echo the earlier futurist and Proletkul't impatience that nothing had changed: "I am afraid that we are preserving too anxiously and too much of what we have inherited from the courts". He directs his reproaches at the poets themselves, criticizing their ability to adjust themselves only too willingly, like the policeman in Čexov's "The Chameleon", to the new conditions. We have, the article goes on, preserved not only old furniture from the previous epoch, but also the tradition of court poets, the "smart" poets who know when it is time to write about the double eagle and when the time has come for the hammer and sickle. These smart poets, "jurkie", as Zamjatin calls them, are around everywhere now, while the other ones, "nejurkie", are silent. The reason for this silence is that "real literature can only exist where it is written not by reliable executive functionaries but by madmen, hermits, heretics, dreamers, rebels, sceptics".

These ideas Zamjatin elaborated in several other articles from the same period and also in his novel *We*, where the problem has the following well-known formulation: "There are two powers in the world—entropy and energy. One leads to blissful rest, to a happy equilibrium; the other—to the destruction of equilibrium, to a tormentingly endless movement" (Shane 1968: 47). His articles and especially "I am Afraid" (*We* was not, as is well known, published

19

in the Soviet Union) evoked several replies, among others from Konstantin Fedin, one of his colleagues and pupils at the House of Arts. It is plausible to assume that this article was one of the main reasons why the by now rather hackneyed question of the silence of the writers was brought up for public discussion.

The debate took place on November 14, 1921, in the House of the Press (Dom pečati). There are apparently very few newspaper reports from this meeting, which may be due to the simple fact that the topic was by then too familar and that the discussion did not produce anything new of special interest. Usually only Majakovskij's contribution is quoted. He pointed out that the pessimistic view was overstated: new books and new talents were now, in fact, appearing (Katanjan 1961: 158). Although Zamjatin's views where still valid in principle, Majakovskij's remark was, of course, correct in the immediate perspective. In June 1921, for instance, the first Soviet "thick" journal, *Red Virgin Soil*, a revival of a famous tradition, began publication. The start of the literary section was a bit slow, but it was received with enthusiasm by readers and writers and quickly grew in size and quality (Maguire 1968: 12 f.). 1922 was to witness the appearance of many new and young talents. Just a few months after the public meeting the whole previous debate about the silence of Russian literature was out of date.

It was a discussion provoked—as the quotations have suggested—by impatience, great expectations, a traditional belief in literature as a leading star and consolation in hard and turbulent times, but also by fear of a new bureaucratic apparatus, an official state art, a general stagnation of literary life. One usually neglected reason for the often rather gloomy comments in those years on the future of Russian literature should be pointed out especially. This was the persistence of concepts of art which historical developments rapidly made obsolete. What the critics were asking the writers to produce was nothing less than "masterpieces" in the old sense, personal visions emanating from the "souls" of "geniuses". Great epic novels in the traditional style, more poems like Blok's *The Twelve*!

Most of them did not see that the special demands of a unique historical situation had created new genres and art forms. New functions of art emerged, the poet's task changed, the very concept of art expanded. It was in the beginning easy to overlook certain tendencies and experiments and maintain that from an established point of view this was not art but forms of agitation and propaganda. In actual fact, however, these experiments should be considered as a testing of new semiotic possibilities: Majakovskij's poems and his "Misterija-Buff", the Rosta windows, the decoration of cities on the anniversaries of the revolution, the agit-trains, the new films, the "living newspapers", the attempts being made in "folk theatre" and agitation on the stage.

Back to Normal?

One response to the revolution from the part of the intellectuals was, as we have seen, an appeal to the writers to break their "silence" and fulfill their traditional role as the conscience of Russia. Another, as the quotations from *The Evening Lights* have suggested, was simply a cautious sigh of relief that things were returning to normal again.

The first phase of the Revolution, so it seemed, had come to an end. From November 1917 to February 1918, the newspapers had almost daily reports (*Everybody's Newspaper, Gazeta dlja vsex*, ran a column entitled "P'janye razgromy") of what one of them called "our shame, the still unhealed shame of our Great Revolution" (ZT 1918: 23.2): searches, arrests, vandalism and, above all, the plundering of state and private wine cellars, that continued for weeks and months (cf. Korolenko 1979). Now, in April, the streets were safer, the mob under control. The food situation was constantly difficult (the press reported daily on food rations and arriving supplies), city traffic was irregular, fuel costs increased and in spite of the peace treaty with Germany political prospects were cloudy. Russia had another four years of revolution and counter-revolution, of civil war and foreign intervention ahead. But unaware of the future and with spring on its way people seemed to be able to breathe a bit more freely (see further Charles Rougle's article).

This was also reflected in the field of art and literature. A characteristic sign—in addition to those mentioned by the reporters of *The Evening Lights*—was the opening of new literary cafés, especially in Moscow. The *Daily News* (*Novosti dnja*), which took a special interest in this phenomenon, mentioned during April and May cafés with names like "Pittoresk", "Trilistnik", "Muzykal'naja tabakerka", "Kuranty poèzii", "Venok iskusstvu".[3]

Another sign was a series of works—mostly poems—dedicated to the revolution by some well-known poets and published in *The Banner*

21

of Labor in May (Pasternak's dramatic scenes, the first one printed May 1, Belyj's "Christ has arisen", May 15, Esenin's "Inonija", May 19, Kljuev's "The Republic", May 22, and Mandel'štam's "Hymn", i.e. "Sumerki svobody", May 24). Mandel'štam's call "Well, let's try" ("Nu čto ž, poprobuem") seems to express something of the general attitude at this particular moment. It was easy to see the recent demonstrations and discussions around the former imperial theatres and the Academy of Art as a tempest in a teacup and overlook the movements and changes going on below the surface.

Let us now take three important fields—the theatre, art and literature—and see to what extent this superficial impression of normalization holds true upon closer examination.

The Theatre: Three Different Pieces

At the end of the winter theatre season, in April 1918, one newspaper (RU 1918: 7.4) interviewed some representatives of theatre life in Petrograd and Moscow. They all pointed to the difficulties of the past winter but mentioned at the same time an unusual interest on the part of the public, to whom the theatre had been "the only consolation". A recurrent theme in the answers was an emphasis on the "freedom" attained by the theatres and a hope that it would remain. "Freedom" referred to the liberation from censorship and "imperial grace" after February 1917, and the hope for the future was clearly a hope that the previous political and bureaucratic control would not return. A. I. Južin, director of the Malyj theatre in Moscow, held up the traditional idea of art as a defense against the utilitarian demands of the day. Only if art was lifted above the political struggles as a reflection of "eternal spiritual beauty", could it be of help and comfort to a distressed Russia:

> Театр завоевал себе свободу — пусть далеко еще не совершенную, пусть еще не умело использованную, но все-таки свободу в высшем понятии этого слова, если еще не высшем его воплощении, и если он сумеет ее укрепить, ставя выше политических доктрин и тенденций, выше подчинения партийным и всяким иным влияниям, если он найдет в себе силы быть только тем, чем он должен быть — высшим отражением лучших вопросов человечества и вечной духовной красоты, то он никогда не утратит своей первенствующей роли в деле сохранения жизненных сил измученной родины.

22

The Moscow stage director N. V. Ivancev approached the problem of "freedom"—"state control" from a different angle. Facing a possible "socialization" of the theatres, he raised the question which dependence was harder to endure, that of a capricous audience or that of the state bureaucracy, even when the latter offered in return a steady income. For him the choice was a simple one:

Театр, всегда стремившийся к свободе, не должен и не может бороться против частной инициативы и не должен быть вмещён в государственный департемент. Только свободное творчество и соперничество двигают искусство, а потому всякое закрепощение теперь гибельно.

Некоторые говорят, что для того, чтобы свободно творить, надо быть обеспеченным. Но они забывают, что опеку сопровождает зависимость. Так уж лучше зависимость от публики (какова ни была эта публика), чем от чиновников, как бы они себя ни называли.

The general problem the Bolsheviks had to face in the reorganization of the theatres was that they consisted of three different pieces—the state, the private and the "democratic" sections, each with a tradition, structure and ideology of its own. How were they to be fit together and gradually merged into one common form?

In the beginning the private theatres continued as before, addressing themselves to their usual audience and retaining the traditional entrepreneur system. They were still clearly in the majority: immediately after the October revolution, for instance, Moscow had 32 theatres. Two were state theatres, one was supported by the city council and the rest were private (Jufit 1968: 373).

But behind this "bourgeois" facade a gradual democratization was taking shape. It was partly a continuation of a trend which had started already at the turn of the century (in which P. Gajdeburov had been one of the pioneers) under such labels as "folk" ("narodnyj"), "public" ("obščedostupnyj"), "mobile" ("peredvižnoj") and "workers'" theatre. ("The worker's theatre" was the oldest of these currents, tracing its beginnings to the founding of the "Theatre for workers" on Vasil'evskij Island in 1887.) After February and especially after October 1917 they were relabelled "proletarian", "proletkul't", "socialist", "soviet". These changes in name were accompanied by and reflected different notions as to the function and organization of these theatres.

Formerly dedicated to "philantropic performances" they were now, in P. Keržencev's words, to become a "creative theatre". This important trend is discussed in Lars Kleberg's article.

The immediate problem concerned the former imperial theatres. Their reorganization had been under discussion since February 1917, and the question became acute immediately after the Bolshevik takeover. The debate was accompanied by several protest meetings and demonstrations against the new regime: the Mariinskij ballet went on strike, a group of actors from the Aleksandrinskij theatre staged a spectacular walk-out, F. D. Batjuškov, in charge of the Petrograd theatres, refused to accept his dismissal (Fitzpatrick 1970: 116 f.). The flexible and persuasive Lunačarskij eventually succeeded in bringing about a temporary settlement. At a meeting on 22 February 1918 it was agreed that the state would provide financial support but would leave artistic direction to a special "artistic soviet", attached to a supreme body, called "The Supreme Soviet of State Theatres" (Verxovnyj sovet gosudarstvennyx teatrov, see NVČ 1918: 23.2).

The situation remained unstable throughout the spring, however. Reports on the theatres in the newspapers often used general headings like "The Theatrical Anthill" ("Teatral'nyj muravejnik") or "The Disorder in the State Theatres" ("Razruxa v gosudarstvennyx teatrax"). In an interview the famous actress Ermolova related her impression of the changes that had taken place:

Для нас театр был храмом ... А теперь ... Пришли молодые люди с поднятыми воротничками, громко кричат, спорят, никого не признают, ролей не учат и все шумят, все шумят ... Актеры ли они, нужны ли они театру — не знаю. Знаю только, что театр опускается все ниже и ниже.

(PÉ 1918: 3.4)

Majakovskij's remark that the repertory had not undergone any changes since the October revolution was no doubt correct, but he consciously or unconsciously overlooked one obvious reason. The big change had already occurred. The abolition of the state and church censorships in March 1917 opened up a new repertory of plays which had not been permitted for political, religious or "moral" considerations. Many of them were still on the repertory at the end of 1917. It is true that there was a noticeable fondness for French farces and erotic comedies. The genre was not limited to its more trivial forms, however, but also included such plays as Arthur Schnitzler's *Reigen* and Oscar Wilde's *Salome*—the latter opened in Moscow on three stages simultaneously and the performance in Petrograd, directed by Mardžanov, was considered to be the best production of 1917 (Rafalovič 1933: 21). The demand for a more contemporary repertory was at first appeased by farces ridiculing the Czar and the old regime (the most popular theme was Rasputin). This reflected a natural interest in two previously tabooed areas—church morals and the Czar's family.

Gradually the theatre also began to produce plays with a "revolutionary" or "critical" content, such as Andreev's *Savva* (prohibited before 1917), Gerhardt Hauptmann's *Die Weber*, John Galsworthy's *Strife* and Gorkij's plays. Most of these plays appeared in small theatres of the "narodnyj" or "rabočij" type, while the state theatres were slow to change course.

The absence of contemporary plays was after October 1917 still conspicuous. There is no contemporary repertory "for the contemporary stage", complained one critic among others in 1919. "The theatre of our time is based on a heroic, more or less revolutionary repertory and on the classics" (VT 1919: 35, p. 9). Lunačarskij himself took part in this topical discussion on the demands for "political", "socialist", "contemporary" plays. "Easier said than done", was his first comment. His next was that the theatre should not "chase after the revolution". The French revolution showed that the theatre was unable immediately to reflect what had happened. The few attempts that were made were not successful. It was better right now, Lunačarskij suggested, to try indirect approaches, to search for similar periods in the past and depict them, or to write fantastic or symbolic plays charged with a revolutionary spirit. He did not mention here a play whose content he had earlier characterized as "the first among recent works of art to reflect the events of real life" (Majakovskij 1956: 506), namely Majakovskij's *Misterija-Buff*, one of the very few original examples of such a repertory.

In its special manifesto ("Manifest letučej federacii futuristov") *The Futurists' Newspaper* singled out one play in particular as a typical anachronism: *The King of the Judeans* (*Car'Iudejskij*), written in 1912 by the Grand Duke Konstantin Konstantinovič. The manifesto gives the impression that here the theatres continued to play, by inertia or on purpose, an old-fashioned religious play which on top of it all

25

was written by a former member of the czarist court. A double challenge to the Bolshevik revolution!

As a matter of fact, this was one of the plays that before 1917 had been forbidden for public performance (there had been a few private ones; see Rafalovič 1933: 13). Although Christ does not appear on the stage and the play instead illustrates his impact on various people, the Church censorship apparently objected in principle to any staging of Biblical themes. By a mere coincidence the play had its opening night just a few days after the Bolshevik revolution. Its considerable success, however, can hardly be interpreted simply as reflecting a protest against the Bolsheviks, but was more likely due to general curiosity about a prohibited play by a former member of the court. It played in various cities besides Petrograd and Moscow up to 1920, which speaks for the assumption that it was not considered as "antirevolutionary".

If it had been, the special commission for combatting "antirevolutionary activity", which was formed very soon after the October revolution, would certainly have interfered, as happened in other cases. Several such incidents were reported in the press. In January 1918, for instance, members of the commission visited a theatre and prohibited the actress M. S. Maradudina from reading (apparently provocative) stories by Tèffi and Averčenko from the stage. On another occasion a patrol interrupted a performance, forbidding the play on the grounds that it was "clearly directed against the Council of People's Commissars". The play was entitled "The Salesmen of Freedom", but, a newspaper remarked, the Bolsheviks were apparently ignorant of the fact that the play was not a new, topical satire but had been written decades ago (*La Trahison* 1918: 4.1).

Such incidents occurred during the first months after the Bolshevik revolution. Later the censorship began to work through the usual bureaucratic channels. If the target at first was "antirevolutionary" plays (see VO 1918: 16.7 which reported on the "isključenie celogo rjada p'es, kak kontr-revoljucionnyx, iz repertuara narodnyx i kommunističeskix teatrov"), the attack was soon focused on the popular erotic comedies. A play by A. P. Kamenskij, *Leda*, in which the heroine appeared more or less undressed on stage, was forbidden in the summer of 1918 by the Moscow Soviet, acting on a request by its theatrical and musical section. A notice in the press reported that this was the first example of repression in Moscow after the revolution and added: "One may assume that this lesson will serve as a sufficient warning to all those who under the banner of art offer nothing but concealed pornography" (Rafalovič 1933: 375). In other words, the former state and church censorships appeared again in new guises, availing themselves of the labels "antirevolutionary" and "pornographic".

There was also trouble of a more practical kind. The urban transport system functioned poorly; the streetcars stopped running at 9 p.m., making it difficult for people to attend theatres and concerts. Another problem was the prohibition of private advertisments in the newspapers (allegedly due to the paper shortage). A short notice, "Today in the theatres", was still included on the last page, but playbills were the only other means of informing those interested. Competition was keen, however—in April 1918 Petrograd was a town of posters, placards and appeals which quickly transformed the houses in the center of the city into gigantic announcement kiosks:

С каждым днем город приобретает все более гнусно-крикливый вид. Стены всех домов сплошь залеплены всевозможными афишами, плакатами, объявлениями, воззваниями, повестками на заседание и чорт знает что. Залепляются уже не только стены, но и драгоценные зеркальные окна магазинов, дорогие вывески. Объявители, стремясь к возможно полному использованию затрат на плакаты, вывешивают их все выше и выше. Скоро дома будут оклеены бумагой до самых крыш ... Запрещение газетных объявлений превратило наружные стены домов в сплошное объявление.

(VO 1918: 9.4)

But things soon got worse. The winter season 1918/19, one critic later pointed out, was probably one of the most difficult in the history of the Russian theatre. Sheer hunger often caused faintings on stage. The temperature sometimes fell to 7–8° Centigrade during the performance. The electricity supply was erratic and petrol lamps had to be kept in reserve. The streetcars now stopped already at 6 p.m. (*Birjuč* 1919: 173).

The reorganization of theatre life thus proceeded slowly for what we have seen to be obvious material, administrative and political reasons. An article in *Izvestija* in September 1918 emphazised that the necessary changes must be introduced step by step. This sounded like an answer to the impatient futurists:

Было бы легкомысленно требовать немедленных результатов от организационных попыток перестроить веками созидавшиеся формы театра. На театре — больше чем на других видах искусства — наслоилось много накипи — античной, феодальной и буржуазной. Нужно с величайшей осторожностью удалять наросты изжитых эпох, чтобы не повредить основного стержня, на котором зиждется театр.

(*Izvestija* 1918: 5.9)

As late as November 1920 a critic ended his negative ("Komu èto nužno?") review of a play by the French writer Paul Claudel with the comment that "it is doubtful whether there is any other country, besides Soviet Russia, in which theatrical activity is so glaringly contrary to the country's vital needs" (KT 1920: 17.11).

By the end of the civil war the problem of "the three pieces" was consequently not yet solved. The relationship between the pieces, however, had changed considerably. And the discussion concerned not only the administrative questions debated in the spring of 1918 (the reorganization of the state theatres, the existence or non-existence of private theatres) but more general matters of principle such as the function of the theatre in the new society, new relations between the stage and the audience, between the stage and reality (see Fitzpatrick 1970: 139 ff.; Rafalovič 1933: 127 ff.).

Art: "It's Cold in the Old Academy"

Artistic life also seemed at first to be following its usual course. In January 1918 the annual exhibition of art students opened in the halls of the Academy of Art. *The Banner of Labor* could not find anything of particular interest and even less of a connection with the world outside the walls of the Academy. Due to the general shortage of fuel the halls were cold and it was easy enough to find their coldness symbolic:

Холодно — в залах старой Академии.
  Холодно.
  Холод сфинксов — с набережной — проник в залы нашего "Institut de beauté". Жизни здесь нет.
  Жизнь — за стенами Академии. Она бьет ключом.
  Она творит новое искусство, новую красоту.

(ZT 1918: 23.1)

A few weeks later the *Mir iskusstva* group opened its traditional exhibition. Here as well art critics could not find anything new, here as well they were reminded of the contrast between this art with its roots in the past and a different, dynamic reality outside:

Каталоги с маркой "Мира Искусства" — одноглавым орлом, печатанные старинным, давно знакомым, неизменным александровским шрифтом — все уносит если не очень далеко назад, то по крайней мере в прошлый, такой тихий и безбурный, по сравнению с нынешним, год

И самое содержание выставки, если не считать фотографически-картинного полотна Кустодиева "27 февраля" — заставляет забыть о том, что над Россией пролетел один из роковых годов.[4]

The process of democratization had begun, however, also here. It progressed along the same two lines we have observed in the theatre: Make museums, palaces and art treasures available to the masses! Stimulate spontaneous activities among the proletariat! Every spectator could also be a performer! The newspapers reported in February and March the appearance of a whole series of "academies", "groups", "workshops" and exhibitions for the workers. An "Ambulatory Academy ABC" ("Brodjaščaja akademija ABV") offered to instruct broad circles of the impoverished population in the fundamentals of art (ZT 1918: 28.1). One group calling itself "Freedom" ("Svoboda") announced an exhibition of paintings done exclusively by workers and dedicated to the following themes: "Men of fire and iron" and "Love of art". An ambulatory exhibition with works by well-known artists such as Petrov-Vodkin, Benois and Boris Grigor'ev, toured the workers' suburbs in Petrograd (ZT 1918: 25.1).

A notice in *The Banner of Labor* in March 1918 offers a particularly good example of this enthusiasm for democratization and spontaneous activity: workers were invited to take part in art circles which were organized in one of the recently opened places for "proletarian activity" which in spite of its democratic ambitions was given the old-fashioned name "Palace of the Arts" (Dvorec iskusstv) (perhaps because it was situated in one of the halls of the Winter Palace):

Во Дворце искусств организуется Объединенная Народная Мастерская Живописного творчества. Одна из задач Мастерской — дать рабочим всех видов труда возможность свободного творчества в искусстве. Поэтому занятия продолжаются с утра до вечера, в будни и праздники. Можно работать совершенно независимо, а также пользоваться руководством художников Нового Искусства, работающих в самом близком общении. Программа и методы работы не предопределяются заранее, но зависит от возможностей и творческой инициативы каждого.

(ZT 1918: 3)

The interesting point here is the mention of "artists of the New Art" (spelled with capitals). Since the Palace of the Arts belonged to Narkompros one may assume that avantgarde artists active within Narkompros at this time had been engaged as instructors. Such activating courses were otherwise the special branch of Proletkul't, but here was apparently an attempt to teach amateur painters cubist techniques!

This was probably no easy task. A notice on an exhibition in the Petrograd socialist club "Red Star" may be rather significant. Three different types of art were brought together there: futurist and proletkul't paintings intermingled with the "slogans" ("lozungi") of the left Socialist Revolutionaries. It was a meeting characteristic of this period: posters, banderols and slogans of direct agitation side by side with avantgarde and proletarian art.

The reaction of the visitors to the futurist canvases was, however, negative. The critic's comment is of a certain interest: while the public found this art too "new", he himself considered the cubist style "out of fashion":

Изломанные, лихорадочно-безпокойные футуристические образы и фигуры-полотна художников из "Пролеткульта" прихотливым образом сочетались со здоровенными, смело угрожающими лозунгами: "Да здравствует великое Знамя Труда", "Истинный рабочий контроль над производством". И темы рисунков: "Да здравствует социализм!" — темы новые для этих, по устаревшему уже, футуристическому шаблону нарисованных полотен. И не случайным кажется это родство между певцами Будущего — футуристами и творцами Будущего — революционерами. Но если наши старые революционеры, "вожди", оценили этих "творцов несотворенного", приняв их в лоно "Пролеткульт", то, во всяком случае, посетители клуба далеки еще от понимания не только "архи-современных" футуристов, но даже и более "устаревших" наших современников.

(ZT 1918: 17.2)

The big problem, however, was—as in the theatre—the heritage from the Palace Ministry, here the Academy of Arts. A commission attached to the Arts Union (Sojuz dejatelej iskusstv), the influential organization formed in May 1917, had been working on a plan of reorganization and in February 1918 a proposal for new statutes was published. The answer from Narkompros was quick and surprising. Pointing out that the SDI commission had been appointed by the former governement and had no authority in the new situation, the IZO department (Otdel izobrazitel'nyx iskusstv) of Narkompros published a different solution—which had the character not of a proposal but of a decree. The Academy was dissolved and the reorganization of the art schools under the supervision of the Academy—the essential part of its activity—was left to be decided by the art students themselves.

This solution was formulated by certain former members of SDI who had joined Narkompros immediately after the October revolution. They soon formed an executive collegiate of IZO known as "the board of seven". The most active member was Nikolaj Punin; the other names were N. Al'tman, S. Čexonin, G. Jatmanov, A. Karev, A. Matveev and P. Vaulin. It was Karev, a former member of the Mir iskusstva group, who was entrusted with the supervision of the reorganization of the Academy.[5]

The reaction was dramatic. SDI immediately called for a protest meeting under the slogan "Everybody to the defense of art" ("Vse na zaščitu iskusstva"). A proclamation was issued, directed above all against the board of seven, accusing them of intrigues and monopolistic designs.[6] It is worth quoting in full:

Как и год тому назад, искусство России в опасности. Уже не толпа, объятая мятежом, — теперь на искусство посягают наши товарищи, на словах они за свободу искусства, на деле требуют свободы только для себя. Они стараются уверить, что именно их искусство понравится пролетариату, что они "левые" в искусстве, хотя многие из них работают в весьма традиционном направлении. Все, что им не нравится, они хотят разрушить, пустить на дым. Не хотят на словах привиллегированного искусства, а сами требуют покровительства одному направлению. Разделяют искусство на буржуазное и пролетарское, и этим демагогическим разделением, совершенно произвольным, возбуждают недобрые чувства против большей части произведений искусства. В стране, свергнувшей иго произвола, они пытаются образовать коллегии по делам искусства не на выборных началах, а по назначению. Варварские воззрения, высказываемые ими, грозят опасностью искусству, сулят разрушение автономным учреждениям, дезорганизацию художественным школам и развал художественной жизни.

(VZ 1918: 6.4)

The meeting took place on April 7. A journalist from *The Evening Lights* began in the ironic tone typical of newspaper reports on the many meetings during the spring of 1918:

По поводу возмутительного сборища буржуев, заполонявших долгие годы русское искусство таким хламом, как музей Александра III, всякие Третьяковские галереи, с нами беседовал один из этих врагов народа, рисовавший буржуазной кистью своей беднейшее крестьянство и все такое не пролетарское, не в пример "семерке" пролетарской с ее народным кубизмом и футуризмом по-азиатски.

(VO 1918: 9.4)

A. Tamanov, architect and president of the Union, opened the meeting by saying that the Union with its 200 different organizations was the only democratic organ in the fields of art and literature. "For that reason it is fair that matters of art be directed by an *Arts* union and not by a wilful collegiate at the Ministry of Enlightenment". Fedor Sologub, the poet and head of the literary section, pointed out that the now common division of artists into "right" and "left" was arbitrary and did not correspond to the political usage of the terms, since the works of the so called "left" artists were "totally incomprehensible to the broad masses".

Lunačarskij was depicted as almost a prisoner of this dictatorial group ("they have forbidden him to sign any papers without their approval"). He was also supposed to have said that in this question he would be on the side of the majority. But against the actual majority of the Arts Union, said one of the members, the avantgardists had mobilized the street. The interesting point in this interpretation is the picture it gives of Lunačarskij as a well-meaning, almost neutral but weak person (corresponding to the label "our soft-hearted Anatolij", issued by *New Life*, see Fitzpatrick 1970: 131) and the avantgarde artists as a malicious junta, striving for power at any cost. What upset the Union was apparently not so much Narkompros' undemocratic way of making decisions above their heads or the solution as such (it had a great deal in common with the proposal suggested by SDI itself) as the "treachery" of their own comrades, the dissenting members of the left bloc.[7]

This group was present at the meeting. One of them took the floor, not—judging from the reports—to defend their actions but just to say that the discussion was of little interest to them. Whatever the opinion of the executive board of SDI on the decision of Narkompros, they were convinced that the students were on their side. These students were supposed to vote on the decision during the next few days, and that was the only thing Narkompros was interested in. Here the speaker was interrupted by voices shouting "Enough", followed by a mixture of applauses and whistles. But everything, the journalist assured his readers, still proceeded "quite decently" and "the scandal was an elegant one".

The meeting of the art students took place on April 14, but contrary to prediction the delegates (with a majority of 63 votes against only 7) decided to support the protest of SDI. The press (VZ 1918: 15.4) noted that part of the delegates (supporting the collegiate of "the seven") left the hall demonstratively after the voting.

Consequences followed close after. When the students met again on April 16, this time to discuss professional matters, they found the hall of the Academy locked and were informed that Karev, who was responsible for the reorganization, had prohibited all meetings in the Academy. A delegation was sent to him but he simply explained that his order was valid: no further meetings in the Academy or the police would be called in. *New Life* (NŽ 1918: 17.4) made a comment that there could be different opinions as to the positions and intentions of the Arts Union and those who support it, but there could not be two different opinions on the "polemic methods used by the comissars and the student's minority behind them in their struggle with opponents holding views different from their own".

Three days later, April 19, a new meeting with the executive committee of SDI took place, this time in Gor'kij's apartment (DN 1918: 21.4)—it had been used for such purposes earlier (see Charles Rougle). Lunačarskij answered a special invitation and showed up. If this was supposed to be a meeting of reconciliation, its results were meager, as the report in *New Life* (1918: 21.4) shows.

The representatives of SDI began by pointing out the abnormal relations between the artists and the government and blamed certain irresponsible groups:

> кучка "безответственных" комиссаров, — невежественных "оппортунистов", готовых служить всякому правительству, игнорируя мнение художественных организаций, на свой страх производит и готовится произвести ряд весьма опасных опытов, грозящих нанести неисправимый урон делу русского искусства. Уничтожение Академии, подтасовка голосов и "сыск" на заседаниях конференции учебных художественных заведений, полицейские покушения на самую свободу заседаний (инцидент Карева), варварский и безграмотный декрет о снятии памятников — вот те преступления в коих повинны правительственные комиссары.

All this, Fedor Sologub said, was at variance with Lunačarskij's own statements; the only possible explanation was that the people's commissar was not aware of what his "assistant commissars" were doing. The best solution was to dismiss the "board of seven" and entrust art matters to the Arts Union.

Lunačarskij's answer, the newspaper emphasized, was met with special interest since it evidently had the character of a declaration of the new government. He began by repeating what he had been saying at almost every meeting with the representatives of art and the theatre since the very first days of the October revolution: the government was in favor of a total separation of art from the state. But this implied, Lunačarskij added, that all official diplomas, privileges, titles and offices must be abolished—for which simple reason the Academy could not be preserved in its present state. A preservation would further give the impression that the government favored certain art groups (since the Academy was undoubtedly dominated by certain,

mainly conservative groups) while the government "was against supporting any existing art group or organization". He was surprised
that the Arts Union, which advocated autonomy, could at the same
time claim official authority over art life. The recent proposal to call
a constituent assembly ("učreditel'nyj sobor xudožnikov") would,
in his opinion, merely lead to domination by mediocrities. For that
reason the government was not afraid of taking a stand which could
be termed "undemocratic":

> Нам не впервые идти против демократии; опыт Европы и
> Америки показал, что большинство ее — буржуазно. Мы
> стоим за активное меньшинство, в искусстве — за союз с от-
> дельными талантами, и готовы в этом смысле пополнить
> состав правительственной "коллегии".

Lunačarskij here introduced in cultural affairs the principle of "the
dictatorship of the minority" which was by necessity already operating
in politics. In the fall of 1918 it would become a leading slogan of
IZO's journal *Art of the Commune* (*Iskusstvo kommuny*; see Jangfeldt's
article in this volume, and Kleberg 1977: 42).

In conclusion Lunačarskij addressed the members of the Arts
Union, scornfully inciting them to continue their self-destructive opposition—and left the hall:

> Продолжайте оставаться в оппозиции, это вам больше к лицу,
> теперешние же попытки художественного объединения и да-
> вления на власть — вызваны не столько заботами об искусстве,
> сколько просто чувством личного самосохранения.

A few days later a new conference of the art students, this time
under the guidance of IZO, met in Petrograd. Only those students who
were in favor of reorganization on the terms proposed by "the board
of seven" were called. The meeting approved a general resolution to
that end (published in the Narkompros journal *The Flame* (*Plamja*)
1918: 2). It did not even mention the earlier majority, which was now
deprived of the possibility of arguing their point of view. The resolution could consequently pass for the official opinion of all art students
—just as the board of seven wanted. Some newspapers made sarcastic
remarks to that effect but there was not much else they could do.

Lunačarskij appeared at the conference and told the students about
the meeting in Gor'kij's apartment. According to his version the

members of the executive council of SDI had offered to cooperate
with him, and Fedor Sologub had the following day even paid him
a complimentary call (PĖ 1918: 22.4). When SDI learned about Lunačarskij's speech and his version of the meeting they were infuriated—
in their opinion the purpose of the meeting had been to hold Lunačarskij responsible in the name of all artists for what the little irresponsible group had done with the Academy of Arts, rather than
to offer him any cooperation. The executive council decided at a
special meeting to break further personal contacts with Lunačarskij
and maintain a policy of confrontation. Since it was important to
coordinate their strategy with that of their Moscow colleagues the
council decided to send a special delegation to the new capital (NŽ
1918: 25.4). The meeting in Moscow was probably not quite so succesful as the council had hoped. A group of left artists appeared, for
instance, with a special declaration supporting the "board of seven":

Совет левой федерации художников приветствует революционные победы Петербуржцев над косностью уклада жизни
искусства. Мы с вами в борьбе против застенков искусства
академии художеств. Приветствуем упразднение академии.
Ваш успех дает нам силы в Москве, где хотят запрятать его
в гроб. Мы утверждаем, что только истинные революционеры
искусства имеют право на строительство новой жизни. Товарищи, мы пойдем вместе с вами в борьбе против затхлости
и засилия буржуазного искусства. Мы верим, что новые руле-
вые сумеют вывести корабль искусства в широкое море.

(NŽ 1918: 1.5)

SDI's idea of calling a general all-Russian conference in June or
July in order to coordinate the struggle against Lunačarskij's cultural
policy was never realized, the reason certainly beeing the rapidly
changing political climate.[8]

Recalling the struggle a few years later, in 1921, Nikolaj Punin
used the same explanation as Lunačarskij for the action of the "board
of seven", namely a distrust of democratic procedure. The line of
"the dictatorship of the minority" was under the circumstances the
only possible tactic to get things moving the way the Bolsheviks wanted
them to: "A congregation of 200–300 artists at which the delegates
begin voting on everything will not get any work done whatsoever"
(ŽI 1921: 8.11). This was the reason why "the seven" had settled for

a radical solution over the head of SDI. When he now asked himself whether he and his group had actually succeeded, he answered briefly: "Broadly speaking—no". Who was to blame? The civil war, partly, but also the fact that "we are human and subject to human errors".

Literature: From "King of Poetry" to LITO

On February 27, 1918 a meeting was arranged in the polytechnical museum in Petrograd to choose "a king of poetry". Poets were invited to come and read their own poetry and actors would fill in and recite for those absent. Very few poets appeared in person, as it turned out. Majakovskij's contribution was *A Cloud in Trousers*, but it gave him only second place. Instead, Igor' Severjanin was elected "king of poetry" and Bal'mont (who was not present) came in third.

Thus the evening would seem to indicate that no sudden change in people's literary taste had occurred after the October revolution (how representative the audience was, is, of course, an open question). Besides, the whole idea of arranging such an evening at this particular moment looks rather out of date. It is also somewhat surprising that Majakovskij should take part in a show, which, although it recalls the futurists' prerevolutionary activity, hardly corresponded to the calls for a "revolution of the spirit" that would be issued just a few weeks later in *The Futurists' Newspaper*. One newspaper (*Mysl'* 1918: 19.2) pointed out that the evening was arranged by a well-known organizer of concerts and lectures. The whole matter was simply a commercial affair and the futurists were paid to appear. To make it more serious the critic P. S. Kogan had been invited to act as chairman but the effect was partly spoiled by the clown Durov who had been seated next to him.

At this time, the end of February, the actors of the state theatres had after several demonstrations and protest meetings reached a temporary agreement with Lunačarskij and Narkompros on questions of autonomy and democratization. Representatives of the Arts Union were drawing up new statues for the Academy of Arts, unconscious of the fact that some former members of the Union, having "deserted" to Narkompros, were preparing quite a different solution which would sidestep them and provoke all artists to violent protest meetings. In other words, while artists and actors were engaged in a serious struggle for their professional interests, the poets amused themselves with

37

farcical jokes, reminiscent of the prerevolutionary bohemian atmosphere.

Such a comparison suggests a clear difference between literature, on the one hand, and art and theatre on the other at this particular time, the beginning of 1918. One reason is obvious. No literary organization had been under the direct control of the Palace Ministry. There were no administrative problems of the same complex kind to be solved here and consequently no need for demonstrations and protest meetings like those that exploded around the Academy of Arts. The question of state control versus autonomy and independence, of vital importance to those sectors which had experienced beside the usual censorship also the pressure of "imperial grace and disgrace", did not seem pertinent to the writers at this stage.

This did not mean that the writers were an easier problem for Lunačarskij and Narkompros. The first approaches, through the Arts Union or through direct invitations, failed. Very soon, however, cracks appeared in the wall of resistance: proletarian writers (Serafimovič, Gastev), the peasant poets (Kljuev and other poets, attached to *The Banner of Labor*), avantgarde poets (Majakovskij), members of the old intelligentsia (Blok). The poems published in *The Banner of Labor* during the month of May 1918 seemed to indicate readiness to cooperate (Mandel'štam: "Well, let's try"). But these were "poetic declarations" and did not necessarily mean that old views on the individualistic or "autonomous" nature of poetry had been abandoned (cf. Fitzpatrick 1970: 135). One characteristic example is Majakovskij who in spite of a personal invitation from IZO in April 1918 did not join Narkompros until the fall (see Jangfeldt).

Literature was certainly a special case in the beginning, compared with art and the theatre. For the leftist artists in IZO and their supporters it was natural to discuss art in terms of "propaganda and education" (as the common slogan then ran) and promote closer relations between art and society, for instance by giving preference to art schools training specialists in the production of porcelain, glassware, furniture etc. (see VŽ 1919: 3/4, p. 107), instead of the old easel art. At the same time even conservative artists and art critics like Aleksandr Benois could find in the protection of art-treasures a field for close cooperation with the Bolsheviks.

Very soon also a theatre department (TEO) was attached to Narkompros. In the fall of 1918, in connection with the changed attitude towards the intelligentsia, it attracted some well-known people. Mejerxol'd became head of the Petrograd section, with Blok as director of the repertory department. The Moscow branch included among others Brjusov, Belyj and Vjačeslav Ivanov. TEO contained a special section on theoretical questions and the discussion focused also here on the theatre as a means of education and propaganda.

It seemed natural that the next move should be a literary department. The publishing house "World Literature" (Vsemirnaja literatura), founded in September 1918 as an independent part of Narkompros, was a step in that direction (Sherr 1977: 258). But it provided first of all—as did TEO—a temporary refuge for the literary intelligentsia.

The first issue of *The Art of the Commune* in December 1918 published a letter from "a group of left poets" ("gruppa levyx poėtov") entitled "Organize literary sections" ("Organizujte otdely slovesnogo iskusstva"; see Jangfeldt 1976: 38). All literary activity, the letter stated, still depended on Lunačarskij personally: "If Lunačarskij catches a cold for four weeks, there is no Russian poetry for four weeks". An organization like IZO and TEO was in their opinion badly needed. But another year passed before a LITO—after some unsuccesful attempts—was finally constituted in December 1919, two years after the other sections. Although names like Brjusov, Gor'kij, Blok and Serafimovič appeared on the board, the main task was rather to take care of strictly professional questions which were becoming more and more topical. The private section shrank rapidly in 1918–20 and was dependent on Narkompros for paper. The new state publishing house (Gosizdat) did not yet work efficiently and gave no priority to literary publications. The book trade and book distribution had also undergone considerable changes (PiR 1921: 2, p. 236).

The aims were clearly more limited than those of IZO and TEO. LITO did not try to tackle theoretical questions of the social and public function of art with the same intensity as the other departments. It was apparently easier to discuss such functions concretely in the case of art, the theatre and cinema. These were media with a more immediate relation to their audience and to society. The writers held on to traditional views of the "individualistic" nature of their work and were sensitive to anything reminiscent of bureaucratic claims or control. Any interference easily evoked parallels with the czarist censorship.

One characteristic example: In May 1918 a commission of Narkompros headed by Lebedev-Poljanskij called a meeting to discuss a "nationalization of the classics". The intention was to make books cheaper and distribution better by means of a state monopoly. 37 writers, critics and literary scholars were invited, but only 9 showed up. All of them—with one exception: Brjusov—opposed the idea. Pavel Sakulin pointed out that a state monopoly would place "an official stamp" ("kazennyj štempel'"') on books and make possible manipulation by means of official, tendentious comments. One newspaper drew a parallel with the czarist censorship and concluded that the old system, in fact, had an advantage:

> Отныне, следовательно, классики могут дойти до народа, в единственном официальном издании, с официальными комментариями. Это не только возвращение к традициям старого режима, который допускал в школы и народные библиотеки только "одобренные" ученым комитетом министерства народного просвещения издания, но и нечто худшее. "Старый режим" затрудняя доступ в народ и школу вольной книги и вольного издания лучших авторов (даже подцензурные) все же не лишал никого права издавать, за пределами ведомственных установлений и в пределах цензуры, какие угодно сочинения, и в том числе и классики.

(NS 1918: 25.5)

The literary field was further sharply divided into sections, which often opposed and overlapped each other in such confusing ways that no one administrative, ideological or artistic frame could include them all (Fitzpatrick 1970: 136f). In the theatre there were three pieces—state, private, "democratic". In literature there were more, and they were different and difficult to puzzle together. This became evident when, at the end of the civil war, journals and publishing houses started to function as before and writers broke their "silence".

The Monumental Propaganda

The Futurists' Newspaper, published in March 1918, had demanded a new and fresh art. What Russian culture needed was "a leap into the future", not "a back to normal" which the bourgeois public, judging from the reports in *The Evening Lights*, was hoping for. Majakovskij's letter was addressed to the new consumers, the workers, but it clearly referred to the new governement as well.

The first moves of the Bolsheviks in the cultural field, however, did not concern "new art" or "avantgarde art", but were political or administrative. The press decree of November 9, for instance, was a typical political measure. It closed down the bourgeois press, i.e. the press of all parties which did not recognize and join the new governement, and provided the Bolsheviks with much needed offices and printing-works for their own propaganda (Dewhirst & Farrell 1973: 6 f.). This take-over of the "enemy press" caused considerable alarm not only among journalists but also among writers, who saw it as general threat against free speech. They gathered around a "Protest-paper" ("Gazeta-protest"), published on November 26 and including contributions by among others, F. Sologub, E. Zamjatin, A. Kuprin, V. Korolenko, V. Zasulič. As might easily have been anticipated, it had no effect. But it apparently gave the intelligentsia the feeling that they were at least trying to defend what they considered the most important accomplishments of the February revolution: the abolishment of the censorship and the beginning of a free press.

The administrative measures were, as we have seen, connected with the reorganization of the former imperial theatres, academies and museums. Direct artistic initiatives were, for obvious reasons, few. There was one, however, a spectacular and from many points of view interesting one. Among other things, it clearly demonstrated certain problems which faced—and in the future would continue to face—the Bolsheviks in the field of arts. It emanated, — and this was, of course, characteristic—not from the artists themselves, but from above, from the very top of the hierarchy, from Lenin himself—quite contrary to the general art policy of, for instance, SDI after the February revolution.

Lunačarskij provided later the background to this idea in an article written after Lenin's death. In a personal conversation with him in March or early April 1918 (Drengenberg 1972: 186) Lenin took up the question how art best could serve Bolshevik propaganda. He proposed two things which could be done on short notice: to decorate the cities with revolutionary posters and slogans and to erect statues and busts of political leaders and progressive writers, artists and philosophers.

Lenin's inspiration was, as he told Lunačarskij, Tomas Campanella's well-known book *The Society of the Sun* (Lunačarskij 1967: 121). In this utopian town the houses are covered with big paintings and statues are erected to dead heroes and leaders so as constantly to confront the people with inspiring models. A Russian translation of Campanella was published in 1918 (there were even two editions). Lenin's impression of the role of art in this utopian city may for that reason have been quite fresh.[9] An article by V. Friče in *Pravda* (1918: 25.4), entitled "The Creators of a New Beauty" ("Tvorcy novoj krasoty"), also has a distinct flavor of such utopian dreams: "Our towns should be not only towns and gardens but also art museums. Throughout the day the worker should be surrounded by beauty. The buildings of workers' cooperatives, of trade unions, of houses of the People should be wonders of architectural art and indoors they should be decorated with statues and pictures."

Lunačarskij could have informed Lenin that his idea was far from original even in a short perspective. The whole idea of monuments to the precursors of freedom appeared, in fact, very soon after the February revolution. Parallels with the French revolution were in those days popular (the Marseillaise served for some time almost as a Russian anthem instead of the old czarist hymn) and J. Tiersot's well-known book on the songs and festivities of the French revolution (*Les fêtes et les chants de la revolution française*) was translated into Russian (a review appeared in ZT 1918: 27.2.). A proposal for new monuments was discussed in the so called "Gor'kij's commission" (see Charles Rougle's article) but was rejected due to the strong opposition of some leftist artists. They saw in monuments and the cult of personality connected with them a typical bourgeois institution that was all too reminiscent of recent czarist days.

The problem of a personality cult was actualized very soon after the October revolution. In an editorial entitled "A new year—a new age" *The Banner of Labor* greeted the new year 1918. Under a collective leadership people were now marching towards a happy future. For the first time the masses had their fate in their own hands. There could be no cult of personality any more, as in the days of the czars or of the Provisional government: "There could be a Miljukov or a Kerenskij epoch, but there can never be a Lenin or a Trockij epoch. The day the revolution begins to dissolve into names, it is drawing near its close" (ZT 1918: 3.1).

42

At about the same time, the beginning of 1918, another journal took up the same question: "The cult of personality is contrary to the whole spirit of Marxism, the spirit of scientific socialism" (VŽ 1918: 2, p. 8). So far, the journal noted, Marxism had never tried to evaluate the personality, its role in social and political development, the importance of the personalities of the leaders. The proletariat, the collective had always been in the foreground. And this is as it should be. But Lenin is a special case. He is inseparable from the party as the party is inseparable from him. As a consequence—so the author tried to solve the dilemma—"to study Lenin as a literary and political person, means to study in a unique personality the tremendous revolutionary, proletarian collective".

Lunačarskij later declared that he had liked Lenin's proposal of a "monumental propaganda" "tremendously" ("črezvyčajno"). But the reaction in IZO was apparently rather cool, especially among the radical artists (cf. Vinogradov 1939: 44). And for obvious reasons— they had fought against monuments as well as against a "Ministry of Fine Arts" in March 1917 and had opposed the recent idea of creating a "Commissariat of the Arts" (Fitzpatrick 1970: 113). A revolution was to them a time for taking down statues, not for creating new ones. The toppling of the Vendôme colonne during the Paris communard rising was often referred to and in March and April 1918 there were attempts to follow this example in Moscow and Petrograd. Taking down statues only to put up new ones instead seemed to the left artists as a meaningless change of labels.

Lenin himself, on the other hand, embraced his idea with an energy and persistency which is indeed astonishing, considering that he had other and more urgent things to do. On April 12, 1918 he signed a decree on "monumental propaganda". By chance or on purpose— another decree, also signed by Lenin, decided the fate of the Academy of Art on the very same day. Very soon a list of persons worthy of statues was suggested. It was a large and generous list, including no fewer than 63 names, among them 17 writers (even such an exclusive poet as Tjutčev).

The decree and the following official comments stressed and specified the educational and political purpose, while the aesthetic aspect was hardly even mentioned. The monuments were meant to serve as "street rostrums from which fresh words encouraging minds and hearts should reach the masses" (*Izvestija* 1918: 24.7). The inaugurations were to have the character of festive occasions and take place on Sundays when people were free to attend. The significance of the revolutionary hero was to be explained in speeches with music accompanying the ceremony. Special concerts and theatre performances would be arranged the same evening. Pamphlets and books describing the man's life and work should be distributed to the people, etc. (*Plamja* 1918: 11, p. 14).

Lenin's impatience with Lunačarskij's difficulty in getting things moving fast enough soon found rather drastic expressions. In a telegram of May 13 to Lunačarskij Lenin expressed his astonishment and indignation ("udivlen i vozmuščen") over the inefficient and slow handling of even such a simple matter, in his opinion, as slogans and posters. In further telegrams and letters to various people Lenin even threatened to bring the responsible parties to trial, calling them "saboteurs and dullards" ("Pozor sabotažnikam i rotozejam", Lenin 1971: 84).

Lenin apparently did not want to accept the obvious reasons for the delay. This gigantic project was simply unfeasible in a country suffering from wars and revolutions. Money was not the big issue, since Lenin personally saw to it that it was granted. But there was a lack of material, of workshops, of artists, of time. It is easy to understand that only part of the ambitious project could be completed by the first anniversary of the revolution. On November 7, 1918 Lenin inaugurated several statues and memorial placards in Moscow, and Lunačarskij spoke in Petrograd in honor of, among others, Marx, whose statue was erected in front of the Smolnyj.

Afterwards Lenin expressed to Lunačarskij his disappointment with the "monumental propaganda" (Lenin 1956: 526). Reality apparently did not match his vision. Lunačarskij found the arrangements in Petrograd rather successful but those in Moscow a complete failure (Lunačarskij 1967: 264). As to the reasons for the failure, it was later common to blame the "leftist" artists (Elkin 1967: 168) or even "saboteurs" ("sledstvie rasxljabannosti, sabotaža, a inogda i prjamogo vredistel'stva vragov", Vinogradov 1939: 39). There were few immediate comments in the newspapers but some of them are of interest since they saw from the beginning the difficulties of the whole project and raised some fundamental questions.

One such question was that the idea itself lacked all democratic foundation. The decree was not preceded by any discussion, either

44

in Narkompros, or among the artists. It was a one-man idea, emanating from the top of the political hierarchy. The "democratic procedure" was instead placed at the other end. First of all, young artists were to be invited to take part in the project, not—as in the old days—merely the already established and well-known "generali-xudožniki". No old-fashioned jury would decide on the models and no prizes be distributed. Made for the present in non-permanent material like plaster, wood or concrete, the provisory models were to be exposed to "the judgement of the masses" ("na sud mass", *Izvestija* 1918: 14.4). The "masses" would decide which model deserved to be preserved in bronze or granite or even such a "bourgeois" material as marble.

To make this more than an empty phrase was not an easy matter. The attempts revealed only too clearly the difficulties involved. In September 1918 Mossovet put to the vote some memorial tablets made by a group of invited artists. Since more young intellectuals ("intellektual'naja molodež") than workers took part in the voting, however, it was declared invalid and the jury reserved for itself the right to make a choice (Drengenberg: 250). Another attempt was no more succesful. The models for a monument to Marx in Moscow were exposed publicly in March 1919 and "all workers" (to avoid the previous mistake) were urged to give their opinion. Since the votes, however, were very few ("kazalos' ne tak mnogo") the jury decided not to distribute any prizes (Vinogradov 1939: 41; Drengenberg 1972: 274).

This was from the beginning a serious question and one of the few direct comments on the decree of April 12 took up exactly this matter (*Rodina* 1918: 16.4). We must, the critic argued, find a solution that will allow for democratic influence, otherwise we will find ourselves back in the well-known procedures of the old regime:

Иначе и новые революционные памятники будут воздвигнуты по существу в том же одностороннем "официально-домашнем" порядке, в каком воздвигались памятники "царей и царских слуг" при режиме бюрократической академии художеств, которая весьма не беспристрастно "поощряла" одних и не давала ходу другим. Где уверенность, что теперь не будет поощряться "футуристический академизм"? В жюри должны быть не назначенные Луначарским коллегии художников, а выборные от всего объединенного художества. Все это, конечно, немыслимо при столь "спешно" назначенном сроке для постановки новых моделей, как ближайшее 1 мая, — сроке, едва ли достаточном для шитья хороших сапог.

In a following article the critic Ja. Tugendxol'd (NR 1918: 15.5) commented on a competition for a monument "to the victims of the proletarian revolution" to be erected on Red Square in Moscow. His first remark concerned the composition of the jury: should it consist of the "komissija xudožestvenno-prosvetitel'nogo otdela Moskovskogo soveta", headed by Malinovskij or of the "kollegija po delam iskusstva", recently set up by Lunačarskij? Or should perhaps the often cited "sud mass" get a chance? Whatever the decision be, the critic continued, history teaches us to be very cautious with official competitions and orders of works of art from state authorities. The best works of art depicting the French revolution—to take an example close at hand—were not those by the official artist David but those by artists like Delacroix or Daumier, made against rather than with official approval.

The critic brought up another noteworthy point. Monumental art had never been a Russian specialty and those who were able successfully to tackle such difficult tasks could at the moment be counted on the fingers. Would it not be better to take a more modest attitude?

… Скульптура, да еще "Монументальная", претендующая на вечность, требует помимо "нутра", "самобытности" и "черноземности", которыми отличаются русские люди, еще и культуры — знания, опыта, умения согласовать возводимый памятник с характером места и фона. Иначе — лучше ограничиться голой стеной, как стена коммунаров в Париже, которая так много говорит чувству зрителя своей безмолвной скромностью о трагедии коммуны. Эта внутренняя скромность особенно нужна нам, русским, далеко еще не имеющим права в нынешний момент возводить в честь нашей пролетарской революции памятники "триумфальные" и ликующие. История венчает героев и мучеников, но не прощает нескромности — ее ничем не обманешь.

As things drew near to the celebrations for the first anniversary and the idea of the project clarified more comments appeared. One of them is of special interest since it touched upon another question of fundamental interest. Allowing that a proletarian society ought to have some kind of "monumental art", should it just adopt the institutions and symbols of the bourgeois one? The decoration of the cities was apparently partly inspired by similar festivities during the French revolution and the painting of houses is a Russian folk tradition. But statues? And, above all, obelisks?

There was, for instance, a plan to put up an obelisk on the Field of Mars in Petrograd for the first anniversary of the revolution. The local Proletkul't organization protested and the article agreed: "An obelisk ... A monument of Egyptian absolutism on the graves of the combatants for freedom ..." The idea, the article joked, must have emerged in Narkompros when it was faced with the problem of what to do with the old obelisks of the Romanov dynasty. "And how easy to adopt them! The only thing needed would be to remove the eagles and paint over the inscription (or nail them up with red boards)— and there you have a fine obelisk of the Revolution."

In a P.S. the author mentioned that he had just learned that an obelisk also would be erected in Moscow to replace the former statue of general Skobelev. And the old Romanov obelisk in the Aleksandrovskij park should also be preserved: only the names of the czars would be replaced by names of the socialist leaders. This, he concluded, should indeed be the subject of new Proletkul't protests:

И старый романовский обелиск в Александровском саду не пропадет без пользы: имена царей будут заменены именами вождей рабочего класса.

Какая глубина замысла, какой размах!

Октябрьская революция, заменяющая надписи на старых царских памятниках!

То, что мне казалось невозможным, становится фактом.

Молчит Московский Пролеткульт, а между тем, кричать, кричать нужно!

(VI 1918: 16.10)

The best known of these new obelisks was that erected on the square before the Mossovet building, replacing a statue of general Skobelev. It was inaugurated on November 7. The day before another obelisk had been put up and publicly unveiled on the Theatre square near by. But this obelisk had a quite different function and symbolic meaning than the traditional monument on the Mossovet square. Entitled "The red wedge" ("Krasnyj klin") and made by N. Kolli, it showed a big red wedge splitting a socle in the shape of a truncated white obelisk. According to the artist the wedge represented the red and the obelisk the white army (Speranskaja 1971: 82 f.). It was a monument with a meaning made obvious to everybody by means of some well-known symbols, in fact, a double pair of contrasting symbols: first of all the colors ("red" versus "white"), then the wedge (a worker's tool) versus an obelisk (an imperial emblem).

These two statues in Moscow emphasized a dilemma which was—as we have already seen—characteristic of the cultural discussion of these years. On the one hand previous forms and symbols were simply taken over and provided with new labels in order to give them a new content, on the other there was an attempt to create something new and original, to radically oppose the manifestations of the old art.

The first issue of IZO's new journal *The Art of the Commune* appeared in December 1918. It contained a short comment by Nikolaj Punin on the October festivities and the monuments. His main objection was that these celebrations did not differ from those of czarist days:

Прежде всего Октябрьские празднества по своему заданию, мало чем отличались от всего того, что в свое время устраивала буржуазия всего мира. Те же декорированные материей улицы, деревянные арки, гирлянды, электрические и даже просто цветные фонарики, как-то тупо напоминавшие пресловутые 'царские дни" с газовыми вензелями и звездами.

Instead of "decoration" ("ukrašenie") artists should at this moment rather favor "destruction" ("razrušenie"), a destruction—real or symbolic—of the old art and the old monuments. This would mark the difference between the previous regime and the new era.

In a later article Punin returned to the question (IK 1919: 9.3). He began by pointing out that "the whole idea of erecting monuments to the great heroes of the revolution is not quite a communist idea. There exist no heroes and certainly no great heroes. The time for a heroic conception of history has gone, never to return". But if a communist society is to build monuments the idea must be approached quite differently. The old artists discussed the matter in terms of realism, in terms of the human body. The modern artist—and Punin takes as an example Tatlin—sees the problem from a quite different angle:

> По его мнению, необходимо раз навсегда покончить с человеческими фигурами; памятники современные прежде всего должны отвечать тому общему стремлению к синтезу отдельных родов искусств, какое мы сейчас наблюдаем. Нет живописи без пространственного (и как частный случай, пластического) понимания формы, нет ваяния без архитектонической и живописной культуры, нет архитектуры без живописи и пространства. Архитектор, живописец и скульптор должны в одинаковой мере принять участие в разработке и выполнении современного памятника. Из этого не следует, конечно, что архитектор должен построить дом, живописец его раскрасить, скульптор украсить. В этом, в сущности, не было бы никакого синтеза. Самый план, проект памятника, не в частях, в целом должен одновременно удовлетворить архитектора, скульптора и живописца.

Tatlin's famous tower, his monument to the Third International, was never realized. Monumental propaganda, on the other hand, produced during the following years new sculptures, busts and reliefs. After a short pause in the 1920's the idea was, as Drengenberg has shown, taken up and developed further in the propaganda art of the Stalin period.

Literary Debate and Struggle for Power

It would seem that a political and social revolution like the Bolshevik revolution should work in the cultural field as well with a set of simple oppositions like "new" versus "old", "radical" versus "conservative", "left" versus "right", "proletarian" versus "bourgeois", "democratic" versus "undemocratic", etc. In art and literature, however, these oppositions did not function quite so simply during the months following the October revolution.

One reason was that they had already been introduced in the cultural debate—by the February revolution. The February revolution abolished the double—state and church—censorship and the Palace ministry with its control over academies, museums and theatres,

An attempt to "reorganize" the Tret'jakov Gallery by discharging I. Grabar' and his assistants provoked several articles in the press at the same time (see NS 1918: 27.4: "Poxod na Tret'jakovskuju gallereju"). It was finally stopped by the newly founded "kollegija po delam iskusstva" in Moscow (Tatlin, Konča-lovskij, Korovin, Konenkov).

9. By his proposal Lenin—as he told Lunačarskij—also had the good intention to keep some—as he imagined—otherwise unemployed artists active. A parallel is Lenin's idea in 1920 to let some scholars make a dictionary of the contemporary Russian Language. In a letter to M. N. Pokrovskij he pointed out that for this work one should, "of course", gather people, "not suitable for other purposes":

Засадить на паек человек 30 ученых или сколько надо, взяв, конечно, не годных на иное дело, — и пусть сделают.

(Lenin 1965: 192)

References

Dewhirst, M. & Farrell, R.
1973 *The Soviet Censorship*. Metuchen, N. J.
Drengenberg, H. J.
1972 *Die sowjetische Politik auf dem Gebiet der bildenden Kunst von 1917 bis 1934* (Ost-Europa-Institut an der freien Universität Berlin. Historische Veröffentlichungen. Bd. 16). Berlin.
Elkin, A.
1967 *Lunačarskij* (Žizn' zamečatel'nyx ljudej). Moskva.
Fitzpatrick, S.
1970 *The Commissariat of Enlightenment*. Cambridge.
Jangfeldt, B.
1976 *Majakovskij and Futurism 1917–1921*. Stockholm.
Jufit, A.
1968 *Sovetskij teatr. Dokumenty i materialy: Russkij sovetskij teatr 1917–1921*. Leningrad.
Katanjan, V.
1961 *Majakovskij. Literaturnaja xronika*. Moskva.
Kleberg, L.
1977 *Teatern som handling*. Stockholm.
Korolenko, V.
1979 "Iz dnevnikov 1917–21 gg.", *Pamjat'. Istoričeskij sbornik*. Vyp. 2. Paris.
Krasnaja Moskva
1920 *Krasnaja Moskva 1917–1920* (sb.). Moskva.
Lenin, V.
1956 *Lenin o kul'ture i iskusstve*. Moskva.
1965 *Polnoe sobranie sočinenij*, T. 51, Moskva.
1971 *Literaturnoe nasledstvo. V. I. Lenin i A. V. Lunačarskij. Perepiska, doklady, dokumenty*. Moskva.

Lunačarskij, A.
1967 *Sobranie sočinenij.* T. I. Moskva.
Maguire, R.
1968 *Red Virgin Soil. Soviet Literature in the 1920's.* Princeton.
Majakovskij, V.
1956, 1959 *Polnoe sobranie sočinenij.* T. II, XII. Moskva.
Mandel'štam, O.
1971 *Sobranie sočinenij v trex tomax.* T. II². New York.
Men'šutin, A. & Sinjavskij, A.
1964 *Poèzija pervyx let revolucii 1917–20.* Moskva.
Rafalovič, V,
1933 *Istorija sovetskogo teatra.* Leningrad.
Shane, A. M.
1968 *The Life and Works of Evgenij Zamjatin.* Berkeley & Los Angeles.
Scherr, B.
1977 "Notes on Literary Life in Petrograd, 1918–1922: A Tale of Three Houses", *Slavic Review* 2 (June), Vol. XXVI, pp. 256–67.
Speranskaja, E. (ed.)
1971 *Agitacionno-massovoe iskusstvo pervyx let Oktjabrja.* Moskva.
Vinogradov, N.
1939 "Vospominanija o monumental'noj propagande v Moskve", *Iskusstvo* 1939: 1.
Vinogradov, S.
1977 "Diskussii o jazyke pervyx poslerevoljucionnyx let", *Russkaja reč'* 1977: 2, p. 37 ff.

The ease with which the Tsar was deposed contributed for a time to concealing the profundity of the contradictions that lay just beneath the surface of Russian society. Intellectuals were led to believe that the Revolution signalled the beginning of the national unity and harmony of which they had been dreaming for decades. Moreover, there was a widespread belief that it was they and their noble tradition that deserved the most credit for the event. "The Russian literary consciousness gazes upon events with a sense of the sweetest spiritual satisfaction, joyfully noting that the seeds first sown by Russian literary thought have sprouted luxuriantly" (Reč' 12.3.1917). Although the propagation of democratic humanistic principles contributed at least indirectly to the fall of the autocracy, events would soon show that intellectuals, including some of the politically best schooled among them, were shortsighted in their analysis and premature in assuming leadership of the historical process.

The Need to Organize

Borne up on the first wave of enthusiasm, intellectuals plunged into the activity that under the autocracy had been either prohibited or severely circumscribed, namely organizing. Only through organization, it was felt, could they, the intelligentsia, break out of their isolation and integrate themselves into the society that had for so long ignored or rebuffed them. Political party activity was one main channel for this released energy. Of more concern to us here, however, are the efforts of what is often termed the "artistic" intelligentsia (*xudožestvennaja intelligencija*) to organize and coordinate cultural activity.

> Братья художники!
> Все организовано, все организуются. Только мы, художники идем вразброд и не сплотились еще в единую семью. Мы должны немедленно организоваться, дабы жизнь не выкинула нас за борт. ... необходимо создать прочную организацию, ближайшей задачей которой должно явиться создание Все-российского союза художников.
>
> (BV 1917: 7.3)

Similar initiatives were observable among practically all professional groups during the first weeks of March. On the 9th, for example, writers met with the object of resurrecting the Union of Russian

Writers (*Sojuz russkix pisatelej*), which had been closed by decree in 1901 (Reč' 1917: 9.3, 12.3). By the end of the month, painters, sculptors, theatrical workers, film makers, architects, musicians and others had all held meetings in the capitals and many provincial centers as well to establish local organizations intended in the near future to expand and unite on the national plane.

Organizational Goals

Most of the organizations that sprang up at this time had two aims. One might be described as defensive, arising from the fear that "otherwise life will throw us overboard". The trade union was the model here, the object being the protection and advancement of artists' professional and material interests. One delegate to the writers' meeting mentioned above, for example, noted that the proposed national union "... will be the competent organ deciding questions of importance to the culture of the nation such as copyrights, the signing of literary agreements with foreign powers, etc." (Reč' 1917: 9.3).

On the other hand, in the view of many of the intellectuals who took the initiative in forming these unions, narrowly professional objectives were secondary to a much broader and more positive function. The same delegate stated of the Writers' Union:

> ... задачей его будет не столько охрана интересов самих писателей, как интересов категории трудящихся, сколько дальнейшая борьба за коренное обновление русской жизни в связи с высшими интересами русской литературы.
>
> (Reč' 1917: 9.3)

Organizations, in other words, were to be harnessed to the accomplishment of what the intelligentsia had long regarded to be its historical mission, namely "the renewal of Russian life" in accordance with its own enlightened principles as these were reflected in the heroic tradition of Russian literature. This is a typical expression of the intelligentsia's dominant *kulturträger* attitude, which conceived the preservation of the cultural heritage and its transmission to the masses as one of the intellectual's major tasks. Writers, to continue the above extract, now had the opportunity to pursue unhindered this all-important pedagogical activity:

March the Society of Architects and Artists (*Obščestvo arxitektorov–xudožnikov*) met to protest against Gor'kij's Commission, which it felt was insufficiently representative of the artistic community. A followup meeting on 9 March was attended by some 46 different groups and institutions, ranging from the Academy of Art to the editorial boards of various journals (*Reč'* 1917: 12.3). The following day, 42 of these representatives elected an organizational committee whose task it was to arrange a mass meeting of intellectuals on 12 March. The object of this latter gathering was the establishment of a "union of unions" (*Sojuz dejatelej iskusstv*, hereafter SDI) that would include representatives of all the cultural professions—literature, scenic arts, painting, sculpture, architecture and music.

Although the attendance at these preparatory meetings was diverse, what soon came to be known as the "leftist" bloc within the SDI was able to secure influence disproportionate to its numerical strength and prestige in cultural life as a whole. In the organizational committee, for example, 4 of the 12 members—Majakovskij, Punin, Mejerxol'd and Al'tman—were "leftists". While this figure is significant enough, it does not wholly justify the insinuations of some Soviet observers that the organizational work of the SDI was altogether dominated by leftist elements (cf. Muratova 1958: 27–28). The other 8 members of the committee, after all, included much more moderate names, such as M. Fokin, K. Somov, and A. Ziloti. But the leftists were clearly more energetic and vociferous than their opponents, and this increased their relative strength. On the eve of the SDIs founding meeting, 11 March, a gathering was arranged on their initiative, now as an organization calling itself "The Union of Artistic, Theatrical, Musical and Poetical Societies, Exhibitions, Publishing Houses, Journals and Newspapers, 'Freedom for Art'" (*Svoboda Iskusstvu*) (Pravda 1917: 11.3). Precisely which groups were represented is unclear. At any rate, *Svoboda Iskusstvu*, with N. Punin, I. Zdanevič and N. Al'tman as secretaries, became one hard core of resistance within the SDI to both Gor'kij's Commission and the proposed Ministry of Fine Arts. Its protests against these projects and its demands that the SDI be established on the principle of universal franchise and be given full authority in the organization of cultural life won the qualified support of many who did not share the leftist, "futurist" orientation of the initiators. Thus, in the list of candidates advanced by the March 11 meeting for the leadership of the SDI one finds such "bourgeois" names as K. I. Arabažin, Mix. Kuzmin, S. Prokof'ev and V. N. Solov'ev (Dinerštejn 1958: 546). Sergej Makovskij, editor of *Apollon*, expressed considerable sympathy for the 14 theses developed by *Svoboda Iskusstvu* proposing a decentralization of cultural institutions on a municipal basis (Makovskij 1917: xv. Cf. below p. 67). It can safely be assumed that his attitude was shared by many other intellectuals. In addition to these men, who stood somewhere left of center in the debate, there was an influential group referred to as the "rightist" or *delovoj* bloc unofficially headed by F. Sologub, which supported the same principles of autonomy, decentralization and full authority for the SDI, but refused to recognize *Svoboda Iskusstvu* and the "futurists".

The Revolution, then, had hardly begun, and already the stage was set for a major conflict among intellectuals on the nature of organized cultural activity in Russia. At one pole were the partisans of cooperation with the new regime; at the other, a "left" and a "right" group both adamantly opposed to any sort of official interference. In the middle was a numerically probably rather significant grouping with wavering bloc preferences. The inevitable clash occurred at the March 12 gathering, a mass meeting at the Mixajlovskij Theater that attracted some 1 400 persons (Dinerštejn 1958: 546). Judging by the reports, it can only be described as lively bordering on the chaotic. Debate centered almost exclusively around Gor'kij, the Ministry, and questions of authority and organization, and it proved impossible to reach any acceptable compromise. List after list of candidates to the SDI Presidium failed to attract sufficient support, with the result that at the end of the meeting control of the formally still unborn organization remained in the hands of the temporary founding committee (Mokul'skij 1933: 52).

The meetings of the subsequent two months failed to break the deadlock. Both the "autonomists" and the "conciliationists" noted partial victories, but the profile and policy of the Union as a whole was destined to remain unclear. The major accomplishment of the former group was the destruction of Gor'kij's Commission. The Commission's appeal on 1 April to cease all projects involving monuments dedicated to the Romanovs brought a new wave of protests, not so much against the letter of the decision as against its spirit. The Commission was accused of vandalism and dictatorial presumptuousness at the SDIs meeting on 4 April. A conciliatory proposal from the

The SDI Controversy as a Rift in the "Intelligentsia"

It is obvious, from the account sketched above, that the SDI was rent asunder from the very beginning by factional strife, and that this very soon rendered the organization practically impotent. It is tempting to leave it at that and explain the failure solely in terms of petty group egotism. This is the dominant Soviet view, which regards the dispute as one between "democratic" and "anti-democratic" tendencies, represented by Gor'kij's Commission and the pro-ministry faction, on the one hand, and the "autonomists" (an unholy alliance of "aesthetes" and "futurists"), on the other. Following this line of reasoning, one is soon led to the conclusion that the conflict was between those who cared about culture and were capable of doing something about it, and those who were more or less indifferent and pursued only their own interests (cf. Muratova 1958: 44).

This, of course, smacks of oversimplification. The battle for and against Gor'kij and the Ministry was not merely a question of egotism, even if similar motives are almost always present in such contexts. What was really at stake was a matter of principle involving different conceptions of the nature of culture and the artist's or intellectual's role in cultural activity. In the connection of most immediate interest to us, the conflict might be described as a kind of intellectual "generation gap" (more with respect to attitudes than to the chronological age of the participants, although a fairly neat distinction can be made on the basis of this criterion as well). The "older" generation—the majority and certainly the most influential—had, as has already been noted, a *kulturträger* notion of themselves and their cultural role. This is clearly evident in the attention Gor'kij's Commission and the proposed Ministry devoted to the preservation of art treasures and popular cultural enlightenment. Now it can be argued—and was of course argued—that it is precisely in these two domains that state interference is not only justified but necessary. Even staunch opponents of an official ministry were sometimes willing to concede the government a certain function here (cf. Makovskij 1917: xvi). The pro-ministry faction, however, saw these tasks as central rather than peripheral and therefore in need of large-scale and centralized funding and coordination. Themselves opponents of the tsarist cultural bureaucracy, they did not fear official institutions as such, provided that these were staffed with people like themselves, who in most cases undoubtedly had the best interests of the nation and culture at heart. A. Benois is reported to have said some five years before the Revolution:

> ... стоило бы ей [the bureaucracy] познать свое назначение, прийти к самосознанию, почувствовать свою душу ..., найти настоящих двигателей, которые сумели бы из этого громадного инструмента извлекать все заложенные в существе его, но до сих пор латентно в нем пребывающие симфонии.
>
> (Makovskij 1917: iii)

This was of course a somewhat naive belief, as even Benois himself was forced to admit later. Bitterly disillusioned by the opposition he and Gor'kij encountered in the SDI and disappointed over the half-hearted support they received from the Provisional Government, he wrote at the end of April:

> В этот-то момент многим наивным людям (и в том числе мне) и показалось, что теперь настала возможность, отойдя от этой груды [the tsarist bureaucracy], которая, к счастью в своем развале не задела ничего ценного, соорудить рядом свободный, светлый и прекрасный храм. Самые несбыточные мечты теперь могли быть реализованы. Казалось, только иди, кто хочет, на работу, и всякого с радостью встретят "свои"! Казалось еще и то, что "ссыльные" и "эмигранты" художественного режима имеют преимущественное право на то, чтобы заняться тем делом, от которого их десятками лет отстраняли. Явилась иллюзия, что и здесь повеяло благотворным дыханием революции, что занесет гору рухляди земля, что вырастет на горе травка и будет гора одним лишь безвредным памятником отживших и более уже не страшных времен. Но не тут-то было! И приходится ныне с горечью в сердце признать, что в искусстве революция отложена на неизвестный срок.
>
> (Benois 1917: 140)

Russia's cultural elite, as Benois rightly notes, did not greet these idealists with open arms. A surprising number of the most prestigious figures, for some reason especially writers, said little or nothing. Others, the "younger" generation, proved to be downright hostile. Their resistance cannot be explained as a lack of concern for the preservation of cultural continuity or for cultural dissemination, even

if these objectives do not occupy the same exalted position in their
set of priorities. On the first point, preservation, the "leftists" were
predictably less worried than the rest. Majakovskij's well known comment at the March 12 meeting of the SDI that a handful of soldiers would
surely suffice to protect the art treasures in the palaces is often cited
as evidence of their nonchalance (Dinerštejn 1958: 546). It can also
be argued, however, that the remark is an expression of trust in the
masses, whom the "preservationists" tended to fear. Secondly, with
the exception of some extreme manifestations of "futurist nihilism"
(cf. Majakovskij 1959: 150), the important point was not so much
hostility toward the cultural heritage as such as the apprehension that
an excessively protective attitude toward the past would inhibit new
creation (cf. Jangfeldt 1976: 61). This fear was by no means exclusively
"leftist", but was shared by many who otherwise stood near the
center in the debate. One observer, for example, noted in terms that
any futurist would probably have found acceptable that it was fine
to surround the Hermitage and other museums and monuments with
bayonets, but what of the future?

> ... теперь все мчится бешено в будущее, когда все творчески
> напряглось, ища новых решений; в дни когда все зовет к риску,
> к великодушному размаху, к молодой щедрости, — туда же к
> этому непонятному грядущему неизбежно должны двинуться и
> "деятели искусства", если они не хотят остаться в странной и
> темной роли боязливых "охранителей" ненужных скряг.
>
> (BV 1917: 30.3)

The questions of preservation and dissemination alike were not a
matter of whether, but how and by whom. The fear of both "left"
and "right" (and evidently a sizable number in the middle) was that
a centralized bureaucracy, for all the expertise and good will in the
world, would end up contributing to the creation of pseudoart serving
its own inflated self-image. A warning example was to be had in
France, which in this respect had gone even further than the old
Russian regime (cf. Makovskij 1917: viii–xii). What the autonomists
pleaded for instead was a network of organizations at a much lower
level. Sologub observed:

> Пусть охраняющие организации возникают снизу и на местах
> посредствам постоянного и свободного возникновения разно-

образных обществ, кружков, собраний, которые так же свободно могут соединяться в местные и международные союзы.

(BV 1917: 13.4)

Svoboda Iskusstvu elaborated on a very similar model in a set of 14 theses adopted on 21 March. Most matters, including funding, would be taken care of at the municipal level. National questions would be decided at congresses on the all-city or all-zemstvo model composed of representatives from all groups and currents. Artists would be trained, not through academics and a centralized school system, but more on the workshop model—the new "universities"— where the artist rather than the professor would be the supreme pedagogical authority. The other major point in the more traditional attitude—the spread of culture to the masses—was by no means ignored, either. Thesis 10 reads:

Для общеобразовательных по вопросам искусства целей формируются кадры чувствующих призвание преподавателей, которые, получив соответствующую подготовку в художественных университетах, должны давать лишь элементарные сведения, грамоту по сущности истории и техники каждого вида искусства. Не всякий обладает даром, чтобы стать художником, но всякий может развить в себе сознательное отношение к созданным другими произведениям.

(Makovskij 1917: xiii–xiv)

Here again the emphasis is on an individual teacher-pupil relationship, where the artist rather than the institution is in the center.

Obviously, then, none of the "autonomists" were indifferent to either the preservation or distribution of culture. What their insistence on a decentralized organizational form reflects, however, is a shift of emphasis from the artist seen as the bearer of already established cultural values, an essentially distributive function, to a view that stresses his right to create new values. Each attitude, in other words, selects the type of organization that best serves its priorities. There is nothing very new or original, for us at least, in either view. For a great many Russian intellectuals, however, the break that the SDI controversy represents with the traditional *kulturträger* ideal came as something of a shock, as can be seen in, for example, Benois' complaint above. The intelligentsia that so many of them had hoped would now join forces and "renew Russia" proved to contain a wider variety of notions as to its proper cultural role than had previously been realized. This was not the last time reality would refuse to conform to established expectations.

Summer and Early Fall 1917: The Agony of Irrelevance

Already before the first governmental crisis in April, it was becoming apparent that the unity that had almost universally been presumed to exist on the nature and goals of the Revolution was in need of revision. The most immediate point of discord was the war with Germany. A surprising number of intellectuals had deluded themselves into believing that one of the main reasons the Revolution had occurred was a desire on the part of the entire Russian people to wage the war more effectively. Many seem to have agreed with Prince Trubeckoj, who declared confidently in early March: "There have been bourgeois revolutions and proletarian revolutions. But a *national* revolution, in the broad sense of the word, like the present Russian one, has never occurred before ... *Faith in Russia and her victory has returned*" (Reč' 1917: 5.3; emphasis in original).

It soon became obvious, however, that a significant and growing section of the population did not fully share this enthusiasm. Demands for an end to the war and the redress of social and economic inequities were now being articulated more and more clearly among the rank and file, both at the front and at home. The split between the leadership and the masses that would culminate in October had begun.

The Persecution of the Intelligentsia

Rightly or wrongly, the immediate result of the radicalization of the masses that accompanied their impatience was that intellectuals, with little regard for the fine points of their actual political attitudes, were increasingly identified with the class enemy, the bourgeoisie; *intelligent* and *buržuj* soon became almost indistinguishable synonyms. This is of course unacceptable from a strictly sociological point of view, but as one observer has noted of similar accusations levelled against the Kadets, they referred not so much to involvement in commerce and industry as to general social values (Rosenberg 1974: 123).

It was not long before intellectuals began to feel the concrete effects of this popular unrest. Signs that they were beginning to review their situation appeared quite early. Thus, in the midst of the turbulence in April the Literary Fund (*Literaturnyj fond*) met and elected a committee to arrange a public discussion on the role of the intelligentsia in the Revolution(Reč' 1917: 25.4). If such a gathering actually took place, it seems strangely to have been ignored by the press, but the mere fact that the theme was felt to be urgent seems to reflect an uncertainty that was little in evidence just a few weeks before. A fortnight later, lively arguments were reported to have raged in the Moscow Literary and Artistic Circle (*Literaturno-xudožestvennyj kružok*) around the complaint of one member that the intelligentsia was neglecting its task of protecting spiritual and cultural values (RV 1917: 14.5). As had often been the case in the past, such laments were a fairly sure indication that something was amiss. By the end of May the situation was openly regarded as critical. One observer commented with frank bitterness:

Травля против интеллигенции ведется широко и в городе и в деревне ...

Живя в такой высоко-культурной стране, мы, конечно, не особенно дорожим интеллигенцией и можем обойтись и без этой породы "буржуев", получающих деньги за какие-то там знания и науки.

(Reč' 1917: 24.5)

The crisis only continued to deepen in the aftermath of the July Days. So recently at the head of the Revolution, its brain and soul, as intellectuals themselves tended to regard it, the intelligentsia was now declared an irrelevant vestige of the hated past, to be hunted into oblivion. Petr Ryss, a prominent left Kadet, who toured the provinces at this time, expressed a sentiment that was broadly shared within and outside his own party's ranks:

Интеллигенция как бы не существует. Ее отмели в сторону, либо, видя невозможность работать, она ушла, спряталась и надеется, что когда "выболтаются", вспомнят и о ней. Какое бесконечное поприще для работы — и как третируют старых, опытных работников! Ими созданы просветительные и разного рода культурные общества, они несли свет и здоровье в тьму. И теперь — они "буржуи", ибо их руки без мозолей, а воротничок рубашки стянут галстухом.

И под шум и назойливую болтовню тысячи ораторов медленно угасают культурные общества, и интеллигенция, основывавшая их для народа, остается без народа, в экстаз непонятных слов поклоняющегося новым богам. Преемственность знаний, традиции интеллекта, то, что и есть культура, на что должна опереться революция и в ней почерпнуть силы — все это сдано в архив, как преступления буржуазии, как отрыжка старого строя.

(Reč' 1917: 30.7)

Aside from the purely physical threat that being indiscriminately branded as the enemy implied, intellectuals' responses to the new situation were conditioned by what they correctly perceived to be a challenge to one of their most cherished notions of themselves.

"What is the Intelligentsia?"

The various definitions of the intelligentsia formulated in the 19th century by men such as I. Aksakov, N. Stronim and N. Mixajlovskij had as one of their major common denominators the thesis that the intelligentsia was a formation above or outside other social estates or classes (cf. Müller 1971: 252–307). This non-estate, non-class or super-class quality (*vnesoslovnost'*, *vneklassnost'*, *nadklassnost'*) implied that membership in the intelligentsia was determined by ethical or ideological rather than sociological criteria. An aristocrat, a *raznočinec* or even a peasant could be reckoned as an *intelligent*, provided that he abandoned his narrow group interests in favor of principles that set "the common good" of society above those of any particular class. The nature of the principles was the subject of a lively debate; they could be conservative, as in the case of the Slavophiles, liberal and evolutionist, or radical, involving the violent overthrow of the autocracy. But all were agreed that what gave their respective notion of the intelligentsia cohesion was an ideological or "spiritual" bond. The role of intellectuals was that of a kind of "cement" (Stronim's term), a non-partisan superstructure that arbitrated in social disputes and bound the nation together in a common will.

Müller (1971: 313) observes that economic and social realities made the inadequacy of such notions increasingly obvious, and that with the beginning of modern party life after the 1905 Revolution the intelligentsia fell into more distinct political factions. This is basically correct, but must be qualified. Marxism attacked the concept in the 1890s with the opposite contention, namely that intellectuals were very much the representatives of different social classes. The renegade Marxists that dominated the *Vexi* symposium represented another deviation, objecting to the altruistic elements in the dominant liberal and radical view. Though no longer monolithic, however, the ideology was far from dead even in the politically more diversified reality after 1905. The principle of non-partisanship was incorporated almost *in toto*, for example, into the program of the Kadets, the party towards which an impressive number of intellectuals (perhaps for just that reason) gravitated. One of the Kadet ideologists described the party's goals as follows:

> The Kadet party—the Party of People's Freedom—is distinguished from all other parties in that it struggles for all citizens, and not for one particular social class. For example, our party struggles not only for workers and peasants, but for the welfare and prosperity of all classes, of the entire Russian state ... In other words, the Party of People's Freedom has a non-class /vneklassovyj/ character, neither bourgeois nor proletarian, but national /vsenarodnyj/.
>
> (Rosenberg 1974: 13)

The Kadets may have been the only party with non-partisanship written into its program, but the fact is that a majority of intellectuals —liberals, populists, and even some who claimed to be Marxists— whether or not they formally belonged to a political party, still subscribed to a greater or lesser degree to the traditional notion that the intelligentsia was an essentially super-class formation working for the good of all society. The manner in which the Revolution was almost universally greeted as a national phenomenon seems to testify to the viability of the tradition. As late as February 1918 one still occasionally encounters statements of the old creed such as the following, pronounced on the 25th anniversary of the populist-oriented journal *Russkoe Bogatstvo*:

> ... в борьбе мы всегда чувствовали широкий, объединяющий всю русскую интеллигенцию круг идей ... "Русское Богатство" является своего рода символом преемственности прогрессив-

71

ных идей, символом верности старому знамени. Для нас это — не партийный флаг, а стяг русской интеллигенции, стяг, на котором написано: служение народу только чистыми средствами, правда–справедливость и правда–истина.

(NV 1918: 14.2)

Revisions

Classical concepts of the intelligentsia as an ideologically cohesive community, classless, non-partisan, and bound together by unselfish dedication to a set of predominantly democratic, progressive principles, were thus alive well into the Revolution. Events in the main, however, were working against their preservation. Unexpectedly rejected by society at large, intellectuals tended to move toward positions that entailed revisions of their conventional self-image, and it is to some of these shifts in outlook that we now turn.

Nadklassnost' as Patriotism

The first such modification is more a natural elaboration of the traditional position than a radical deviation from it. It is but a short step, after all, from the "common good" posited as an abstract ideal, to the immediate interests of the nation-state, especially in a situation of crisis. Before the war with Germany, all but the most conservative intellectuals were reluctant to accept nationalism as a viable alternative to their traditional altruistic humanism. The statist theories developed by Struve and others after the 1905 Revolution, which had strongly nationalistic and even chauvinistic undertones, met with overwhelmingly negative criticism (cf. Zimmerman 1976 and Brooks 1972: 199).

In peacetime, nationalist aspirations may have seemed not quite lofty enough to command most intellectuals' wholehearted allegiance. In war, such distinctions often become blurred. Dedication to the cause of mankind was not rejected—it was simply identified with the short-range aims of the nation. "Russia" came before all else, even the Revolution. Many felt with Dmitrij Merežkovskij that

Русская интеллигенция несла ... не классовую, а общенациональную идею революции. ... Не Россия для революции, а революция для России; поэтому надо спасать сначала Россию и потом уже революцию.

(RSI 1918: 22.8)

This does not necessarily mean that intellectuals achieved any great degree of cohesion in practice. As might be expected, there was a good deal of competition as to who was the most patriotic revolutionary or most revolutionary patriot. From especially conservative quarters one often hears the lament that the whole of Russian society, from the *mužik* on up to all but a small group within the intelligentsia, had been corrupted by the pernicious spirit of cosmopolitanism and partisanship:

> Русский интеллигент, русский крестьянин, русский рабочий забыли Россию ... У русской интеллигенции осталось лишь привязанность к доктрине, партии, классу с царящей над ними и их органически не сплачивающей, непонятою фигурой единства человечества, отвлеченно и безжизненно материализующейся в образ интернационального союза пролетариев всех стран.
>
> (Reč' 1917: 20.8)

One response to social disintegration was thus a renewed appeal to all classes and groups to unite under the banner of Russia. The effort was given a certain organizational nucleus in the League of Russian Culture (*Liga russkoj kul'tury*), founded in the midst of the patriotic wave that accompanied the June offensive. The leaders of the League were anxious to stress that they were a "non-class and non-political" organization dedicated to the good of the cultural tradition that united all Russians (Reč' 1917: 22.6). In reality, it was a right-wing Kadet project, numbering men such as P. Struve, A. V. Kartašev and V. A. Maklakov among its initiators. Its appeal was accordingly simple: for Russia, against Marxist internationalism:

> Основатели лиги убеждены, что тем, кто более любит "свободу и права человека", тем, кто живее ощущает "вселенскую правду человечества", тем решительнее он должен стать на защиту "родной культуры", ибо "только через национальное сознание создается союз равных и свободных народов". Единство человечества осуществимо не через международный союз рабочих, борющихся против остальных классов в разных государствах, а через братство народов, воспринявших каждый всю внутреннюю цельность.
>
> (Reč' 1917: 20.9)

In terms of practical activity, the League was limited to a series of patriotic rallies and does not seem to have played any substantial role in cultural life as a whole.

As a response to the critical situation in which intellectuals found themselves by the beginning of the summer of 1917, their emphasis on an already ardent patriotism can be regarded as an attempt to reassert their role as the leading and unifying stratum in Russian society. Alongside this trend of nationalist classlessness there was another that superficially may seem to contradict it but which in fact involved a similar shift or identification of values and was represented by some of the same people.

The Bourgeoisie Reconsidered

Russian intellectuals, including many whom we would now regard as fairly conservative and others of a more liberal or radical persuasion, had traditionally incorporated an anti-bourgeois attitude in their general ideological stance. This should not be construed in too precise a sociological sense; the middle class as we know it in Europe had in Russia only begun to establish itself by the end of the 19th century. But hostility to the narrow provincialism and timidity of creative purpose that became associated with the "bourgeois way of life" was very much present in the Russian intellectual's outlook, and he often perceived this uncompromising antipathy toward "philistinism" (*meščanstvo*, as it was most often called) as a factor that distinguished the idealistic Russian intelligentsia from its European counterparts. Ivanov-Razumnik's definition, in which most intellectuals could find something that was congenial to them, stressed this noble spiritual profile:

> Интеллигенция есть этически-антимещанская, социологически-внесословная, внеклассовая, приемственная группа, характеризуемая творчеством новых форм и идеалов и активным проведением их в жизнь в направлении к физическому и умственному, общественному и индивидуальному освобождению личности.

> (Ivanov-Razumnik 1906: 20)

The idealism in this attitude was not accepted by all as eternal, however. As early as the *Vexi* compendium, Petr Struve had noted that the intelligentsia was bound to become "bourgeois". That is,

74

with the social modernization and diversification of Russia, intellectuals would be forced to adapt themselves to the existing social structure and take their places in various social classes (Struve 1909: 173), and the bourgeoisie would presumably be the dominant class in the emerging order. The Revolution, in this line of thinking, was the handmaiden of just such a process. Struve, for example, spoke of its task as "the creation of a new, national-bourgeois (*narodnoburžuaznaja*) Russia", which he understood to be founded in practice on the stimulation of "bourgeois desires for ownership among the masses". The duty of the intelligentsia, and the penance by which it could expiate its enormous sin of socialism, was accordingly the "creation of universal (*obščečelovečeskaja*) culture in bourgeois forms" (Struve 1917: 59–60).

This is an interesting but by no means unique attempt to reconcile the traditional view of the disinterested intelligentsia with what was becoming a very partisan outlook indeed. The interests of a particular class are simply equated with "history" or "culture", thereby resolving the contradiction, at least in theory.

Before the Revolution, the pleas of Struve and others for the *embourgeoisement* of the intelligentsia were for the most part little heeded, and intellectuals' anti-philistinism remained virtually monolithic. During the course of 1917, however, significant cracks began to appear in this façade. In practical politics, they were manifested in attempts by the right wing of the Kadet party to break with the policy of the majority and form an alliance with merchant and trade-industrialist groups espousing an openly bourgeois philosophy (cf. Rosenberg 1974: 34–35). A chronologically somewhat later article that is best treated here formulates the shift in conventional intelligentsia terms. The distinctive feature of the Russian intelligentsia ever since Herzen, the commentator signing himself "Sobesednik" noted, was its instinctive hate of the Philistine, "the high priest of private property". The Revolution, however, had shown that this attitude was in need of revision.

Нельзя не увидать, что сейчас мобилизованы все силы мещанства ... сейчас происходит не водворение социализма, не борьба за иные принципы общественного устройства, а за то, чтобы при прежней сохранности института собственности большим собственником был я, а не мой сосед.

(RV 1918: 10.2)

In other words, the deepening Revolution "had revealed philistinism in everyone". Consequently:

> ... интеллигент должен изменить свое отношение к мещанству ... к самой идее мещанства нельзя уже относиться с былым презрением. Мещанство — увы! — свойство человека ... неприятное это свойство — что говорить? — но нельзя же одним ругательством и отрицанием против него бороться. Надо его признать, надо признать лежащее в его основе чувство и право собственности, — только неприятные стороны его надо уметь направить так, чтобы они служили на пользу, а не вред другим.
>
> (RV 1918: 10.2)

"Sobesednik" thus arrives from his ethical starting point at the same conclusion as Struve, who based himself instead on an historical analysis: the intelligentsia must recognize the bourgeois drive for enrichment as universal and hence legitimate. If he stops short of advocating an alliance with the bourgeoisie, he is at least favoring a reconciliation with it.

"The Third Class"

The final revision in intellectuals' self-image that we shall consider here is in some respects the most interesting, for it has certain affinities to the tendency already noted in connection with the cultural debate within the SDI. One of its principal representatives is also the same, namely Fedor Sologub. At an SDI meeting on 31 March Sologub had declared that in an organized society it was prohibited to do anything that was harmful to others, but that he, as an artist, strove to do just that. By this he meant that the task of art was to "disturb" those who supported a bourgeois order as well as those who would establish a proletarian one (Muratova 1958: 36). This is in other words a rather familiar statement of the critical, as opposed to the partisan, function of art, and as such needs little comment.

What is intriguing in our context, however, is that Sologub went on some three months later to elaborate his demands for creative autonomy for the artist into a much more ambitious definition of the intelligentsia as a whole. The defiantly defensive tone of his article, which appeared shortly before the outbreak of the "July Days" crisis, suggests that the extremism of his position was stimulated by the increasing general hostility toward intellectuals. His argument, which deserves to be quoted at some length, defined the intelligentsia as a

> ... третий класс, который для себя ничего не требует и который является объектом эксплуатации обоих враждующих классов. Этот злополучный класс — интеллигенция. Та самая интеллигенция, которая подготовила, создала и воодушевила революцию, та самая интеллигенция, на которую свысока смотрит буржуазия, та самая интеллигенция, которую рабочий относит к буржуазии за привычку чистой жизни.
>
> Когда буржуа и пролетарий, наконец, составят один класс, занятый изготовлением и распределением товаров, интеллигенция к этому классу не присоединится. Она уже не производит товаров, а идеи и формы — не товар.
>
> Интеллигенция станет угнетенным, низшим классом. Разрозненная теперь, жалко приписавшаяся ко всем чужим приходам, тогда она осознает свой классовый интерес и поведет борьбу за свое место под солнцем. Как и пролетариат она найдет наипрочнейшую для себя опору в международных единениях, во всемирных союзах поэтов, врачей, адвокатов, артистов, архитекторов, инженеров. Соединив все таланты, все знания, весь свет разума, вдохновения, мечты дерзающей и зовущей, она вызовет на бой завладевшие благами мира производителей материальных ценностей, на бой во имя высших интересов человеческого духа, и тогда мы посмотрим, чем кончится борьба между грубою силою и озаренным дерзновением человеческого гения.
>
> (BV 1917: 23.6)

Aside from the glimpse Sologub's remarks give us into the psychological processes at work among Russian intellectuals, they are also interesting from a theoretical point of view. The kind of hostility to both the proletariat and the bourgeoisie that he drives to an extreme is not new in the Russian intellectual tradition and was long before him well established in the European one. One observer has noted of French intellectuals' view of industrial society in the 19th century that from their rather aristocratic "spiritual" standpoint "it often appeared to literary men that the only important difference between the bourgeoisie and the proletariat was the capacity of the first to exploit the second. Aside from this the two seemed one in their common devotion to material gratifications" (Graña 1964: 69). To, for example, Stendhal, "persons engaged in the machinery of production ... were all dealers in things, thing-handlers and thing-makers, inherently disqualified to render decisions in which the higher aims of men were at stake" (Graña 1964: 98).

Sologub and, it may well be supposed, many others in what we have chosen to call the "younger" generation of intellectuals, are in line, philosophically and to an extent aesthetically, with this broad current of European thought. There is, however, another and more specifically Russian influence at work here as well. The key concept in this connection is Sologub's use of the term "class". When he speaks of the intelligentsia as a class, he is not doing so in the loose sense of "group" or "formation", but obviously attributes to the notion a much more solid sociological content. The intelligentsia no longer stands above the class struggle, but will participate in it on a par with the other two antagonists to defend its own class interests. Here he comes dangerously close to the arguments of a strongly anti-intellectualist thinker by the name of Maxaev. Maxaev (Russified form of W. K. Machajski) was a Polish socialist who wrote under the pseudonym A. Vol'skij and attracted a certain following in Russia around the 1905 Revolution. One of his principal theses was that the intelligentsia was a parasite class living on the labor of the proletariat, and that intellectuals strove to use their monopoly of knowledge to secure for themselves world dominance. At the same time that Sologub protests against the "thing-makers'" contemptuous view of the intellectual, he accepts their premise that the intelligentsia has class interests that are at variance with those of other classes, and maintains, quite in agreement with Maxaev, that it will seek global hegemony. Anti-intellectualism is, as it were, "turned inside out" to become super-intellectualism.

If the trend of which Sologub is perhaps the best known spokesman had been limited to him and a handful of other modernist artists, it could be considered a marginal phenomenon of little consequence in the broader context. But there is evidence that the attitude was both widespread and growing. It was noted in a review of the year's events at the end of 1917, for example, that

В Москве даже образовалась "федерация союзов работников умственного труда" — вчерашние, вероятно, все "народники", — этот союз предлагает интеллигентам отбросить традиционный "сентиментализм" и навязанные замашки "благотворительности" и во всеуслышение объявить "свою классовую волю". Осуществляется утопия Махаева: интеллигенция организуется в класс и будет добиваться господства.

(NŽ 1917: 31.12)

The history and composition of this federation have proved difficult to establish; it was probably just one of the many loosely knit societies that sprouted up and almost as quickly disappeared during this hectic period. Its mere existence is nevertheless significant when placed in the context of a tendency we have seen developing since the very first days of the Revolution, and we shall have occasion to return to manifestations of similar attitudes below, when intellectuals for the last time returned to a broad public debate of their nature and role. First, however, we shall briefly consider some of the events in the interim that set the stage for that discussion.

Fall and Winter 1917/1918

The seizure of power by the Bolsheviks in October, as far as intellectuals were concerned, could only mean a further deterioration of their situation. They had for some months been identified with the class enemy in the popular mind. Now one of the most extreme and best organized parties made class war a tenet of official policy. That boded ill for anyone who was not a soldier, a worker or a peasant, for in an inflamed atmosphere such as this one the cut of a man's coat often meant more than the subtleties of his actual political views. Newspapers had even before the coup abounded in protests against cases of real or alleged violence perpetrated on the "intelligentsia" (by which was meant both intellectuals in the proper sense and "white collar workers"—*intelligentnye truženiki*; cf., for example, RV 1917: 8.10). By December, there was frequent talk of a formal "crusade" against intellectuals:

Объявлен безумный поход против культурной России; под ударами кулака, — в прямом и переносном смысле слова — гибнут культурные ценности, веками накопленные страной.

Объявлен поход против создательницы этих ценностей — русской интеллигенции, обреченной на жестокие удары и во времена самодержавия, и при торжествующей демагогии.

(RV 1917: 9.12)

The familiar complaint that the intelligentsia was "disappearing" was more relevant than ever before, now increasingly in the concrete, physical sense. Food and fuel were in desperately short supply. Manual laborers and soldiers naturally received more substantial rations. This not unjust discrimination, however, probably brought many of those entitled to smaller portions dangerously close to the bare subsistence level. One newspaper account, objecting to the popular belief that intellectuals were continuing to live in relative comfort, maintained that 76 % of all cases of typhus reported in Petrograd afflicted the intelligentsia (SSl 1918: 30.1). Such statistics are extremely difficult to verify, but they were evidently widely accepted by intellectuals at the time, which in itself is indicative of the prevailing mood.

Whatever optimism may have survived the turn of the New Year was promptly dispelled by the events of the first week. Many continued to cling stubbornly to the belief that the convening of the Constituent Assembly would return Russia to the path of legitimacy. That somewhat unrealistic hope was forthwith laid to rest. Still more frightening evidence that the "crusade" was going to continue and even be intensified, however, came two days later. On 7 January the former Kadet ministers Fedor Kokoškin and Andrej Šingarev, who had been seized by the Bolsheviks on 28 November in a wave of arrests of Kadet leaders, were dragged from the Mariinskij Hospital and summarily executed by a group of Red sailors. The act was not officially sanctioned and the perpetrators were later tried, but whether or not the Bolshevik leaders were believed innocent, the overall effect of the brutality was numbing. The full gravity of the moment had perhaps finally become apparent to all. In the words of one commentator:

Мучительная гибель Кокошкина и Шингарева недаром вызвала в русском мыслящем обществе взрыв чувства близкого к отчаянию. Она как будто впервые открыла многим всю глубину бездны в которую свалилось несчастное наше отечество.

(RV 1918: 17.1)

Paralysis

Concretely, there seemed to be little intellectuals could do to remedy their situation. Plans for issuing appeals and pleas for moderation were reportedly widely discussed in Petrograd, but it was recognized from the outset that such a traditional approach had little chance of success. The gap between the intelligentsia and the people was proving unbridgeable:

> ... но все это — от интеллигенции к интеллигенции ... народ, масса здесь ни при чем — до них эта литература не доходит, а если бы и доходила, то ее тон, способы ее аргументации, самая фразеология не в состоянии затронуть живые силы страны.
>
> Слишком далеко мы отошли от масс, чтобы наше интеллигентское понимание общественных дел и вопросов переживаемого момента могло подействовать на людей, думающих по-простецки ...
>
> (RV 1917: 31.12)

The most common tactic was instead, as far as was physically possible, simply to ignore the new rulers and try to carry on as if nothing had happened. Strikes on the part of such groups as civil servants, bank employees, teachers, etc., were also usual (cf. Fitzpatrick 1970: 35). While such actions had a certain harassment value, they depended for any measurable degree of real success on support from broader sectors of the population, which at least in the capitals was not forthcoming.

Intellectuals in the cultural professions also used the boycott strategy, although their economically marginal nature made the results even less noticeable. The Bolsheviks, represented especially by Lunačarskij, made several efforts in the first few months after October to enlist the cooperation of artists and writers, but all such initiatives were rebuffed. Lunačarskij's proposal to the SDI in November to establish a state soviet on cultural affairs was rejected unanimously. A later appeal for cooperation with Narkompros to safeguard art treasures met with a similar refusal, with the exception of some individuals such as Count Zubov (cf. Fitzpatrick 1970: 28). In late December a pro-Bolshevik rally was organized by Rjurik Ivnev, a minor poet. Blok, Mejerxol'd, Petrov-Vodkin, Esenin and others attended. *Izvestija* reported on 28 December that the gathering was an important sign that part of the intelligentsia had decided "on the necessity of working under the direction of the Soviet regime" (Fitzpatrick 1970: 119). This was a premature conclusion. Ivnev himself wrote a letter to the paper protesting this formulation and declaring his own adherence to the principle of free art, and Blok and Petrov-Vodkin are also known to have been less than enthusiastic about Soviet "direction" (Fitzpatrick 1970: 120). A followup meeting arranged for early January was even less successful. It was announced on 30 December, slated speakers being Lunačarskij and Kollontaj on the part of the Bolsheviks, Kamkov and Spiridonova, from the left SRs; and Blok, Ivanov-Razumnik, Petrov-Vodkin, Esenin and Ivnev as representatives of the cultural community. The meeting would evidently have had something of a populist flavor, as most of the non-Bolsheviks had more or less definite leanings in that direction. As things turned out, however, it had no flavor at all. The majority SR daily *Delo Naroda* could gleefully report already on 31 December that Blok, Ivanov-Razumnik and Petrov-Vodkin, the most important intellectuals, had been included as speakers without their knowledge. Probably as a result, none of the three men attended (Blok 1965: 381).

The Bolsheviks were thus unable to raise more than sporadic and rather shaky support from among the most important intellectuals. But the intellectual community itself was ineffectively organized and incapable of offering any coordinated resistance. Political opposition was hampered by divisions within the parties themselves, arrests of leaders, and the liquidation of the Constituent Assembly. The level of activity within cultural organizations, which at least potentially provided a base for action, had failed to develop any clear profile or sense of direction. The Writers' Union, for example, which as we have already seen was intended to expand into an effective and nationally representative organization, was still musing on such projects some nine months after its creation. A meeting in the middle of December seems symptomatic. The main topic was no longer ambitious plans for "renewing Russia", but the creation of a literary center on the West European or American club model, which would afford writers a place to meet and comfortable housing accomodations. (Something of the sort actually was established and partially financed by the State about a year later; cf. Scherr 1977.) Otherwise, the only thing this gathering in the middle of the crisis seems to have accomplished was an election of members to its administrative council and a by now rather stale declaration of solidarity with the Allies (NV 1917: 19.12). The SDI had continued to run in the same downhill direction noted in May. The most concrete proposal that seems to have been worked out during the fall was that the SDI be given representation in the Soviet of the Russian Republic (BV 1917: 6.10). The idea was discussed only among the Presidium, however, as due either to the Bolshevik coup or internal difficulties or both it does not appear to have been voted upon by a plenum meeting. Other actions were of a more negative character. On 3 December, for example, there was a lively discussion of rumors that Lunačarskij was about to create a section of proletarian art within Narkompros to seize control of all cultural institutions in the capital (NV 1917: 2.12). The SDI issued a protest, reiterating the long familiar demand that cultural questions be decided through the competent artists' organizations (NV 1917: 5.12). The force of such protests, however, was diminished by the fact that the SDI itself could only subjectively claim to be truly representative of the Russian cultural community. An article in the left Menshevik *Novaja žizn'* provides a generally believable description of the development of the Union. The SDI, it noted, was intended in the beginning to unite all cultural intellectuals to defend their common artistic, material and juridical interests, but had instead degenerated into the ordinary type of literary and artistic circle or club. Although membership was officially over 800, a normal meeting drew 20–30 (12, or almost half of these were on the Presidium). The statutes of the organization had yet to be presented to a plenum assembly for discussion. The article agrees with the criticism expressed by the "leftist" bloc that the SDIs chief function had become that of an "artistic bureau" which recommended members for various official posts. It was admitted that the Union had at any rate done something positive by serving as a forum for the discussion of cultural questions, but that is a weak compliment which hardly counterbalances the general conclusion (NŽ 1918: 24.1).

Spring 1918: Revaluations, Recriminations

The atmosphere in the final months of 1917 was not one congenial to discussion or analysis. Russia's intellectual elite was with few exceptions still too shocked and too unorganized to respond articulately to the challenge of events. Even at the darkest hour, however, some consolation could be had in the thought that complete distrust of all educated people could not reasonably last forever (RV 1917: 13.12). Blok was one of the rare true optimists. In a telephone interview with the Petrograd daily *Petrogradskoe èxo* he stated confidently on 14 January that the hostility of the intelligentsia toward the Bolsheviks was "superficial" and already decreasing, and that a "musical" reconciliation was bound to occur (Blok 1962: 8). This was of course a considerable overstatement, but Blok was right in predicting that change was already on the way. With it would come reviews of the past year and a renewed discussion of the intelligentsia, dominant themes in the early spring months of 1918.

A Year of Revolution

A convenient date for summarizing was soon at hand. On 7 March (New Style) a group of prominent Menshevik and somewhat less well-known populist-oriented intellectuals arranged a public dispute on the theme "The First Anniversary of the Russian Revolution". Much of the discussion seems to have been devoted to partisan political wrangling, but on one point there was broad general agreement—the Revolution was over. "Actually", the chairman opened the meeting, "what we are celebrating now is not an anniversary, but a requiem service, a funeral banquet" (VZ 1918: 9.3). Another characterized the period after October as the final rout of the Revolution.

These were not novel laments; the Revolution had been anointed and buried before, as early as the summer of 1917 (cf. RV 1917: 14.7). Then, however, it was by conservative intellectuals who regarded the inclusion of socialists into the government as a betrayal of revolutionary objectives, above all the establishment of a bourgeois parliamentary republic. Now these same socialists found themselves in much the same position as their "bourgeois" rivals. From the point of view of the socialists themselves, it was even worse, for there was evidence that the Bolsheviks were manoeuvering to secure the support of non-socialist intellectuals and experts at their expense. In a decree concerning the Commission of Supply issued in the middle of February it was established that there would be "no negotiations with the saboteurs" (meaning all those engaged in strike or boycott actions), but that commissars were free to employ, *as individuals*, experts who were willing to recognize the Soviet regime (NŽ 1918: 15.2). This was an appeal to politically less conscious elements that was evidently calculated to exclude non-Bolshevik socialists, who at this stage at least were generally not willing to make ideological compromises. The fear among these intellectuals, as they summed up a year of revolution, was that the old tsarist bureaucrats were well on their way to reaching a *modus vivendi* with the new Bolshevik ones. Instead of establishing a unified revolutionary front with the other socialist parties, the Bolsheviks seemed to be allying themselves with the bourgeois sharpers (*del'cy*) who were more and more intensively penetrating Bolshevik organizations, thus forming a united reactionary front (NŽ 1917: 17.2). Vjačeslav Polonskij observed in an article on intellectuals and the Revolution:

> Любопытнее всего то обстоятельство, что именно в стане октябрьских победителей сразу как-то оказалось многое множество людей, которые вчера еще открыто пировали за столом буржуазии, открыто поносили и рабочий класс и так называемую демократию.

> (VZ 1918: 13.3)

The Revolution, according to Polonskij, had in fact come full circle. In the beginning, it had sifted out those intellectuals who had been socialists in word but not in deed. October represented the reversal of this process: the new rulers had done what the socialist intelligentsia had held unthinkable. They had excluded it and were now turning back to join hands with the old jailers, who shared their mentality and methods. "The people have changed. Otherwise things are the same" (VZ 1917: 13.3).

A Change in Course

The criticism and fears expressed already in February evidence a growing awareness that a shift in Bolshevik strategy was imminent. Lenin had made it known that an end to the war with Germany would give Russia the "breathing space" necessary to repair her war-torn economy. The signing of the Brest-Litovsk treaty on 3 March and its ratification on the 15th marked the beginning of this new period of revolutionary history.

If Polonskij and many other socialists looked upon the coming change as a threat to the socialist intelligentsia, there were others in the same quarters who were roused to a cautious optimism. "Half of the Russian Revolution is already over", one observer noted hopefully. "The destructive period is over, or at least drawing to a close." What this meant for intellectuals was that the "class war", which, because it had developed into a war against the intelligentsia was the "saddest misunderstanding" of the Revolution, could now be settled peaceably. The time had come for the intelligentsia and the people to be reconciled (VO 1918: 27.3).

General sentiments such as the above were fanned by the increasing conviction, heralded on the right, that Lenin's "breathing space" in effect signified a return to the past and implied a tacit admission that the party's policy had failed. One commentator perceived evidence of this in the fact that the Bolsheviks changed their name from Social Democrats to Communists in March: "The Bolsheviks have become 'Communists' because they no longer believe that Communism is at hand" (RU 1918: 21.3). The causal connection is disputable, but the Bolshevik leadership was in fact split between "Leninists", who were in favor of re-establishing authority in production on rather traditional hierarchical lines, and the "Leftists", who advocated developing the more spontaneous system of workers' control (cf. Daniels 1960: 81–87). Lenin's immediate goal at this time was not Communism, but state capitalism, and retention for the time being of the old administrative structure was of some importance to intellectuals. It meant that a head-on conflict with the "bourgeoisie" was no longer being sought, and that greater emphasis would be placed on the intrinsic value of education and skills. Hints and rumors to this effect circulated throughout March without any official confirmation or denial. Then, on the 29th, Lunačarskij let the cat out of the bag in an interview with *Novaja žizn'*. There he stated quite frankly that "The Soviet regime has nothing against trying to find a certain *modus vivendi* with the most intelligent and creative strata of the bourgeoisie" (NŽ 1918: 29.3).

Lenin immediately characterized Lunačarskij's remarks as "nonsense" (VO 1918: 1.4), and there were even rumors that the commissar would be forced to resign for his indiscretion (VO 2.4, 6.4.1918), but the interview nonetheless produced a "tremendous sensation" among intellectuals in Moscow (VO 1918: 1.4), and most newspapers carried new reports and opinions during the following week. Lenin's irritation becomes more understandable in light of the fact that the question of the relationship of the Soviets to the "bourgeois specialists" was being prepared at that very moment for discussion at a Central Committee meeting on 31 March. It was a delicate matter on which the feelings of the Bolshevik Left ran rather high, and Lunačarskij's disclosure can hardly have made things easier for the Leninists. In the end, at any rate, Lenin won out. The "new course", largely due to the escalation of the Civil War later in the spring, did not go as far as some had hoped and others feared, but for a short time the "anti-intelligentsia" crusade had abated.

"The Tragedy of the Intelligentsia"

In the atmosphere of qualified thaw that followed Brest-Litovsk intellectuals returned to a discussion of their past and future that had been interrupted by the events of October. The center of the debate was a meeting organized by the Petrograd Union of Russian Writers on the theme "the tragedy of the intelligentsia". It may well be possible to consider the gathering as a kind of response to Lunačarskij's announcement of a policy change. It was first announced on 30 March, to take place the following day. Public discussions of this sort were generally advertised at least a week in advance; one easily gets the impression that the organizers were anxious to stimulate debate while themes relating to the intelligentsia were still the issue of the day. Whether or not this was their express intention, the moment appears to have been well chosen, at least in the opinion of many intellectuals themselves (cf. NV 1918: 5.4).

The composition of the audience and the list of speakers is of some interest. The correspondent of the left Menshevik daily *Večernie ogni* characterized the gathering, which was evidently quite large, as follows:

Те же лица на эстраде и почти та же публика.

За председательским столом те же спокойные, уравновешенные Венгеров и Батюшков, несколько сотрудников Русского Богатства и Русских Ведомостей ... задумчивое, утомленное лицо "бабушки" Брешко-Брешковской ...

Вместо студентов — больше защитные куртки прапорщиков.

Много почтенных дам и курсисток и той типичной публики, которая непременно посещала все вечера союза и литературного фонда и из года в год "поминала" Чернышевского, Некрасова и Надсона, облюбованных нашей интеллигентской кружковщиной.

(VO 1918: 1.4)

S. Vengerov was a well known liberal literary historian and critic; F. D. Batjuškov had been an editor of the "legal Marxist" journal *Mir Božij* and head of State Theaters under the Provisional Government; *Russkoe Bogatstvo* was a prominent populist journal; *Russkie Vedomosti* was the Moscow Kadet daily; E. K. Breško-Breškovskaja was the grand old lady of the "People's Will" movement, recently returned from ten years of Siberian exile.

The liberal-populist coloring of the audience corresponds to what might be termed the ideological nucleus of the traditional intelligentsia. The reporter, who stands several degrees to the left, understandably maintains his somewhat ironical distance. Examining the list of speakers, we find this same nucleus, with the addition of other elements. It included A. M. Red'ko, the keynote speaker, who was an editor of *Russkoe Bogatstvo*; V. K. Agafonov, earlier in the left opposition in the SR party and a contributor to *Mir Božij*; A. A. Gizetti, biographer of Lavrov and Mixajlovskij, P. Ryss, a leading Kadet and contributor to *Naš Vek* (formerly *Reč'*); V. A. Bazarov, co-editor of the left Menshevik *Novaja Žizn'*; L. G. Dejč, editor of the Plexanovite *Edinstvo*; A. S. Potresov, the right-wing Menshevik editor of *Den'*; and M. P. Nevedomskij, formerly an editor of *Mir Božij* and now a prominent Menshevik (VO 1918: 30.3).

The meeting thus had a fairly clear political profile. With the possible exception of Bazarov, whose (recently adopted) "internationalist" position places him slightly to the left, all of the speakers were somewhere on the liberal to moderate socialist spectrum, with a predominance of populists and right Mensheviks. Most of them were in addition active party leaders or publicists. This is not to suggest that the gathering should be interpreted exclusively as a political manifestation, but it does reflect a certain political reality. The parties of the "left center" represented in this discussion of intellectuals' problems would some two weeks later formally establish a coalition known as the Union for the Regeneration of Russia (*Sojuz Vozrož-*

denija Rossii), dedicated to a reassertion of state authority and a reunification of Russian territories, through renewed war with Germany if need be (cf. Rosenberg 1974: 291–292).

"Who is to Blame?"

Judging by the two lengthy reports we have of it, the March 31 meeting was a typical intelligentsia gathering—lively and somewhat inconclusive. Observers not immediately involved in the debate tended to look upon it as just another cliquish squabble with little bearing on real life. "*Tragikomedija*", the title of one report, says something of its reception in these quarters (PÈ 1918: 3.4). Another journalist on the same newspaper commented a few days later:

> Вообще все эти споры и разговоры об интеллигенции чрезвычайно симптоматичны для нашей истории, когда интеллигенция загоняется в тупик, и вместо дела, начинает разбираться в своем паспорте.
>
> (PÈ 1918: 6.4)

The reporter from *Večernie ogni* concluded his account:

> Вместо того, чтобы спасать Россию, каждый отгородился своими загородками и в своих мечтах и теориях создает свой собственный строй и свое государство.
>
> Сегодня сошлись, немного поспорили и поволновались, а завтра как вчера будут снова ругать друг друга "дураками".
>
> Вот она русская, безысходная трагедия.
>
> (VO 1918: 1.4)

As we look back upon the 1918 debate, however, we can see that the analyses presented there were not as much at variance with one another as they may have seemed in the polemical heat of the moment. Most of the viewpoints aired at the meeting and in the subsequent discussion in the press rested on certain common observations and assumptions. The first of these was a universal disillusionment with the masses and a consequent revision of the intelligentsia's traditional altruistic social committment. A. M. Red'ko developed the point, beginning with a by now familiar lament:

> Сто тридцать лет существовала русская интеллигенция [Dating from Radiščev's *Putešestvie* in 1789?] и в награду получила шапку-

невидимку. Вдруг ничего не оказалось: кроме пролетариата и буржуазии так таки и нет никакой интеллигенции.

(VO 1918: 1.4)

Two factors were responsible for this extinction. The first was an irreconcilable antagonism between the intellectual and the crowd:

Тут докладчик делает большое отступление. Он обобщает трагедию русской интеллигенции с трагедией мировой интеллигенции, противопоставляет два класса — простаков и интеллигентов ... Еще больше внимания уделяет он знахарству, кузнецам, к которым во все века, начиная с мифического Прометея, похитившего небесный огонь — народ относился с подозрением и недоверием.

(VO 1918: 1.4)

The masses looked upon the intelligentsia as a parasite, since intellectuals did not participate directly in the production of material riches:

У интеллигенции спрашивают, что она создает? Она не может ответить на этот вопрос на понятном для массы языке и ей отвечают, что трудятся только те, которые стоят у станка: об остальных говорят трафаретной фразой: "довольно вы нашей кровушки попили".

(VO 1918: 1.4)

Here we are back on familiar ground. Sologub, it will be remembered, had begun from similar premises and postulated an inherent conflict of interests between the "intelligentsia" and the "thing-makers" (see above p. 77). And by the same twist of argumentation, Red'ko also concedes the contentions of his anti-intellectual adversaries. One of the intelligentsia's greatest mistakes, he continued, was that it had scorned industry, preferring instead to work in professions that were of more immediate benefit to the people—teachers, agronomists, doctors, etc. In other words, and this was the second sin, in idealizing the people and sacrificing itself for the people the intelligentsia had ignored its true calling, which must be concluded to be intellectual labor, with or without any immediate social application:

Во имя верховенства народа русская интеллигенция сама отказывалась от своей роли, от своего обаяния и приняла деятельное участие в разрушении культуры России. Трагедия русской интеллигенции в том, что она сама себя не уважала, что провозглашая "все для народа" идеализировала этот народ и довела до того, что он не сознает размера переживаемых бедствий.

(VO 1918: 1.4)

The same point was made later by one of those present at the meeting. The tragedy of the intelligentsia, the observer maintained, lay in its constant self-effacement and self-humiliation, its readiness to declare its own nothingness and bow down before the "mighty peasant" or the "mighty proletariat" to beg for salvation. The growing mood now, however, demanded "more faith in the power of knowledge, in culture, in ourselves" (NV 1918: 2.4). We have seen similar demands before. The claims for autonomy that arose in connection with the SDI dispute in March 1917 ultimately rested on much the same rejection of tradition, much the same feeling that the intrinsic worth of artistic and intellectual enterprise had been insufficiently recognized in Russia. Then, however, such demands were advanced by a relatively small group of artists insisting on control over their professional sphere. What we are witnessing a year later is a much broader revaluation of tradition by intellectuals who until recently had been among its most ardent supporters. Enlarging the historical context somewhat, the shift can be seen to be highly reminiscent of the criticism expressed earlier in the *Vexi* collection, a similarity which is probably due more to common experiences than to direct influence. Intellectuals who had earlier tended to regard the *vexovcy* as both alarmist and elitist were now drawn toward many of the same conclusions.

The rest of the meeting seems to have been largely dominated by two Mensheviks, A. N. Potresov and M. N. Nevedomskij. The Mensheviks, in particular the right wing, were prey to much of the same disillusionment with the Russian people as their non-Marxist colleagues. If the Populists had idealized the peasant, they had been guilty of the same naivety with respect to the proletariat. As one speaker at a slightly later gathering noted:

На рабочий класс возлагалась особая миссия: существовал предрассудок, что на каждого рабочего, лишь только он ста-

91

новится к станку — мистически нисходит сознание. Но этого не оказалось. Бернштейн свидетельствует, что германские рабочие находятся в состоянии отупения после войны. А у нас в рабочих, крестьянских и иных комитетах повсюду вытесняются лучшие, а остальные приспособляются к звериным инстинктам.

(VO 1918: 8.4)

There was general agreement, then, that the masses had proven themselves ignorant and savage, incapable of appreciating higher cultural values. Where Potresov differed with Red'ko (and Ryss, who supported Red'ko) was that he did not subscribe to the same eternal antagonism between the intellectual and non-intellectual, but regarded the rejection of the intelligentsia as resulting from the backwardness of Russian society. In the West the situation was different:

В Европе ничего подобного нет: там все рабочие дисциплинированы, все несут тяготы войны, но в то же время и в той же Германии существует серьезное движение оспаривающее социалистическое движение рабочих.

(VO 1918: 1.4)

"Discipline" is the key word here. According to Potresov, the whole of Russian society—the masses, the intelligentsia and even the bourgeoisie—were undisciplined. What this meant in terms of concrete reality was insufficient support of the war effort. Instead of uniting in a solid front against Germany, Russia disintegrated into a myriad of warring factions, each pursuing its narrow class interests. The radical intelligentsia bore a great deal of responsibility for this decomposition of national consciousness. M. Nevedomskij lashed out:

Интеллигенция совершила страшное преступление, да преступление! (взрыв апплодисментов) именно тем, что долбила народу, что война эта — дело рук буржуазии.

Что война — антинародна, народу не нужна. Долбили темному, невежественному мужику — ну и додолбились. Произошла революция — стал мужик искать виновников. За все и платит буржуазия.

(VZ 1918: 2.4)

The Mensheviks at the meeting thus emphasized the intelligentsia's proper nature as the repository of national consciousness, a trend we have observed from very early in the Revolution. Whereas the notion of "patriotic classlessness" was, as we have noted, a minor adjustment for a liberal or a populist, for a Marxist it implied a rejection of that critique of the intelligentsia notion and a return to more traditional concepts. In the Marxist model, each class had its own intelligentsia, its leadership, quite simply, which was an organic part of the class in question (cf. Polonskij 1924: 15). The notion of one unified Intelligentsia was illusory. Potresov's observation that in Europe "there is no detached intelligentsia crowned with a halo of political struggle" would seem to follow this line of reasoning. Each class has its interests and its intelligentsia to lead it in pursuing them. The workers' movement defends proletarian interests, and the bourgeoisie is naturally conservative. European intellectuals, however, being better disciplined in the performance of "national tasks" than their Russian counterparts, have been able to reconcile these narrow class interests with the needs of the entire nation. This, of course, is a very un-Marxist rejection of the primacy of the class struggle, and was at the heart of the dispute between "internationalist" and "defensist" Mensheviks.

Red'ko's and Potresov's viewpoints taken together provide a fairly representative picture of the dominant attitudes among intellectuals at this time. On the one hand, there was an increasing tendency to reject the intelligentsia tradition that had insisted on the primacy of social commitment and selfless devotion to the people as its ethical code. Red'ko reflects a trend we have seen earlier that insisted instead on the need for a new "selfishness" on the part of intellectuals, a demand that they attend to their own interests, which were often in conflict with those of the masses. On the other hand, there was a call—which we have also seen before—for more patriotism, "discipline" or "state consciousness" ("*gosudarstvennost*'") as it was sometimes termed. The two reactions differ in emphasis rather than substance. Both are based on the conviction that intellectuals have been denied the leadership of the country that they rightfully deserve. Both blame the situation on the "uncultured" people and their leftist political opponents, for whom, in the words of one conservative commentator on the debate, "Russia and Russian culture do not exist as a living fact, as a permanent value of a non-class, universal essence" (NV 1918: 10.4). The "left-center" intellectuals who spoke at the March 31 meeting and in the press afterwards presented for the most part only variations on this theme.

"What Should be Done?"

Intellectuals opposed to the Bolshevik regime were universally aware that they had come to a *cul-de-sac*. The very title of the March 31 discussion, "the tragedy of the intelligentsia", is indicative of this consciousness. The "change of course" was a mixed blessing: if it meant a certain relaxation of the general hostility toward intellectuals, it also seemed to conceal the risk that many would be absorbed as docile servants of the new regime.

> Выйти ... надо, по возможности скорее. Жизнь не ждет. Пока одни погрузились в раздумье, так или иначе приспособляются: бессознательно, инстинктивно. Или под тем или иным благовидным предлогом, идут на "казенную службу" или ... становятся "газетчиками", "дворниками" и т. д.
>
> (NV 1918: 13.4)

But could intellectuals recapture anything of the role they had hoped to play in the first months of the Revolution? Were the only alternatives capitulation or rejection?

Politically, there were some hopes of establishing a viable opposition. The Union of Regeneration was just such an attempt. It came to little, however, partly because of internal discord and partly because the escalating civil war soon rendered all organized opposition illegal.

The cultural sphere was perhaps a shade brighter. For one thing, the Bolsheviks had not yet succeeded in consolidating their control over cultural life, and March and April witnessed a number of attempts to resist the extension of their power. One such initiative came from the SDI, which was roused into active opposition by Lunačarskij's decision of April 12 to abolish the Academy of Art. The decision stood firm, however, and the debate ended abruptly in May (cf. N. Å. Nilsson's article, this volume). F. Sologub headed another attempt to organize the literary section of the SDI into a trade union capable of defending writers' "material and spiritual interests" (NŽ 1918: 12.3). This Union of Belletrists (*Sojuz dejatelej xudožestvennogo slova*) also met with limited success. Although it continued to exist for over a year, it never attained quite the power its founders had hoped for (cf. Scherr 1977, Širmakov 1957). There was, however, another and much broader organizational effort that deserves mention, if only because it has largely been ignored.

"Culture and Freedom": A New "Going to the People"

We noted at the beginning of our survey that a great many intellectuals greeted the February Revolution as an opportunity to realize their traditional *kulturträger* ideals—a "renewal of Russia" through education and the diffusion of humanistic cultural values. We have also seen that these hopes soon ran aground, partly due to differences among intellectuals themselves, partly because of the rapidly deteriorating political situation. After a year of revolution, there was still no organization independent of the Bolsheviks that was capable or willing to set about the enormous task of enlightening Russia.

Finally, however, the first steps toward creating such an organization were taken in the spring of 1918. On 7 April a large gathering of predominantly socialist intellectuals met in the Činzelli Circus in Petrograd and formally founded the society "Culture and Freedom" (*Kul'tura i svoboda*). The name itself tells us a good deal about the ideas and ideals that motivated the founders. First of all, it has a rather familiar ring to it. One is reminded of the short-lived journal *Svoboda i Kul'tura* of 1906, edited by S. Frank. The dominant theme in that publication, which appeared in the wake of the Kadets' electoral successes, was that the Revolution was a cultural triumph, meaning that liberal ideals were taking root among the people (cf. Brooks 1972: 84). "Culture and Freedom" was founded on exactly the opposite conclusion, namely that the 1917 revolutions had failed to advance the spread of humanist values in Russia. Gor'kij, chairman of the new organization, summarized the situation in his speech to the first public meeting:

> Можем ли мы по совести сказать, что за год революции русский народ, освободившийся от насилия и гнета полицейско-чиновничьего строя, стал лучше, добрее, умнее, честнее?
>
> Нет, ни один правдивый человек не скажет этого ... Своекорыстие, жадность и злоба, воспитанные старым строем, остались с нами. Люди так же грабят и обманывают друг друга, как всегда обманывали и грабили. ...
>
> Все дурное в человеке освобождено, человек оголился изнутри, и бесстыдно показывает срам своей души ...
>
> (VZ 1918: 10.4)

The full name of the organization, "Culture and Enlightenment Society in Commemoration of February 27", is expressive, being at once an admission that the ideals that had inspired the February Revolution had been betrayed, and a declaration that it was still not too late to revive them. Intellectuals had been pressed into silence and internal exile by the course of events. Under this pressure, as we have seen, many of them revalued their traditional self-image and role, turning to ideals that were openly bourgeois and/or nationalist and elitist. What we are witnessing now is an organized resurgence of the old mission. The editorial in the first issue of the organization's publication *Vestnik Kul'tury i Svobody* spoke in familiar terms of "resurrecting" Russia through the "quantitative expansion of culture, its penetration into the depths of the masses, and the transformation through culture of the native talent of the Russian people" (VKS I 1918: 3).

The non-partisan, super-class nature of this great cultural task was emphasized. Gor'kij wrote of the organization in May:

> Задача демократической и пролетарской интеллигенции — об"единение всех интеллектуальных сил страны на почве культурной работы. Но для успеха этой работы следует отказаться от партийного сектанства ... та часть интеллигенции, которая настроена наименее сектантски ... начинает чувствовать необходимость широкой культурной работы ... Об этом говорит попытка представителей различных политических взглядов организовать внепартийное общество под девизом: "Культура и Свобода" ...
>
> (NŽ 1918: 1.5)

"Culture and Freedom" was indeed open to all who shared its goals, but in practice it was an almost exclusively socialist undertaking. While one finds the names of liberals such as S. A. Vengerov, Countess Panina, S. Ol'denberg and F. D. Batjuškov among those active in the organization, the bulk of the leadership were Social Democrats or populists of varying shades. Among the latter can be mentioned Vera Figner, V. G. Arxangel'skij and V. I. Zasulič, among the former L. M. Bramson, V. A. Bazarov and G. V. Plexanov (VKS I 1918: 50). This in itself is indicative of the split that had occurred among intellectuals during the first year of revolution: most liberals, and even a good many populists and other socialists, were either unable or unwilling to contribute to what was certainly one of the most concerted efforts intellectuals ever made to realize organizationally their traditional enlightenist ideals. The *kulturträger* intelligentsia had by 1918 definitely shifted toward the left.

Just how united this broad grouping was in practice is difficult to determine. There were differences in outlook among its leading members that in the long run might well have proved difficult to reconcile. From the beginning, in fact, "Culture and Freedom" failed to attract the support of many left Mensheviks, who were repelled by what they felt to be an excessively negative attitude towards the people on the part of the well-represented socialist right. *Večernie ogni*, for example, noted in a report from the April 7 meeting significantly entitled "Tragedija socializma":

> Исходная точка и у буржуев и у социалистов одна и та же: народ, не оправдавший себя и тех надежд, которые на него возлагали. Он совершил революцию, но он оказался способным только на разрушение и не сумел ничего создать. Выводы самые мрачные. ... После многих речей с тяжелым чувством расходился народ.
>
> (VO 1918: 8.4)

There was a danger, and many within the organization as well must have been aware of it, that the whole project would revert to the old paternalism. *Večernjaja zvezda* observed of the speeches at the meeting:

> ... в них звучала отчужденность, хоть и невольная, от широкой массы, свойственная всем речам "интеллигентщины", которая не могла не оставить собравшуюся аудиторию довольно холодной. А ведь общество рассчитывает пойти в самую гущу, и об установлении с ней внутренней, не чисто формальной связи (по типу: "я поучаю, а ты слушай"), — ему следует подумать.
>
> (VZ 1918: 8.4)

A second possible obstacle to achieving the broad support Gor'kij hoped for came from another "younger" generation of intellectuals, this time those with a specifically proletarian background. The appeal of "Culture and Freedom" was for a union between the "old" and the "new" intelligentsias. Gor'kij himself was the incarnation of such an alliance, but many of the "younger" elements, those, for example, who gravitated toward Proletkul't, did not agree on its desirability. Polemizing with the article of 1 May quoted above, for example, one critic objected to the notion that the intelligentsia should play the leading role in diffusing culture. Instead of "Culture and Freedom", he advocated creating a "United Workers' Party", stressing the workers' desire to rise upward to culture by their own efforts (NŽ 1918: 15.5). Gor'kij immediately answered the attack with the familiar contention that his opponent did not understand the true, "humanitarian, deeply idealistic content" of the concept "culture". The majority of workers regarded socialism only as an economic doctrine designed to satisfy the egoism of the working class. They failed to realize that socialism was for all mankind, all classes, that it was not merely a political and economic analysis, but the highest stage of human cultural achievement (NŽ 1918: 16.5).

Unfortunately, the thus far limited body of materials at our easy disposal makes it difficult to determine both the full extent of the activities of "Culture and Freedom" and the degree to which differences on goals and methods may have affected it. *Vestnik Kul'tury i Svobody* appeared in at least four issues in July and August, 1918, but only the first of these was available at this writing, requests for the others from the Soviet Union having proved fruitless. Judging from this one report, however, the society appears to have been both energetic and businesslike. The list of organizations that had joined it by July is a long one, ranging from teachers' unions to workers' clubs to consumers' societies to cooperatives (cf. VKS I 1918: 39–40). A network of contacts had been established with other parts of Russia through a special interurban section (*inogorodnyj otdel*) set up already on 22 April, and considerable space was devoted in the journal to reports from the provinces. An advisory bureau was organized in Petrograd, to which other groups could apply for lecturers, aid in organizing courses, concerts, theatrical events, etc. (VKS I 1918: 50–52). A book section was devoted to setting up libraries and establishing a publishing house. A central stock of books was collected in Petrograd in May and June through voluntary donations stimulated by a series of public lectures. The drive yielded some 20 000 books and 900 000 brochures and pamphlets (VKS I 1918: 52–54). The article section included contributions by Gor'kij, "On Civic Education"; V. Zelenko, "Fundamental Questions of Cultural and Educational Work"; V. Arxangel'skij, "Cultural Work in the Provinces"; A. Aleksandrovič, "The Basic Tasks of Cultural and Educational Work in the Area of Art"; I. Kubikov, "Workers' Clubs in Petrograd"; and L. Bramson, "The Origin of the 'Culture and Freedom' Society, its Tasks and First Steps".

Even this cursory summary of a single issue of the society's publication clearly distinguishes "Culture and Freedom" from the organizational attempts that preceded it. It may well have accomplished more in the first two months of its existence than organizations such as the SDI and the Writers' Union managed to do in over eighteen months. This was no doubt facilitated by the fact that the leaders of Gor'kij's organization were, the reservations noted notwithstanding, in far better agreement as to its function and general objectives. In addition and certainly just as importantly, they were spurred by a sense of urgency which we in retrospect can easily see should have been felt a year earlier. We can only speculate on the effects the initiative might have had had it occurred then.

Summer 1918: Silence

The debate on the intelligentsia that blossomed up in the spring of 1918 came to a sudden end in the summer. Faced with a full-scale civil war and with their territory reduced to the center of Russia around the capitals, the Bolsheviks had by July banned practically all oppositional publications, thus effectively terminating public discussion. The one known attempt to continue it, a collection of essays by many of the original *Vexi* group entitled *Iz glubiny*, was printed in July but immediately seized, and did not become generally available until 1969, when it was republished in the West.

The exact fate of "Culture and Freedom" is as yet unclear. Soviet sources are conspicuously sparing in their treatment of the organization and Gor'kij's role in it. As late as October it published his *Untimely Thoughts*, in itself remarkable in view of the general situation. The attempt on Lenin's life in August was followed by the beginning of the Red Terror, when opposition in any form was likely to be interpreted as counterrevolution. Gor'kij himself, partly, no doubt, on personal conviction and perhaps also because he correctly perceived he could exert a moderating influence, made his peace with the Bolshevik regime. On 4 September he and Lunačarskij signed an agreement establishing the World Literature (*Vsemirnaja Literatura*) project. On 6 October he and G. Zinov'ev addressed a mass meeting in Petrograd on the theme "The Intelligentsia and the Revolution", where he appealed to intellectuals to abandon their "ragged umbrella of neutrality" and cooperate with the Bolshevik regime (PP 1918: 13.10). This meeting should perhaps be established as the final point of the discussion we have been considering. The problem of the intellectual's relationship to the new society was not suddenly resolved, but any further discussion of it was forced to proceed on much different premises.

Summary and Conclusions

As Ovsjaniko-Kulikovskij's remark quoted in the introduction to this study correctly notes, Russian intellectuals were throughout their history plagued by questions of identity and purpose which had occupied their Western counterparts much less intensively. If it can be stated that it is to some extent the intellectual's lot in all societies and ages to be at variance with the community at large, which seldom if ever fully shares his ideals and aspirations, in the relatively unsophisticated social structure of the underdeveloped country it becomes possible to speak of mass intellectual isolation and alienation. Such alienation and the conditions producing it are indeed the factors that give the term "intelligentsia" its specific content. Unless by the word is meant a broad and vaguely defined stratum roughly corresponding to "white-collar workers" or the like, it seems inappropriate to speak of a "French intelligentsia" or "English intelligentsia" as equivalent to the 19th-century Russian phenomenon. The more diversified the society, the more developed its political and institutional infrastructure, the less relevant it becomes to refer to intellectuals as an ideologically cohesive entity striving toward a set of universally beneficial goals. Intellectuals choose sides and join parties, and whereas it is perhaps only human to interpret one's own preferences as valid for all groups, they do not generally, on the basis of their activity as intellectuals, claim membership in any superior, classless, selfless grouping held together by adherence to such principles.

In Russia there were considerably fewer natural obstacles to the development of this sort of thinking. Intellectuals were in a sense "united", because there was a lack of effective channels of adaptation. Yet the true substance of this unity can well be questioned. As Müller (1971) has shown in detail, the spread of the term "intelligentsia" in the latter half of the 19th century was accompanied by an often heated debate on what it actually denoted. Practically all intellectuals agreed on the objective existence of such an intellectual superstructure in Russian society, and all those who claimed membership in it generally maintained that the intelligentsia's ideals were some shade of "democratic", "progressive", "anti-Philistine", etc., but beyond this one encounters a myriad of mutually hostile groups, each advocating, often in extremely uncompromising terms, its own interpretation and solution. Hence the eternal accusations of "cliquishness" that mark much of the discussion. Intellectuals themselves tended to regard this love of bickering (*gryzoljubie*, as one commentator dubbed it (VO 1918: 10.4)) as an intrinsic feature of the Russian intellectual's mentality. Perhaps it was, but one is also justified in wondering whether such eternal discord on questions relating to self-image and purpose might not reflect more than a merely psychological reality. In other words, how adequately did the concept "intelligentsia" reflect the objective position of the intellectual in Russian society?

The above survey would seem to argue for the view that it did so but very inadequately. Intellectuals entered the Revolution in the opposite belief, namely that the upheaval was a confirmation of the intelligentsia and its tradition of struggle against the autocracy. For a short time, the "intelligentsia" found itself in the position of leadership it had long claimed by virtue of its intellectual and moral superiority. Now all that remained was to translate ideals into reality—the intelligentsia's reality, in which social and philosophical differences would be resolved in a humanist spirit of mutual respect. The time for squabbling was over, the time for action had come.

This vision of national harmony was as naive as it was widespread, extending from conservatives even to many Bolsheviks, who were willing at the outset to support the Provisional Government and needed dissuading by Lenin to recover their revolutionary purpose. It rested on two interrelated premises: first, that the "intelligentsia" was in broad agreement as to general goals and priorities, and secondly that the people were willing to recognize the legitimacy of its leadership. We have seen that both of these assumptions were belied almost immediately. Concentrating on the cultural rather than the political sphere, where the breakdown was even more obvious, we have seen that the intelligentsia's traditional enlightenist ideals were not nearly as unanimously shared as had been believed. A small but energetic

101

group of cultural intellectuals was adamantly opposed to the official interference which the practical implementation of the intelligentsia's cultural mission almost inevitably entailed, and this disunity on such basic questions was in no small measure responsible for the weakness of organizational efforts in the cultural area during the first months of the Revolution.

The overthrow of the Tsar, then, did not serve to give intellectuals the sense of identity and purpose they had been groping for for so long. They were no closer to knowing what the intelligentsia was than before. When they were subsequently rejected by the masses and branded as enemies, the discussion entered its final phase. Old notions and definitions were rapidly abandoned. Some intellectuals turned to patriotic appeals to re-establish their authority. The humanist, cosmopolitain intelligentsia became a national intelligentsia. Others openly declared their adherence to the bourgeoisie, which implied a break with the non-partisanship and anti-Philistinism that had been important cohesive factors in the traditional intelligentsia notion. Still others rejected the altruism and social commitment that represented other defining characteristics, insisting instead that intellectuals pursue their own interests regardless of whether these coincided with those of other social classes.

All of these trends were present even before the Revolution, but the events of 1917–1918 accelerated and extended them. As Russia plunged deeper and deeper into social strife, the idea of a single intellectual or moral superstructure capable of resolving such conflicts became increasingly less applicable. The notion continued to exist, but reality was quite simply outstripping it. Even without the Revolution, Russia had for some time been evolving toward the same sort of economical, political and social diversity characteristic of modern Western societies, and it was only a matter of time before the "intelligentsia" would have to be exchanged for concepts that would more accurately reflect such sophistication. The Bolshevik Revolution may have put a somewhat sudden and artifical end to a long debate, but the classical question "What is the intelligentsia?" was already giving way to "Is there (a need for) an intelligentsia?" Russian intellectuals were themselves not entirely unaware of the shift. F. D. Batjuškov noted in a contribution to the debate of April 1918 that brings us back to Ovsjaniko-Kulikovskij's distinction between the Russian intelligentsia and Western intellectuals:

Теперешний кризис может привести к тому, что понятие об "интеллигенции" утратит свое специфическое значение, что оно вскоре станет анахронизмом, — ибо раз "классы" сами себя отстаивают, то им и не нужно опекунов и родителей; но в выгрыше останутся и сами "интеллигенты", обратившиеся просто в "образованных тружеников" на разных поприщах умственной жизни, и сам народ, который будет знать своих лучших представителей, — при свободном доступе для всех и каждого, обладающего нужными данными, — в области чистого и прикладного знания, в области искусства и даже спекулятивной мысли.

(NV 1918: 2.4)

An overly optimistic prediction, perhaps, but nonetheless based on a sound observation: the "intelligentsia" had become a mere abstraction and should be abandoned. The sooner Russian intellectuals realized this, the sooner they would find a meaningful identity and role. How and in what measure they succeeded in doing so are themes that belong to the first chapter of their contemporary history.

Bibliography

Benois, A. N.
1977 "Revoljucija v xudožestvennom mire" (14/27.5.1917), reprinted in: *Aleksandr Benua razmyšljaet*, M. 1968.
Blok, A. A.
1962 *Sobranie sočinenij v vos'mi tomax*, t. VI (Moskva–Leningrad).
Brooks, Jeffrey Peter
1972 *Liberalism, Literature, and the Idea of Culture in Russia, 1905–1914* (Unpublished doctoral dissertation, Stanford University).
Brower, Daniel R.
1967 "The Problem of the Russian Intelligentsia", *Slavic Review* XXVI (4), 638–647.
Daniels, R. V.
1960 *The Conscience of the Revolution. Communist Opposition in Soviet Russia* (Clarion Books, New York 1969).
1961 "Intellectuals and the Russian Revolution", *ASEER* XX, 270–278.
Dinerštejn, E. A.
1958 "Majakovskij v fevrale–oktjabre 1917 g.", *Literaturnoe nasledstvo*, t. 65, 541–571 (Moskva).

Elkin, Boris
1961 "The Russian Intelligentsia on the Eve of the Revolution", in: *The Russian Intelligentsia*, ed. by Richard Pipes (Columbia University Press, New York).
Erman, L. K.
1966 *Intelligencija v pervoj russkoj revoljucii* (Moskva).
Fedjukin, S. A.
1972 *Velikij oktjabr' i intelligencija* (Moskva).
Fitzpatrick, Sheila
1970 *The Commissariat of Enlightenment. Soviet Organization of Education and the Arts under Lunacharsky, October 1917–1921* (The Cambridge University Press, Cambridge).
Graña, César
1964 *Bohemian versus Bourgeois. French Society and the French Man of Letters in the Nineteenth Century* (Basic Books, Inc., New York–London).
Ivanov-Razumnik, R.
1906 *Istorija russkoj obščestvennoj mysli*, Čast' I, Izd. 5-oe, pererabotannoe (Revoljucionnaja mysl', Pg. 1918).
Jangfeldt, Bengt
1976 *Majakovskij and Futurism 1917–1921* (Almqvist & Wiksell, Stockholm).
Kim, M. P.
1968 *Sovetskaja intelligencija. Istorija formirovanija i rosta 1917–1965 gg.* (Moskva).
Lampert, E.
1965 *Sons against Fathers. Studies in Russian Radicalism and Revolution* (Oxford University Press, Oxford).
Majakovskij, V. V.
1959 *Polnoe sobranie sočinenij v trinadcati tomax*, t. XII (Moskva).
Makovskij, Sergej
1917 "Ministerstvo Iskusstv", *Apollon* 2–3 (fevral'–mart), i–xvi.
Malia, Martin
1961 "What is the Intelligentsia?" in: *The Russian Intelligentsia*, ed. by Richard Pipes (Columbia University Press, New York).
Mokul'skij, S.
1933 "Petrogradskie teatry ot fevralja k oktjabrju", in: V. Rafalovič (ed.), *Istorija sovetskogo teatra*, t. I, 1917–1921, Leningrad.
Müller, Otto Wilh.
1971 *Intelligencija. Untersuchungen zur Geschichte eines politischen Schlagwortes* (Athenäum Verlag, Frankfurt).
Muratova, K. D.
1958 *M. Gor'kij v bor'be za razvitie sovetskoj literatury* (Moskva–Leningrad).
Oberländer, Gisela
1965 *Die Vechi-Diskussion (1909–1912)* (Doctoral dissertation, Universität zu Köln).

Ovsjaniko-Kulikovskij, D. N.
1908–1911 *Istorija russkoj intelligencii*, vols. 1–3, also in: *Sobranie sočinenij*, t. 7 (1910)–9 (1911) (Prometej, SPb).

Pipes, Richard
1961 "The Historical Evolution of the Russian Intelligentsia", in: *The Russian Intelligentsia*, ed. by Richard Pipes (Columbia University Press, New York).

Polonskij, Vjačeslav
1924 *Uxodjaščaja Rus'. Stat'i ob intelligencii 1920–1924* (Moskva).
1929 *Očerki literaturnogo dviženija revoljucionnoj époxi*, 2-oe izd. (Moskva–Leningrad).

Raeff, Marc
1966 *Origins of the Russian Intelligentsia. The Nineteenth-Century Nobility* (Harbinger Books, New York).

Rosenberg, William G.
1974 *Liberals in the Russian Revolution. The Constitutional Democratic Party, 1917–1921* (Princeton University Press, Princeton N.J.).

Scherr, Barry
1977 "Notes on Literary Life in Petrograd, 1918–1922: A Tale of Three Houses." *Slavic Review* 2 (June) Vol. XXVI, pp. 256–267.

Širmakov, P. P.
1958 "K istorii literaturno-xudožestvennyx ob"edinenij pervyx let Sovetskoj vlasti: Sojuz dejatelej xudožestvennoj literatury (1918–1919 gody). In: *Voprosy sovetskoj literatury*, vol. 7, red. V. A. Kovalev and A. I. Pavlovskij (Moskva–Leningrad).

Struve, P. B.
1909 "Intelligencija i revoljucija", in: *Vexi. Sbornik statej o russkoj intelligencii*, 3-e izdanie (Moskva).
1917 "V čem revoljucija i kontr-revoljucija", *Russkaja mysl'* 11–12, 57–61.

Tompkins, St. R.
1957 *The Russian Intelligentsia. Makers of the Revolutionary State* (Oklahoma University Press, Norman Okla.).

Zimmerman, Judith E.
1976 "The Political Views of the *Vexi* Authors", *Canadian-American Slavic Studies*, 10, No. 3 (Fall, 1976), 307–327.

Bengt Jangfeldt

Russian Futurism 1917–1919

I. An Outline

The task of this review is to analyze the development of Petrograd and Moscow futurism during the first post-revolutionary years: its attitude to the revolution, its relations to the political powers, and its position in cultural life.[1] (For an outline of futurism in other parts of Russia, see Markov 1968, Rappoport 1974, and Jangfeldt 1975 and 1976.)

No matter how the face of futurism changed during these years, there was one person who was always in the front-line: Vladimir Majakovskij. This position he occupied in his broad capacity as poet, playwright, painter, and spokesman for avantgarde ideas. Majakovskij's development is representative—if not in detail, then at least in its general traits—of futurism as a whole. It is therefore both justifiable and convenient to describe "Russian futurism 1917–1919" principally from the point of view of Majakovskij's own development.

The history of post-revolutionary futurism can be divided into two distinct periods. The first one runs from October, 1917, until April, 1918, and can be called "Kafe Poètov futurism"; the second one, which I call "IZO futurism", runs from the fall of 1918 until April, 1919.[2] Between these two periods lies the summer of 1918, which led to fundamental changes in the development of the Russian revolution, politically as well as culturally.

Kafe Poètov Futurism

The first period of post-revolutionary futurism coincided with the militant and anarchistic period of the political revolution. This was the time of "left communism", headed by Buxarin, and of the impatient revolutionism of the left socialist-revolutionaries. But it was also the time of political anarchism, a movement tolerated by the Bolsheviks and, to a certain extent, even enjoying their support, until the middle of April, when the anarchists were raided by the Čeka.

106

The winter and spring of 1918 was also a time of political pluralism within the socialist camp: although most socialists were opposed to Bolshevism, socialist parties and groups were still allowed to exist, and the migration of members between the parties was "still to some extent operative" (Carr 1966: I, 193). This pluralism meant that there existed a freedom of (socialist) thought and expression: one could still be a *non*-Bolshevik socialist without being accused of being *anti*-Bolshevik or *anti*-Soviet. There was as yet no need for anyone with socialist sympathies to make a definite political choice.

It is against this general political background that one must judge the development of futurism as well. The first period of post-revolutionary futurism not only coincided with political pluralism and anarchism; it bore the same traits of revolutionary enthusiasm itself. Immediately after the October revolution, the old cubo-futurists Vladimir Majakovskij, David Burljuk, and Vasilij Kamenskij resumed the café tradition of pre-revolutionary futurism. Disappointed with the cultural program of the Bolsheviks (see section II, "Majakovskij and October"), they chose to continue the *épatage* of early futurism from the stage of the Kafe Poètov in Moscow (hence the designation "Kafe Poètov futurism").

The ideology of "Kafe Poètov futurism" was anti-authoritarian and anarchistic socialism (the three poets gave their group the anarchistically sounding name "Federation of Futurists"). The manifestos published in *The Futurists' Newspaper* (Gazeta Futuristov) on March 15 declared that futurism is the esthetic counterpart of "socialism-anarchism" ("Otkrytoe pis'mo rabočim"), that art should come out onto the streets ("Dekret No 1 o demokratizacii iskusstv"), that the Academy of Art should be abolished and art separated from the state ("Manifest Letučej Federacii Futuristov"), and that only a "Revolution of the Spirit" ("Revoljucija Duxa") can free man from the fetters of old art (Ibidem, and "Otkrytoe pis'mo rabočim"). The manifestos were signed by all three futurists, except "Otkrytoe pis'mo rabočim" which was written by Majakovskij alone.

The separation of art from the state was a demand that had already been presented a year earlier in "Sojuz dejatelej iskusstv" (henceforth SDI), and not only by the futurists but by almost all artists, regardless of political faith. In March, 1918, however, the Academy had still not been abolished, and the issue was as topical as ever.

The "Revolution of the Spirit" was the third revolution that was to come after the political and economical revolutions—a spiritual change without which the revolution would not be complete. The first two revolutions had been successful, but in the cultural field "old art" was till dominant:

Театры попрежнему ставят: "Иудейских" и прочих "царей" (сочинения Романовых[3]), попрежнему памятники генералов, князей — царских любовниц и царицыных любовников тяжкой, грязной ногой стоят на горлах молодых улиц. В мелочных лавочках, называемых высокопарно выставками торгуют чистой мазней барских дочек и дачек в стиле Рококо и прочих Людовиков.

("Manifest Letučej Federacii Futuristov", Jangfeldt 1975, 156)

Against this background Burljuk, Kamenskij, and Majakovskij urged the "proletarians of the factories and the land" to carry through "a third bloodless but cruel revolution, the revolution of the spirit" (Ibidem).

The need for a spiritual change was felt not only by the futurists; the idea was expressed, in more or less identical terms, by people with differing political and esthetical creeds: the scythians (Ivanov-Razumnik, Belyj), Maksim Gor'kij, the anarchists, and others (see Jangfeldt 1976, 68–70). To Majakovskij the "Revolution of the Spirit" was of special importance, and he would return to the idea more than once, during the period of "IZO futurism", and again later (cf. especially the long poem "IV Internacional").

The anarchism of "Kafe Poètov futurism" was not only theoretical but also had a practical side. Thus, for example, in March, at a time when anarchist occupations of private houses were commonplace in the new capital, Moscow, the three futurists occupied a part of the former restaurant, Peterhof, where they planned to organize a "House of free art" ("Dom svobodnogo iskusstva"), a club for what was called in *Gazeta Futuristov* "individualist-anarchism of creation"—"individual'-anarxizm tvorčestva". However, nothing came out of the futurists' occupation—for which the Moscow federation of anarchist groups disclaimed responsibility (UR 1918: 40, 20(7).3)—since they were ousted from the restaurant after only about a week (RU 1918: 43, 21.3). Nevertheless, the anarchist journal *Revolutionary Creation* (Revoljucionnoe tvorčestvo) listed the "House of free art" as one of

Moscow's anarchist clubs and *Gazeta Futuristov* as an organ of anarchism (RT 1918: I/II, 139, 141).

The first period of post-revolutionary futurism ended in April, 1918, when the Kafe Poètov was closed (April 14). The "official" reason for the closing of the café was that the three "whales" of futurism were leaving Moscow in order to propagate futurism in other parts of the Russian republic (see Figaro 1918: 52, 15.4). In fact, the next day Burljuk left the capital,[4] and Kamenskij also disappeared from the Moscow scene; Majakovskij, for his part, spent most of his time from March until June making films.

The end of anarchistic futurism thus coincided with the end of political anarchism; even if the closing of the Kafe Poètov had no direct connection with the Čeka action against the anarchists two days before, the coincidence was by no means accidental—it signalled the end of the "anarchistic" period of the Russian revolution, in politics as well as in culture. The end of "Kafe Poètov futurism" also meant the final dissolution of the "classical" cubo-futurist group.

The Emergence of IZO

Parallel to the anarchistic futurism of Majakovskij, Burljuk, and Kamenskij, the spring of 1918 witnessed the emergence of another group that was to play a decisive rôle in the history of the Russian avant-garde. This was the collegiate formed by the Commissar of Enlightenment, Anatolij Lunačarskij, within Narkompros—IZO, short for "Otdel izobraziteľnogo iskusstva". When, in November, 1917, Lunačarskij had called upon the artists in SDI to cooperate with the new political power, he had met with solid opposition from both the left and the right: art should be autonomous. Given this negative response, Lunačarskij decided to organize, behind the back of SDI, a collegiate that would try to solve one of the most urgent questions facing Narkompros: the reorganization of artistic life, which meant, above all, the abolition of the Academy.

IZO was instituted on January 29, 1918, and initially had seven members (six artists and one art historian): David Šterenberg (head), Čexonin, Aľtman, Karev, Matveev, Jatmanov, Vaulin, and Nikolaj Punin. According to the latter, "these were the only ones to whom the October revolution was not only an inevitable fact, but a necessary fact conditioned by the laws of history" (ŽI 1921: 8.11).[5] The fact that there was at this time only a tiny minority of seven people that was willing to cooperate with the Bolsheviks (and thereby give up the demand that art be separated from the state) is interesting enough; still more significant is the fact that this "semerka" was immediately attacked by SDI for its "treason" against the cause of art. It was not only the conservatives who were against the founding of IZO, but the "left bloc" also "disclaimed responsibility for actions carried out by the persons in question" (NŽ 1918: 9.4./27.3).

The founding of IZO nevertheless had two major consequences: SDI was transformed into a body without any real influence on artistic life; the Academy was abolished, on April 12, and replaced, in October, by the first "free art studies" ("Svomasy").

At the beginning of April, Nikolaj Punin, Natan Al'tman, and the composer Artur Lur'e went to Moscow in order to participate in the organization of an IZO collegiate in the capital, and in connection with this they published a greeting to the Moscow futurists, notably Majakovskij and Tatlin. The tone of the greeting echoed the Moscow futurists' own verbal acrobatics:

> Петербург у вас в гостях эти дни, дорогие товарищи-москвичи, взрывающие станции на дорогах искусства. Осведомляем вас, что академия художеств уже в ящике раз навсегда ... Мы пригнали северную победу, мы — мастера и стальные стержни для ваших красных великих знамен ... Делайте все против охраны буржуазного хлама в искусстве ... Мы у руля. Леворуля! Социалисты великие, ересь, семя, ваши рабочие руки сюда! Вот рычаг, сжимающий прошлое, ненавидимое и вами. Приветствуем вас в Москве, тов. Маяковский и Татлин. Приезжайте к нам в Петербург!
>
> (Anarxija 1918: 39, 9.4. Quoted from Ja. Tugendxol'd, "'Levyj' rul'", Rodina 1918: 16.4)

Two days later, on April 11, a Moscow collegiate was instituted; Tatlin joined it, and even became its head (Xronika 1975, 46). An artist like Malevič, on the other hand, who at this time was very much inclined towards anarchism and wrote articles for the daily newspaper, *Anarchy* (Anarxija), in his reply to the Petrograd greeting accused its authors of being no better than "The World of Art" and "Apollon" (Malevič, 1971, 58–59). As for Majakovskij, it should be noted that he did not join the Moscow collegiate, although he was directly called upon to do so.

110

The Summer of 1918

Several events during the summer of 1918 contributed to the radical change in Russian domestic politics that took place in the fall of the same year. "The Bolshevik Revolution passed through three major crises, three periods when the existence of the Soviet regime was seriously threatened. The first and the greatest of these three crises was during the summer months of 1918, when the area of the Soviet Republic was restricted to a territory which roughly corresponded with that of the Muscovite principality in the fifteenth century [...]" (Chamberlin 1935, 42).

In a couple of months Russia witnessed the escalation of the civil war and foreign intervention; the expulsion, on June 14, of all socialist-revolutionaries of the right and the centre as well as the Mensheviks from membership in the Soviets at all levels, which left only one legal party with the Bolsheviks—the *left* socialist-revolutionaries; the expulsion from the Soviets of the *left* SR's as well, after their attempt during the fifth congress of Soviets, on July 4–6, to overthrow the Bolsheviks; the final closure, in July, of all socialist papers; the assassination of the Czar's family; the assassinations of the socialist leaders, Volodarskij and Urickij, and the attempt, on August 30, to murder Lenin; the beginning of "red terror", by a Čeka decree of September 4.

As a result of this, the Bolsheviks were the only legal party after the summer of 1918. E. H. Carr, the outstanding chronicler of the Russian revolution, concludes: "The events of the summer of 1918 left the Bolsheviks without rivals or partners the ruling party in the state; and they possessed in the Cheka an organ of absolute power" (Carr 1966: I, 177).

This polarization of political life had two important consequences: 1. People had to make a final choice: for or against. The fluidity of membership between the parties that had been conceivable during the spring, was no longer possible. Now there were only two camps, the "whites" and the "reds"; 2. The Bolsheviks, for their part, now needed all the support they could get, and therefore had to make Bolshevik politics more attractive to other socialists. Also, they could no longer afford to challenge the intelligentsia—especially the technical intelligentsia—the way they had done in the spring.

In the political field this meant a more lenient attitude towards the socialist parties which had been banned from the Soviets in the summer. "It was decided [at the sixth All-Russian Congress of Soviets, at the beginning of November, 1918] to hold out an olive branch to the excluded socialist parties—or to accept it when proffered by them" (Carr 1966: I, 179). Even before this decision, the Mensheviks had recognized that the October revolution was "historically necessary", ruled out "all political cooperation with classes hostile to democracy", and promised "direct support of the military forces of the Soviet government against foreign intervention" (Carr 1966: I, 179). In response to this, the Bolsheviks allowed the Mensheviks to resume political activity, and also released all political prisoners "unless a definite charge of counter-revolutionary activities were preferred against them within two weeks of their arrest [...]" (Carr 1966: I, 178). The socialist-revolutionaries soon followed the example of the Mensheviks, and in February, 1919, "decisively rejected any attempt to overthrow the Soviet power by way of armed struggle" (Carr 1966: I, 180). Thus, for a certain period of time a political truce was brought about, even if there could be no doubt as to who dictated the conditions.

The same kind of rapprochement took place between the Bolsheviks and the intelligentsia. When the party reached out a hand, many of those who had previously been critical of Bolshevism accepted the offer. This did not necessarily mean that they had become Bolsheviks; but Bolshevism seemed to many non-Bolsheviks (socialists as well as non-socialists) a better alternative than the ideas for which the "white" side stood.

The example of Maksim Gor'kij is especially interesting in this respect. Until now Gor'kij had been very critical of, and even hostile to the Bolsheviks (see, for instance, his numerous "Untimely thoughts" ("Nesvoevremennye mysli") in *New Life*, Novaja žizn'. On April 9 he had even refused to debate with Zinov'ev before the Petrograd Soviet, the reason being "that the workers are seduced by demagogues like Zinov'ev; that the reckless demagogy of Bolshevism, exciting the black instincts of the masses, puts the working intelligentsia in the tragic position of strangers in their own milieu; and that the Soviet policy is a treacherous policy toward the working class" (NŽ 1918: 9.4/27.3). By September, however, Gor'kij had changed his position, and announced that "the terrorist acts executed against the leaders of the Soviet republic make him embark definitely on the road of close cooperation with it" (IRSL 1967, 698).[6] A month later, on October 6,

112

Gor'kij acted as chairman at a meeting of "the working intelligentsia", at which the representatives of the Bolshevik party called upon the intelligentsia to support the Soviet regime. One of the speakers was none other than Zinov'ev, who formulated the new political situation in this way: "For those who want to work with us, we open the road. [...] In an age like the one we are living through now, neutrality is impossible. [...] School cannot be neutral, art cannot be neutral, literature cannot be neutral. [...] Comrades, there is no choice. [...] And I would advise you [...] to go to the working class" (PP 1918: 13.10). The same kind of appeals were made at this time by other Bolsheviks as well, like Lenin and Radek.[7]

IZO Futurists in Power

The artists were also approached and called upon to side with the revolution. Just as the political leaders had turned to the socialist parties and the working intelligentsia, IZO turned to "the workers and the artists" and welcomed those who had now, one year after the revolution, come to serve "the socialist fatherland"—but only those who supported "contemporary art", who "break and destroy forms in order to create new art" (VNP 1918: 4/5, 14 [September/ October]). The avant-garde character of IZO was further underlined by the fact that the third art debate organized by IZO (on October 24) was devoted to "The futurists and artistic creation". At this meeting the IZO Commissar Punin ardently spoke out in favor of futurism as the art of the proletariat (VNP 1918: 6/8, 89–91).

During the fall of 1918 the IZO collegiates in Petrograd and Moscow—the latter under the leadership of Vladimir Tatlin—were complemented by many of the foremost artists of the day: Kazimir Malevič, Pavel Kuznecov, Il'ja Maškov, Robert Fal'k, Aleksej Morgunov, Ol'ga Rozanova, Vasilij Kandinskij, Baranov-Rossinė, and others. IZO thus became a stronghold of the avant-garde, or the "futurists", as its adherents were usually called.

At this time, the term "futurism" was given a wider and less specific meaning: earlier, the name had been used to designate the "real" futurists, i.e. the cubo-futurists and other groups that called themselves futurists; in the fall of 1918, however, "futurism" became synonymous with "avant-garde", "left art", and so on—all non-realists, regardless of whether they were futurists, cubists, suprematists, constructivists, etc., were called "futurists" by the critics. For the sake of simplicity, the "left-wing artists" themselves gradually accepted this rather imprecise definition.

Majakovskij and Osip Brik also began to work with IZO in the fall of 1918. They were both socialists, but when the Petrograd and Moscow collegiates were instituted in the spring of 1918, they had not joined them. On the contrary, Brik had devoted a number of articles (all printed in Menshevik newspapers) in December, 1917, and January, 1918, to criticism of the Bolsheviks' cultural program (for a discussion of these articles, see the section "Os'ka's noble letter", pp. 121). And, as we have seen, Majakovskij did not join the Moscow collegiate when he was specially invited to do so in April. Nor did he publish the few poems he wrote in the Bolshevik press; "Xorošee otnošenie k lošadjam" was in fact published as late as June 9 in Gor'kij's Menshevik paper, *Novaja žizn'* (Moscow edition).

It was thus in the general wave of rapprochement in the fall of 1918 that Majakovskij and Brik finally joined IZO.[8] This also meant that they abandoned the principle of the separation of art from the state expressed in "Manifest Letučej Federacii Futuristov". However, this manifesto was signed by Majakovskij, not by Brik, who as early as January, 1918, had warned against "the deceitful notion of 'autonomy'", which would only be used by the "old generals of art" in order to control art schools and institutions (VZ 1918: 22.1). From this rather obscure and enigmatic article it is clear that Brik obviously had nothing against state-supported art—as long as this art was the art he himself supported. Brik's dualistic position may, in fact, be traced back to Lunačarskij's unsuccessful November gathering of the artists and writers, at which Brik played the part of the Commissar's personal representative (Dinerštejn 1958, 566).

What Brik criticized was thus not state art *per se* but the fact that it was represented by the wrong people, i.e. the advocates of traditional esthetics. By cooperating closely with Narkompros, the futurists could prevent the "old generals of art" from gaining power and influence. Majakovskij and Brik in fact became more closely tied to Narkompros not only through IZO, but also through their own publishing enterprise IMO (Iskusstvo molodyx), which was financed by Narkompros; IMO's first books—*Misterija-buff* and the "revolutionary anthology" *Rye-Word* (Ržanoe slovo)—were published for the first anniversary of the revolution.[9]

One of the first questions raised in the now numerically and intellectually strong Petrograd collegiate was the need for a mouthpiece for IZO futurism. Brik suggested that IZO needed not only a journal but also an "simpler and more flexible" newspaper (IK 1918: 1), and on December 7, 1918, the first issue of *Art of the Commune* (Iskusstvo Kommuny) was published. In January, 1919, it was supplemented by *Art* (Iskusstvo), a similar paper published by the Moscow collegiate. A journal, *Visual Art* (Izobrazitel'noe iskusstvo), was also planned, but only one much-delayed issue was ever published (the foreword was dated May, 1918, the year of publication was given as 1919, but it did not appear until the beginning of 1920).

The most important paper was *Iskusstvo Kommuny* (Petrograd, December, 1918–April, 1919; nineteen issues), with Brik, Punin, and Natan Al'tman as editors. The main contributors (besides the editors themselves) were Malevič, Šagal, Šklovskij, Boris Kušner, and Majakovskij, who published his poems as editorials (for an analysis of Majakovskij's rôle in *Iskusstvo Kommuny*, see Jangfeldt 1976, 30–71).

The main point in the ideology of IZO—as expressed in Majakovskij's poems, for example—was the struggle against the influence of the cultural heritage on the culture of the new society. As I have tried to show earlier (Jangfeldt 1976, 51–63), the futurists did not repudiate the old culture *as such* but fought against the *influence* of this heritage on the new art and literature. The IZO futurists, however, like other avant-garde groups, had a penchant for provocative formulations, and were themselves at times to blame for being misunderstood—not only by their contemporaries, but by later critics as well.

The "new" or "young" art that was to replace old art was, of course, futurism. According to the futurists themselves, futurism was the most advanced art of the time, and therefore the only art worthy of and consonant with the proletariat, historically the most advanced class. Thus futurism was equated with proletarian art. The IZO futurists never gave more precise definitions of these concepts, which were both positively charged and often used as mere catchwords in the debate. All that was "new" and experimental was declared "futurist" and thereby also "proletarian". In retrospect, one can say that "futurism" was what we today unite under the general heading of non-figurative or objectless art ("bespredmetnoe iskusstvo"). The IZO futurists were against all forms of representative art and spoke out in favor of Tatlin and his "material culture" or Malevič with his

115

suprematism (see Punin's article in IK 1919: 10, 2). They also stressed professionalism, talent, and quality; they detested the tendency, so common immediately after the revolution, to take a favorable view of all attempts to create "proletarian art", as long as the artist had a true proletarian ideology and/or background. So, for example, Majakovskij declared that "the attitude of the poet to his material should be just as conscientious as the attitude of a welder to the steel" (Majakovskij 1959, 454).

In this struggle against the influence of the cultural heritage, the futurists came to challenge not only the Proletkul'tists, who often rejected this heritage in words but who—due to lack of esthetic education—depended heavily on the old culture (see Jangfeldt 1976, 72–91), but also many of the esthetically conservative academicians and critics and, what is more, the whole educational policy of the Bolshevik party.

The position occupied by the IZO futurists at the end of 1918 was very strong.[10] They were in charge of art education in the whole republic; they were responsible for the purchases of new art for the museums; and they were able to propagate their ideas in organs published and financed by the Commissariat of Enlightenment. Nevertheless, they were far from satisfied with the speed of the revolution in the cultural field. Nothing had changed since the publication of the manifestos in *Gazeta Futuristov* in March. In December, 1918, therefore, Majakovskij, Brik, and Punin started performing for the workers of the Vyborg District in Petrograd. No doubt the futurists strongly felt the need for a social base on which to stand; they had to prove to the critics—and to the workers!—that they were as close to the proletariat as they themselves claimed to be.

As a result of these contacts, a Communist–Futurist Collective (Kom–Fut) was founded in January, 1919, consisting of Brik and Kušner and a couple of workers. (Since it was a party collective, Majakovskij, who was not a communist, could not participate.) The Kom-Futers claimed that the cultural policy of the Bolsheviks was not revolutionary at all, that the cultural revolution was lagging behind the political and economic ones by more than a year, and that it was now necessary to subject the Soviet organs of culture and enlightenment to a "new [...] cultural communist ideology", in other words, the ideology of the Kom–Fut, which, in turn, was that of IZO.

However, nothing came out of Kom–Fut. It was supposed to be a

116

party collective within the Vyborg District of RKP (b) in Petrograd, but was refused membership on the grounds that "by endorsing such a collective we may create an undesirable precedent for the future" (IK 1919: 9, 2.2). Thereby the Kom–Fut lost its *raison d'être* and ceased to exist, but from now on "Kom–Futy" became a common designation for communist-oriented futurists (for the history of Kom–Fut, see Jangfeldt 1976, 92–108).

This repudiation of Kom–Fut was just another example of the growing criticism of the futurists, whose position in the eyes of many had become far too strong. Although the IZO futurists' position was formally strong—it depended, in fact, to a great extent on the benevolence of Anatolij Lunačarskij—they had been subjected to harsh criticism ever since they had been able to influence cultural life in Russia.

The criticism had begun as early as the first anniversary of the revolution, when a few avant-garde artists decorated some streets in Petrograd, thereby realizing the demand set forth in "Dekret No 1 o demokratizacii iskusstv". These decorations long remained a cornerstone in the criticism of futurism's alleged "incomprehensibility" (although less than ten of the close on ninety artists taking part could be regarded as "futurists", and although not all of their decorations were particularly radical in form).

The accusation of "incomprehensibility" was coupled with criticism of the futurists' position within IZO. It was said that they had "occupied" IZO—"zasil'e" was the current expression—and were trying to achieve recognition as official "state art". It is true that the IZO futurists believed in the dictatorship of a minority in the cultural sphere (a counterpart to the Bolsheviks' dictatorship in politics[11]) and saw themselves in the rôle of this vanguard. Cf. Punin: "We want to see our October realized, we want to establish a dictatorship of the minority, for only the minority constitutes a creative force capable of walking in step with the working class" (IK 1918: 3). Thus, there was something in the criticism of "zasil'e". But this criticism also contained a strong distrust of the futurists' *motives*: it was suggested that they were not true revolutionaries but had merely taken advantage of the moment in order to gain a position of power. In particular among the representatives of the Proletkul't, every futurist approach to the proletariat was regarded as "an attempt of one class to influence the psychology of the working class in their own interest" (Grjaduščee 1918: 10, 10).

117

At the beginning of 1919 the attacks on futurism became more frequent and intense. One of the driving forces behind the anti-futurist campaign was Vladimir Friče (head of "fine arts" and "popular festivities" within the Moscow section of education), who was also one of the leading figures in the successful attempts to stop the second printing and staging of *Misterija-buff*. On March 1, 1919, the Moscow Soviet asked Friče to give a lecture on futurism before its Executive committee and plenary meeting (VI 1919: 6.3). At the same time, Ol'ga Kameneva, head of TEO (the Theatre section of Narkompros), also took exception to the futurists (VI 1919: 1.3), and futurism was made the subject of a special discussion in the Petrograd Proletkul't (VŽ 1919: 6/7, 72).

The IZO futurists tried to meet the criticism, and more than half of *Iskusstvo* No. 5 (April 1) was devoted to rebutting the attacks. But the front against futurism became both broader and more united. So, for example, the Executive Committee of the Petrograd Soviet decided that the organization of May 1st celebrations for 1919 should "on no condition" be entrusted to the futurists from IZO (Rostovceva 1971, 39), and on April 4 "Sojuz rabotnikov nauki, iskusstva i kul'-tury" adopted a resolution in which Narkompros was prevailed upon to "pay attention to the unlimited dominance of futurism, cubism, imaginism etc. in the Soviet Socialist Republic" and to take measures to support those trying to create "genuine proletarian art in full concord with communism" (Pravda 1919: 9.4). A little later, on May 6, Lenin criticized the futurists for using "the peasants' and workers' institutions of enlightenment" for "their own personal tricks", and for presenting "the most absurd doodles" ("nelepejšee krivljanie") as something new and proletarian (Lenin 1963, 330).

As a result of these attacks, the IZO futurists were dealt a fatal blow: they were deprived of their most important mouthpiece, *Iskusstvo Kommuny*, which was closed after its nineteenth issue (April 13). *Iskusstvo* also began to experience publishing difficulties, officially due to shortage of paper,[12] and No. 6 did not appear until July 8. Majakovskij later spoke of "the persecution of left art, brilliantly completed by the closing of 'Iskusstvo Kommuny' and so on" (Majakovskij 1959, 42).

This was the beginning of the end of avant-garde hegemony within IZO. The last issue of *Iskusstvo* (No. 8) was published in September, and by the end of the year the futurists had lost their previous influence on cultural life. In a speech in December, Anatolij Lunačarskij "dwelled upon the at one time so noticeable predominance of leftist artistic movements in the country". He accounted for this by the fact that these had expressed such a clear sympathy for Soviet power, but that the changing attitude of the intelligentsia had now made it possible to create a "balanced" collegiate within IZO (IRSL 1967, 712).

The Avant-Garde and the State

Futurist hegemony within IZO lasted for a very short period of time, less than six months. The reason why they were given this position in the first place is quite obvious—the Bolshevik party had no elaborated view on cultural matters (not even the party program adopted by the eighth party congress in March, 1919, paid any attention to cultural policy), and the futurists were the only ones who showed any kind of revolutionary enthusiasm and were willing to work with the new government. Lunačarskij later explained:

> [...] они скорей почувствовали симпатию к революции и увлеклись ею, когда она протянула им руку [...] я протянул футуристам руку, главным образом потому, что в общей политике Наркомпроса нам необходимо было опереться на серьезный коллектив творческих художественных сил. Их я нашел почти исключительно здесь, среди так называемых "левых" художников.
>
> (Lunačarskij 1967, 116)

In order to answer the question as to why the futurists lost power and influence, one must take several factors into account. First of all, the general political situation, which left little room for esthetic experimentation: "The year 1919 was the year of Soviet Russia's most complete isolation from the outside world. [...] Throughout 1919 the dominant factor in Soviet foreign policy, as in the Soviet economy, was the civil war [...]" (Carr 1966: III, 117). Majakovskij summarized: "The authorities, busy with the fronts and the destruction, took little interest in esthetic feuds, wanted peace and order behind the lines, and tried to bring us to reason out of respect for 'the men of rank' ('imenitejšim')" (Majakovskij 1959, 42–43).

1919 seems to have been a crucial year for everybody who had greeted the revolution as a first step toward a spiritual rebirth. In a letter to Ivanov-Razumnik in 1927, Andrej Belyj wrote that 1919 was "the most difficult year", "a clear disappointment in the nearness of the *revolution of the Spirit*'" (Nivat 1974, 78; the italics are Belyj's). Also for the futurists, and especially for Majakovskij, the year 1919 was no doubt a year of disappointment—they understood not only that the Revolution of the Spirit was not close but also that it was not wanted in the form in which the futurists presented it.

The curtailment of the influence of the futurists, however, was not only due to the difficult political situation. There is no reason to believe that they would have stayed in power, had the political conditions been more favorable. The failure of the futurists to retain their influence must also be seen against the background of the educational and cultural level of the Russian people. The futurists represented the most advanced esthetics of their time, and wanted their ideas to become accepted as the "cultural ideology" of the uncultured Russian masses. The Bolshevik party, on the other hand, saw its immediate task in trying to eradicate illiteracy, which encompassed more than three quarters of the population. Here was a conflict—between the "spiritual revolution" of the futurists and the "cultural revolution" of the Bolsheviks—that could not be bridged.

This antagonism touches on the essential issue in relations between the state and the avant-garde. By closing *Iskusstvo Kommuny* and curtailing futurist influence within IZO, the government deprived the futurists of their opportunity to propagate, in organs and bodies of the Narkompros, ideas that ran counter to official ideology. One may argue that it was wrong of the Bolsheviks not to adopt futurism as the esthetic creed of the proletariat, but that is another question. The essential aspect of the problem is whether any state—especially a totalitarian one—can tolerate a government body using government-financed organs to advocate ideas which the government itself is opposed to.

From the point of view of the avant-garde, what is at issue is whether an avant-garde movement can ever exercise state power without losing its function as an avant-garde. Any group exercising state power must, in order to stay in power, comply with *raison d'état*. An avant-garde thus has two possibilities: either remain "in opposition" and thereby retain the intrinsic function of an avant-garde—or assume power, yield to state reason, make necessary compromises etc., and in that way abandon its rôle as an avant-garde.

One cannot but agree with Vratislav Effenberger, who contends that "revoluční oficialisace avantgardy směřuje k popření jejích vlastních sociálních a kulturních kritických funkcí" (Effenberger 1969, 157), and that "oficialisovaná avantgarda je komický protimluv" (Effenberger 1968, 54).

The history of IZO futurism seems to support this view: the futurists stayed in power as long as they could propagate their ideas without interference and without regard to state reason; when, faced with hard criticism, they refused to conform with official Bolshevik esthetics, they had to go.

II. Majakovskij and October

When trying to define more closely Vladimir Majakovskij's immediate reactions to the events of October, the most difficult problem is the lack of factual material. The poet himself made no official comments, and the only clue we have are a couple of words dropped at the great discussion about cooperation (or non-cooperation) with Soviet power, on November 17, 1917. Unfortunately, the record of this meeting has not been published in full, and all we know is that Majakovskij agreed with Fedor Sologub—who said that art belongs to the people—and that in order to attain this goal one has to turn to the new power—"prixoditsja obratit'sja k vlasti, privetstvovat' novuju vlast'" (Dinerštejn 1958, 566).[13]

This lack of factual material compels us to scrutinize the existing texts, i.e. poems, articles, correspondence all the more narrowly. I would in this connection like to call attention to a letter from Majakovskij to Lili Brik and the poem "To Russia".

1. "Os'ka's Noble Letter"

In a letter from Majakovskij to Lili Brik, written around Christmas 1917 (not in the middle of December, as is stated in Majakovskij 1961, 28), and sent to Petrograd from Moscow, where Majakovskij had moved at the beginning of the same month, we find the following passage:

Прочел в "Новой жизни" дышащее благородством Оськино письмо. Хотел бы получить такое же.

(Majakovskij 1961, 29)

The letter Majakovskij refers to is a letter to the editor from Osip Brik, published in Gor'kij's Menshevik newspaper *Novaja žizn'* on December 5 (18), 1917. It was written in connection with the elections to the Petrograd City Duma, for which the Bolsheviks had nominated Brik as their candidate.

What, then, was it that Majakovskij found so "noble" in Brik's letter? The commentary to Majakovskij's collected works leaves us without any real answer:

> Оговаривая свое несогласие с "культурной программой боль-
> шевиков, как она выразилась в деятельности ЦК пролетарских
> культурно-просветительных организаций", он [Брик, B. J.] в
> то же время заявил, что считает "преступлением перед куль-
> турой и народом всякий саботаж, всякий отказ от активной
> культурной работы".

(Majakovskij 1961, 303)

The same explanation, word by word, is given in Percov 1969, 339, and LN 1958, 104, a fact which no doubt lends the commentary a semi-official air. Nevertheless, it fails to explain why Majakovskij was so enthusiatic about the letter. In fact, Brik's little article, called "My position", leaves no doubt as to the reasons for Majakovskij's positive reaction to it. I quote it here *in extenso*:

Моя позиция

Кто то из знакомых сказал мне, что я избран в гласные новой городской думы по списку большевиков. Для меня это явилось полной неожиданностью: никто моего согласия не спрашивал и никому я его не давал.

Я не политик, ни в какой партии не состою, я культурный деятель; поэтому я не знаю, хорошую ли политику ведут боль-шевики или нет. Аресты инакомыслящих, насилие над словом, над печатью и прочие проявления физической силы не являются отличительным признаком большевиков: так поступает всякая власть. И в самодержавной России, и в либеральной Англии, и в демократической Франции; так поступали кадеты после 3–4 июля, так же собирался действовать Керенский накануне 25 октября.

Но культурная программа большевиков невозможна. В этом я убедился, присутствуя на конференции пролетарских культурно-просветительных организаций. Если предоставить им свободно хозяйничать в этой области, то получится нечто, ничего общего с культурой не имеющее. Поэтому я считаю преступлением перед культурой и народом всякий саботаж, всякий отказ от активной культурной работы. Сидеть и ждать, пока все образуется — почетная роль обывателя. Обусловливать торжество культуры победой контр-революции могут только безнадежно ослепшие люди. Единственно верный путь — неуклонно вести свою культурную линию, быть везде, где культуре грозит опасность, стойко защищая ее от всякого, в том числе и большевистского, вандализма.

По этим соображениям я не отказываюсь от своего неожиданного избранья, причем заявляю, что я в партии большевиков не состою, никакой партийной дисциплине не подчиняюсь, и ни в каких политических выступлениях участия не приму. Их культурная программа, посколько она выразилась в деятельности Ц. К. пролетарских культурно-просветительных организаций, для меня совершенно неприемлема; именно с ней я считаю необходимым особенно энергично бороться.

Если большевикам моя позиция не подходит, то прошу вычеркнуть меня из числа гласных.

О. М. Брик.

(NŽ 1917: 193 (197), 5 (18). 12, p. 4)

The main elements of Brik's argumentation are thus that although he is not a member of the Bolshevik party, he 1) accepts the nomination on the condition that he will not have to submit to any party discipline or take part in any party manifestations, 2) does this because he does *not* agree with the Bolsheviks' cultural program, which he sees as a threat to culture; therefore he finds it his duty to fight Bolshevik "vandalism" and "defend culture" from within the party.

In other words, to Brik the nomination on the Bolshevik list is not a matter of political conviction, but a matter of tactics: he accepts the nomination in order to *fight* the party line on cultural questions. And he even issues an ultimatum: if the Bolsheviks do not approve of his "position", he will not accept nomination.

Given the full text of Brik's letter, it is not difficult to understand what Majakovskij found so noble in it: Brik's repudiation of the Bolsheviks' cultural policy, as "expressed in the activity of the Central

Committee of the proletarian organizations for culture and enlighten-ment".

The first conference of the proletarian organizations for culture and enlightenment was held in Petrograd a week before the October revolution. This conference, which had been convened in close cooperation with the Bolshevik party and, in particular, with the future Commissar of Enlightenment, Anatolij Lunačarskij, laid the foundations of Proletkul't (as it came to be called in November, 1917; see Gorbunov 1974, 50). It may seem strange that Brik speaks about the Bolsheviks' cultural program "as expressed in the activity" of Proletkul't, when we know that in 1920 the party suppressed Proletkul't as an independent organization because it propagandized a view on culture alien to Bolshevik ideology and demanded independence from the party. But at this time cooperation between the party and Proletkul't was close (Proletkul't was, in fact, directly subsidized by the state), and the contradictions that were to lead to the split were not yet palpable. Furthermore, Lunačarskij always supported the independence of Proletkul't—even against Lenin—and Brik's equating Bolshevik with Proletkul't cultural ideology is therefore fully justified.

It is clear from the letter that Brik attended the conference mentioned. He defended futurism and attacked the traditionalism inherent in the cultural program of Proletkul't:

> Вспомните, как издевались надо мной на первой конференции пролетарских культурно-просветительных организаций, когда я позволил себе заметить, что пролетарский художник будет писать не кистью, а шваброй. Какое поднялось возмущение, когда я произнес слово "футуризм".

(IK 1918: 3)

What Brik, as a spokesman of the avant-garde, could not accept, was the emphasis laid on the culture of the past and the unwillingness to recognize modern art and literature.[14] This conservatism was, of course, alien to the avant-gardists who, during the preceding decade, had effected one of the greatest revolutions ever in the field of art and literature. Here the clash was absolute: while Brik and his colleagues had rejected the esthetic brush in favor of the swab of de-esthetization and were on their way to developing the theory of production art, the task of the party (and Proletkul't) was to help the workers master this very brush.

Brik's letter to the editor was only one of several articles that he devoted to the problem of art in the new society at this time. In one of these (VZ 1918: 25.1), he criticizes Proletkul't for its vague use of the term "proletarian" poet and poetry. If "proletarian poetry" is something written "about" the people, then many bourgeois writers are proletarian. If only writers descending from the people are proletarians, then several Proletkul'tists must be excluded. And if only a "socialist" can be called proletarian, then what about the Mensheviks and the Socialist Revolutionaries?

Brik concludes that one should not try to patronize any indefinable "proletarian poetry" but "give the budding poets and writers (i.e. the futurists—B.J.) a chance to appear before the face of the people". According to Brik, the proletariat itself will understand which kind of poetry is dearer to it, who are its "proletarian poets".[15]

This criticism of Proletkul't was to reach its peak a year later, in the winter of 1918–1919, in the violent polemics conducted mainly in *Iskusstvo Kommuny* (where Brik returned to the problem of defining "proletarian poet") and *Iskusstvo* and in the Proletkul't organs, but also in public debates (see Jangfeldt 1976, 72–91). Two of the main protagonists were none other than Brik and Majakovskij; the latter saw before him the following results of the conservative esthetics preached by the party and Proletkul't:

> Совдепы вычинят в пару лет.
> И в праздник
> будут играть
> пролеткультцы
> в сквере
> перед советом
> в крокет.
>
> (Majakovskij 1957, 101)

Majakovskij's enthusiasm over Brik's article was thus only the first expression, after the October revolution, of an artistic conviction that was fundamental to the esthetics of the avant-garde: there can be no revolutionary content without a revolutionary approach to form.

Majakovskij and Brik in fact followed Brik's formula—to work within the system in order to change it—when they began to work in IZO, in the fall of 1918. The same is true of the decision to organize

125

the Communist–Futurist Collective (Kom–Fut) within the party in January, 1919, and the second attempt to organize such a collective two years later (see Jangfeldt 1976, 92 ff.). All these attempts to formulate an alternative to the official cultural ideology—or lack of it—show the constant dissatisfaction of the avant-garde with the cultural policy of the Bolsheviks. As is shown by Brik's letter to *Novaja žizn'* and Majakovskij's reaction to it, this dissatisfaction goes back to the first months following the October revolution.

2. *"To Russia"*

In the spring of 1917, Vladimir Majakovskij greeted the February revolution with the poem "Revoljucija. Poëtoxronika", published in May in *Novaja žizn'*. The long poem is an expression of revolutionary enthusiasm in general, but above all an actual *chronicle* of the events of February 27. It is clear from the poem that Majakovskij regarded this revolution as his own:

> Мы победили!
> Слава нам!
> Сла-а-ав-в-ва нам!

"Revoljucija" ends with the conviction that this day means the victory of socialism:

> ... днесь
> небывалой сбывается былью
> социалистов великая ересь!
>
> (Majakovskij 1955, 139, 140)

Against this background it is striking that Majakovskij did not dedicate any complimentary poem to the Bolshevik revolution until the fall of 1918—not until the first anniversary of the revolution did he stage "Misterija-buff" and print "Geroi i žertvy revoljucii". It is true that he wrote "Oda revoljucii" and "Naš marš" as early as December, 1917 (Jakobson 1956, 204), but these poems are emotional responses to a revolutionary atmosphere (see Smorodin 1972, 22) rather than expressions of support for the Bolshevik revolution in particular.

In fact, the first two years after the October revolution were a period of uncertainty and reflection for Majakovskij. This indisputable fact has been stressed by the Soviet scholar A. Smorodin, who talks about

Majakovskij's "silence" and his being "shaked by events" (Smorodin 1972, 20, 21). From the October revolution to the fall of 1919, when he began his work at ROSTA, Majakovskij wrote only about a dozen poems, most of which were in fact emotional and abstract revolutionary hymns, like "Oda revoljucii" and "Naš marš", or dealt with the problems of contemporary art and literature and their rôle in the new society (the poems in *Iskusstvo Kommuny*). In a letter to Lili Brik from March, 1918, Majakovskij complained: "Ne pišetsja, nastroenie gnusnoe" (LN 1958, 107).

It would thus seem as if Majakovskij's immediate poetical answer to the Bolshevik revolution was—silence. There is, however, in Majakovskij's PSS a poem that has escaped the attention of the Majakovskij scholars. This poem is "To Russia" ("Rossii"; Majakovskij 1955, 130).

In all of Majakovskij's PSS since the thirties, "Rossii" is dated 1916. However, since no manuscript has been preserved, and the poem has not been found in the periodical press of that year, the dating is said to be "arbitrary" (Majakovskij 1955, 436). In fact, "Rossii" was published only in 1919, in Majakovskij's first collected works, *Vse sočinennoe Vladimirom Majakovskim 1909–1919*, and dated 1915. In this book, however, out of eighty poems and plays, less than a fifth are correctly dated. The reason for this is the collection's rather peculiar genesis. During the first post-revolutionary years Russia experienced a constant paper shortage, and in 1919, with the escalation of the civil war, the crisis became acute. In spite of this, Majakovskij wanted to put out his first collected works, and he therefore invented a fictitious jubilee, the tenth anniversary of his literary début. The story of the publication of *Vse sočinennoe* is told by Lili Brik in an unpublished manuscript:

Маяковскому очень хотелось выпустить свое, тогда еще не обширное, "Собрание сочинений", а придраться было не к чему, и тогда он решился на вполне безобидное жульничество [...], тем более, что стихи он действительно начал писать в 1909, правда не те, которые он пометил этой датой [...]. Ему нужен был этот юбилей для издания — вот он и подписал под стихами из "Пощечины" дату 1909 год. И, соответственно, изменил хронологию и по отношению к [...] другим стихотворениям.

(L. Brik 1951, 34–35)

127

With this in mind, it is easy to understand the irony in the title of Majakovskij's foreword to the collection: "Ljubiteljam jubileev".[16]

The datings in *Vse sočinennoe* are thus of no help in trying to establish the time "Rossii" was written. In fact, several poems from the years around the revolution are also incorrectly dated in Majakovskij's *last* PSS: "Sebe, ljubimomy, posvjaščaet ėti stroki avtor" is said to have been written at the beginning of 1916, but was actually not written until a year later (Jakobson 1956, 204); "Oda revoljucii" is dated November, 1918—when it was published—but, as with "Naš marš", it had already been written by the end of 1917 (Ibidem); the long poem "Čelovek" is said to have been written in 1916–1917, although there is overwhelming evidence that it was actually written between February and October, 1917 (Dinerštejn 1958, 555–556; Jakobson 1956, 204; Spasskij 1940, 98, and Ėrenburg 1961, 391; the latter three speak about the poem as recently finished at the beginning of 1918).

The "arbitrary" dating of "Rossii" thus leaves us with the task of trying to pin it down chronologically according to the contents. Here follows the poem as it was printed for the first time, in *Vse sočinennoe*. As opposed to later editions, it is not divided into stanzas, and it lacks the "academic" punctuation that Majakovskij never cared for. A couple of orthographical errors have been corrected.

России

1Вот иду я

2заморский страус

3в перьях строф размеров и рифм.

4Спрятать голову глупый стараюсь

5в оперенье звенящее врыв.

6Я не твой снеговая уродина.

7Глубже

8в перья душа уложись!

9И иная окажется родина

10вижу

11выжжена южная жизнь.

12Остров зноя.

13В пальмы овазился.

14"Эй

15дорогу!"

$_{16}$Выдумку мнут;

$_{17}$и опять

$_{18}$до другого оазиса

$_{19}$вью следы песками минут.

$_{20}$Иные жмутся

$_{21}$— уйти-б

$_{22}$не кусается-ль. —

$_{23}$Иные изогнуты в низкую лесть.

$_{24}$"Мама

$_{25}$а мама

$_{26}$несет он яйца?"

$_{27}$"Не знаю душечка.

$_{28}$Должен бы несть"

$_{29}$Ржут этажия.

$_{30}$Улицы пялятся.

$_{31}$Обдают водой холода.

$_{32}$Весь истыканный в дымы и в пальцы

$_{33}$переваливаю года.

$_{34}$Что-ж бери меня хваткой мерзкой!

$_{35}$Бритвой ветра перья обрей.

$_{36}$Пусть исчезну

$_{37}$чужой и заморский

$_{38}$под неистовства всех декабрей.

On a general level, "Rossii" is a poem about the poet and his home country. More specifically it deals—as is suggested by the title—with the attitude of the poet to Russia (and *vice versa*).

Through the whole poem, the poet is depicted as an ostrich from the other side of the sea. But the poet is not only compared to an ostrich: the image of the poet and the ostrich merge in a realized metaphor. So, for example, the ostrich's feathers are made up of $_3$*strof razmerov i rifm*. The ostrich is "silly" enough to dig himself into his $_5$*operen'e zvenjaščee*, that is, to occupy himself with poetry, to take refuge in poetry. The reason is that the ostrich does not belong in this $_6$*snegovaja urodina*. Majakovskij uses the word "urodina", meaning a (female) monster but also containing the word "rodina", with which it rhymes. By doing so, he creates a new meaning out of "urodina": a monstrous or hideous motherland.

Then the ostrich calls his soul to turn even deeper into the plumage, that is into poetry, phantasy, dreams. The imaginary southern country Majakovskij sees before him, may be interpreted as the poet's vision of the revolutionary society as the dreamland of poetry; here, at last, he will be at home. But here too imagination is suppressed ($_{16}$*Vydumku mnut*) and the ostrich is thrown off the road ($_{14-15}$"*Èj | dorogu!*"). Once again he has to hurry on to the next oasis, pressed by time (note the masterly expression $_{19}$*peskami minut*, alluding both to the desert sands and to a sand-glass). Even in his motherland, the land of the southern sun/the land of poetry, the ostrich/poet is looked upon as an alien and foreign element, and the attitude to him alternates between confusion and adulation (20–28).

The poet's utopia turns out to be a fiction, and at the end of the poem he is back in the wintry city of the first lines. Nothing has changed, and the poet finally surrenders and turns to his country with the words: $_{34}$*Čto-ž beri menja xvatkoj merzkoj!* The word "mërzkoj" (it must be pronounced "ë", since it rhymes with "zamorskij") is a concoction from "merzkij", loathsome, and "mërzlyj", frozen, and functions as an echo and qualification of $_6$*urodina*. The wind's razor may just as well shave off his feathers, i.e. poetry, and he himself disappear into the furious Decembers—$_{38}$*pod neistovstva vsex dekabrej.*

The theme of "Rossii" is a variation on the theme of the poet as an emigré in his own country. The poet with his phantasy and imagination is always "zamorskij", from the other side of the sea. When he "turns deeper into his feathers "and occupies himself with poetry, people are either confused or flatter him. And the Decembrist Russia is far away from the ideal land of the poet; here poetry has no *raison d'être* at all: $_{35}$*Britvoj vetra per'ja obrej.*

"Rossii" is a central poem in Majakovskij's works, since it is an expression of an essential, albeit not new, problem: the position of the poet in society, and the attitude of society to the poet. From the mood of the poem we may suppose that it was prompted by some specific event(s) that made the poet experience a feeling of total estrangement. The events following the revolution in October, 1917, may have had such an effect on Majakovskij, whereas it is difficult to find anything similar in 1916. It is therefore not impossible that "Rossii" was actually written in December, 1917 (the month is suggested by the last line of the poem).[17]

If we assume that "Rossii" was written then, it must be looked at in conjunction with Osip Brik's letter and Majakovskij's reaction to it. In "Rossii" Majakovskij talks about himself as a poet of imagination and originality. For Majakovskij and other poets, the revolution was expected to create exactly that kind of society in which artistic creation was not only free but also liberated the people; the principles that governed art should govern life as well. This vision was dealt a fatal blow when it became clear that the Bolshevik party had chosen to support the Proletkul't. The Proletkul't challenged Majakovskij's image of the poet and stressed other qualities: the poet's origin was judged to be more important than what he wrote, and form was declared inferior to content. It was more important *what* was written—and *by whom*!—than *how* it was written.

Another important source of disappointment for Majakovskij was undoubtedly the Bolsheviks' appeal to the artists and poets in November. The party's invitation to cooperate with the Soviet power met with total repudiation on the part of the cultural workers, who were tired of state interference in artistic life and had far more anarchistic ideas of artistic freedom than the Bolsheviks were willing to accept. It is true that Majakovskij, according to the transcript, "greeted the new power", but Brik underlines that Majakovskij was "disappointed": "When he could not come to terms ("Ne sgovorivšis'") with the People's Commissar or find any other ways of propagating 'left art', Majakovskij went to Moscow, where, together with D. Burljuk and V. Kamenskij, he tried to talk to the people over the head of Lunačarskij [...] from the stage of 'Kafe Poétov' [...]" (O. Brik 1940, 89).

The "flight" to Moscow at the beginning of December was thus a direct result of the impossibility of coming to terms with the new political powers. It is very plausible that "Rossii" may have been written at this time, when Majakovskij was utterly disappointed with the Bolsheviks' cultural policies. It would then coincide with Majakovskij's letter to Lili Brik, with its enthusiasm over Brik's criticism of the Proletkul't and the Bolsheviks' cultural ideology. Read in this light, the poem becomes a rejection of the utilitarian demands made of poetry at this time and a defense—albeit resigned—of imagination and originality.

In fact, the clash between Majakovskij and Lunačarskij seems to have been serious. Dinerštejn speaks about "some kind of abnormalities" in their relations, and quotes a note dating from 1938 (which,

131

unfortunately, has not been published in full), in which Punin recalls that "there was a conflict between Majakovskij and Lunačarskij [...]. It would be very interesting to reconstruct this [...]. Then it would be possible to explain in concrete terms Majakovskij's and Brik's delay in responding to the October revolution" (Dinerštejn 1958, 563–564).

It may seem a little strange that a poet could write, more or less at the same time, such different poems as "Rossii", on the one hand, and "Oda revoljucii" and "Naš marš", on the other. But, as we have seen, Majakovskij's attitude to the October revolution was highly complex in the initial stages; just as complex as his attitude to life in general. The "Poet of the Revolution" also had another side, the characteristic features of which were a child-like need for love and affection (see, for instance, his letters to Lili Brik), a general disposition towards depression (and suicide), and a strong sense of alienation, of not being understood (see Triolet 1975 and Jakobson 1931 among others). The feeling of estrangement expressed in "Rossii" would be echoed eight years later in the poem "Homewards!", "Domoj!" (the fact that these very lines were later deleted by Majakovskij, is a graphic confirmation of this duality in his character):

> Я хочу
>> быть понят моей страной,
>> а не буду понят, —
>>> что ж,
>> по родной стране
>> пройду стороной,
>> как проходит
>>> косой дождь.
>
> (Majakovskij 1958, 429)

In one of the draft versions (Majakovskij 1958, 428), the "rodnoj" of line four is substituted for "čužoj" (see also Jakobson 1971, VII). This substitution assumes special significance with "Rossii" in mind: Russia ("rodnaja strana") may very well be experienced by the poet as an alien country ("čužaja strana"). The substitution of "rodnoj" for "čužoj" is fully possible within a semantic field in which "rodina" and "urodina" form two interchangeable poles of one basic concept: Russia.[18] There is, as has been pointed out, "kein Gefühl so rein [...], dass es nicht mit einem ihm widerstrebenden Gefühl vermengt wäre (Ambivalenz der Gefühle)" (Jakobson 1972, 399).

With this dialecticism in mind, it should not seem illogical that Majakovskij's reactions to the events of October embraced both enthusiasm and estrangement. Most great Russian poets responded ambiguously to the revolution; and it seems absurd in my view that one should demand of Majakovskij a simple and unequivocal reaction to an event of such universal impact.

1. In Jangfeldt 1975 and 1976 I discuss in detail particular problems which are only mentioned in passing in this outline: *Gazeta Futuristov*; the futurists and IZO; the Revolution of the Spirit; the futurists and Proletkul't; and Kom-Fut.
2. For a discussion of Majakovskij's development between February and October, 1917, see E. Dinerštejn 1958.
3. This alludes to "Car' Iudejskij", a play by the Grand Duke Konstantin Romanov which was prohibited by church censorship before the revolution but could, by a strange paradox, be played in Soviet Russia. See Nils Åke Nilsson's article in this volume.
4. In one of his autobiographical sketches, Burljuk claims that he left Moscow on April 2, 1918 (Burljuk 1924, 45). This dating has since been accepted by the scholars (see e.g. Felix Philipp Ingold's interesting publication /Ingold 1973/ and Helga Ladurner's unfortunately highly inaccurate article on Burljuk /Ladurner 1978/). From the report in *Figaro* we learn that Burljuk participated at the closing of Kafe Poètov on April 14. It is therefore reasonable to believe that he left the capital the next day—which was April 15, new style, but *April 2, old style.*
5. The fact that he received the support of only a minority of artists obviously did not bother Lunačarskij, who is reported to have said in a discussion: "In politics we are for an active minority, in art for a union with individual outstanding talents [...]" (NŽ 1918: 21(6).4).
6. In order to guarantee the support of Gor'kij, who was of tremendous propagandistic importance to the Bolsheviks, and also of the rest of the literary intelligentsia, the writer was promised—and given—a publishing house, "Vsemirnaja literatura" which started up at the beginning of 1919. Here Gor'kij gathered around him many of the most famous writers of the time, who translated foreign literature and thereby got food for the day—not a common privilege in starving Russia.
7. A number of these articles and speeches were later collected in a small brochure called *Intelligencija i Sovetskaja vlast'. Sbornik statej*, M. 1919. Here was printed Gor'kij's address "Appeal to the people and the working intelligentsia" from November 28, in which he formulated the political alternatives in this way: "The proletariat and the working intelligentsia must decide to whom they are closer—the defenders of the old order [...] or those who arouse new social ideas and emotions [...]" (pp. 23–24).
8. Brik states that he and Majakovskij were invited to become members by Šterenberg and Punin in July–August, and that Majakovskij began work in the

collegiate in August or September (O. Brik 1940, 97, 93). It is true that contact between Narkompros and Majakovskij was established at this time: so, for example, Majakovskij is mentioned as a contributor to *Vestnik Narodnogo Prosveščenija* in the September issue of the journal (see also the facts presented in Katanjan 1961, 100). But Majakovskij, in fact, joined the collegiate much later, not before December. Brik worked out the statutes for IZO's "Bjuro xudožestvennogo truda", adopted on September 30, but became a member of the *collegiate* only on November 21 (see VNP 1918: 4/5, 42, and 1919: 1/3 (9/11), 128). Both he and Majakovskij attended the session of the collegiate on November 28, but while Brik is mentioned as a member, it is stressed that Majakovskij was present as a *non*-member: "Besides the members of the collegiate, *Vladimir Majakovskij* also attended the session [...]" (IK 1918: 1). Majakovskij took part in several sessions during the winter of 1918-1919 (see Majakovskij 1959, 216-238; 596-599); that he eventually did become a member is shown by the fact that he was formally removed from the Petrograd collegiate when he moved to Moscow in the spring of 1919 (Majakovskij 1959, 596).

9. One person who objected to the futurists' cooperation with the political powers was Viktor Šklovskij, who formulated the following ultra-formalist creed in an article in *Iskusstvo Kommuny*: "Art was always free from life, and in its colour was never reflected the colour of the flag over the town's castle" (IK 1919: 17, 30.3). When Šklovskij reprinted the article in his book *Xod konja* (Moskva–Berlin 1923), he added a note saying that it had been written "on the occasion of the futurists' assumption of leading posts in Narkompros" (p. 36).

10. One example of the futurists' strong position within IZO and Narkompros is the discussion that followed the staging, on the first anniversary of the revolution, of Majakovskij's play *Misterija-buff*. In a review, Andrej Levinson was very critical of the play and also accused the futurists of wanting to make their art the official art of the masses: "Samye pritjazanija futurizma— stat' oficial'nym iskusstvom očnuvšixsja mass predstavljajutsja mne nasil'stven- nymi. [...] futuristy ne vedut, a sami vlekutsja za momentom, im nadobno ugodit' novomu xozjainu, ottogo oni tak gruby i zapal'čivy" (ŽI 1918: 11.11). This review elicited a violent reaction from nine supporters and friends of Majakovskij, and in an article in the same paper they explained that these kind of accusations should be answered "only by administrative means" ("liš' v administrativnom porjadke" (ŽI 1918: 21.11). The nine people who signed the article were all members of the IZO collegiate. The fact that they openly suggested such a measure shows not only that they felt their position to be very secure, but also that they obviously did not hesitate to use the same kind of "polemical methods" that they had been so critical of in tsarist Russia. (In summing up the discussion, this claim to a monopoly of opinions was denounced by Lunačarskij; ŽI 1918: 27.11.)

11. As a matter of fact, futurism was even regarded—by the futurists themselves— as a *corrective* to communism. In his answer to Šklovskij's article (note 9), Nikolaj Punin stressed that "futurism is a corrective to communism, since

134

futurism is not only an artistic movement but a whole system of forms [...].
And now we are even prepared to assert that communism as a theory of culture
cannot exist without futurism, just as yesterday evening does not exist without
our remembrance of it today" (IK 1919: 17).

12. It is true that there was an acute paper shortage in Russia all through 1919,
but the question of which papers are to be allocated supplies is, nevertheless,
always a question of priority.

13. The edited version of the record has a more definite wording: "[...] nužno
privetstvovat' novuju vlast' i vojti s nej v kontakt" (Majakovskij 1959, 215).

14. Later on, many Proletkul'tists were to ignore the importance of the cultural
heritage, and it was, among other things, this attitude that led to the schism
between the Proletkul't and the party; but at this time Proletkul't had to be
judged solely by its program, and this expressively stated that "the proletariat
[...] must master the whole cultural heritage" (Gorbunov 1974, 50).

15. Brik's other articles of importance include "Bol'ševiki i avtorskoe pravo"
(NŽ 1917: 202(196), 15(28).12), a criticism of the decree on copyright; "Narodnoe prosveščenie" (NŽ 1917: 210(204), 24.12 (8.1.1918)), which criticizes the
Bolsheviks for turning the journal Narodnoe prosveščenie into a pure party
organ and thereby acting contrary to "the fundamental slogan of the socialist
and generally democratic ("obščedemokratičeskaja") cultural program—freedom of spiritual self-determination"; "Rabočij teatr Rossijskoj Respubliki"
(NŽ 1918: 3(217), 5(18).1)—aimed at Lunačarskij and his conservatism in
reorganizing the state theatres; "Neumestnoe politikanstvo" (Knižnyj ugol
1918: 2, pp. 28–29), where Brik sees Blok's poem "The twelve", for instance,
as an example of "neumestnoe politikanstvo"—he is not against political
poetry, but it can exist only alongside other themes (religious, romantic, everyday /"bytovye"/ themes) and is acceptable only if the poet is able to transform
his personal experience (which is of no interest to the readers) into "poetic
material".

16. Majakovskij's biographer erroneously treats the dating "1909–1919" as a wish
on the part of the poet to underline the connection between his "direct participation in the revolutionary struggle" and his first attempts, in the Butyrki prison,
to write poetry (Percov 1969, 108).

17. This hypothesis has been confirmed orally by N. Xardžiev, the editor of the
first volume of Majakovskij's PSS (Moskva 1939), who, in his turn, had it
confirmed by Osip Brik; the poem had been redated in order to make it possible to publish it at all.

18. Marina Cvetaeva, in her article "Poèt i vremja" (1932), writes pertinently
on the problem of the poet's estrangement in his own country: "Every poet is
essentially an emigré, even in Russia. [...] The poet—indeed all people of
art—but most of all the poet—bears a special stamp of discomfort, by which
one recognizes the poet even in his own home. [...] Počvennost', narodnost',
nacional'nost', rasovost', klassovost'—and the very sovremennost' that is
created—all this is only a facade, the first or seventh layer of skin, which the
poet does nothing but try to shake off" (Cvetaeva 1971, 624–625). This
question is treated in Ilma Rakuša's article on the "nad-nacional'nost'"
of Cvetaeva (Rakuša 1978).

References

Brik, L.
1951 [Vospominanija]. Unpublished MS.
Brik, O.
1940 "IMO—iskusstvo molodyx", sb. *Majakovskomu*, Leningrad.
Burljuk, D.
1924 *Avtobiografija i stixi*, New York.
Carr, E. H.
1966 *The Bolshevik Revolution 1917–1923*, Vol. I and III, London.
Chamberlin, W. H.
1935 *The Russian Revolution 1917–1921*, Vol. II, London.
Cvetaeva, M.
1971 *Nesobrannye proizvedenija*, München.
Dinerštejn, E.
1958 "Majakovskij v fevrale–oktjabre 1917 g.", *Literaturnoe Nasledstvo*, t. 65, Moskva.
Effenberger, V.
1968 "Od avantgardní tvorby k dnešnímu umění", *Problémy literárnej avantgardy*, Bratislava.
1969 *Realita a poesie. K vývojové dialektice moderního umění*, Praha.
Èrenburg, I.
1961 *Ljudi, gody, žizn'*, Moskva.
Gorbunov, V.
1974 *V. I. Lenin i Proletkul't*, Moskva.
Ingold, F. Ph.
1973 "Die einzige Kunst der Gegenwart. Eine vergessene Deklaration von David Davidovič Burljuk", *Slavica Helvetica* (Schweizerische Beiträge zum VII. internationalen Slavistenkongress).
IRSL
1967 *Istorija russkoj sovetskoj literatury*, t. 1, Moskva.
Jakobson, R.
1956 "Novye stroki Majakovskogo", *Russkij literaturnyj arxiv*, New York.
1971 *Selected Writings*, Vol. II, The Hague.
1972 "Was ist Poesie?", *Texte der russischen Formalisten*, Band II, München.
Jangfeldt, B.
1975 "Notes on 'Manifest Letučej Federacii Futuristov' and the Revolution of the Spirit", *Vladimir Majakovskij. Memoirs and Essays* (eds. B. Jangfeldt/N. Å. Nilsson), Stockholm.
1976 *Majakovskij and Futurism 1917–1921*, Stockholm.
Katanjan, V.
1961 *Majakovskij. Literaturnaja xronika*[4], Moskva.
Ladurner, H.
1978 "David D. Burljuks Leben und Schaffen 1908–1920", *Wiener Slawistischer Almanach*, Band I, Wien.

Lenin, V.
1963 *Polnoe sobranie sočinenij*, t. 38, Moskva.
LN
1958 *Literaturnoe Nasledstvo*, t. 65 (*Novoe o Majakovskom*), Moskva.
Lunačarskij, A.
1967 *Ob izobrazitel'nom iskusstve*, Moskva.
Majakovskij, V.
1955, 1957, 1958, 1959, 1961 *Polnoe sobranie sočinenij*, tt. I, IV, VII, XII, XIII.
Malevič, K.
1971 *Essays on Art 1915–1928*. Ed. by Troels Andersen, Copenhagen.
Markov, V.
1968 *Russian Futurism. A History*, Berkeley.
Nivat, G.
1974 "A. Belyj. Lettre autobiographique à Ivanov-Razumnik", *Cahiers du monde russe et soviétique*, Vol. XV, 1–2, Paris–La Haye.
Percov, V.
1969 *Majakovskij. Žizn' i tvorčestvo 1893–1917*, Moskva.
Rakuša, I.
1978 "Nad-nacional'nost' poèta: Cvetaeva i Ril'ke (na materiale neopublikovannoj perepiski)." In print.
Rappoport, E.
1974 *Let molodyx našix porox*, Irkutsk.
Rostovceva, I.
1971 "Učastie xudožnikov v organizacii i provedenii prazdnikov 1 Maja i 7 Nojabrja v Petrograde v 1918 godu", *Agitacionno-massovoe iskusstvo pervyx let Oktjabrja*, Moskva.
Smorodin, A.
1972 *Poèzija V. V. Majakovskogo i publicistika 20-x godov*, Leningrad.
Spasskij, S.
1940 *Majakovskij i ego sputniki*, Leningrad.
Šklovskij, V.
1923 *Xod konja*, Moskva–Berlin.
Triolet, E.
1975 "Voinstvujuščij poèt", *Vladimir Majakovskij. Memoirs and Essays* (eds. B. Jangfeldt/N. Å. Nilsson), Stockholm.
Xronika
1975 *Kul'turnaja žizn' v SSSR 1917–1927. Xronika*, Moskva.

Stefani Hoffman

Scythian Theory and Literature, 1917–1924

In the turbulent period of the October Revolution, the scythians not only participated enthusiastically in the transient whirlwind of contemporary literary activity, but also produced works of lasting artistic value. This article will present an historical survey of the scythian group covering its three major phases:

1. Period of the scythian *Miscellanies* (*Skify, sborniki*), 1916–1917.
2. Period of work on the newspaper *Banner of Labor* (*Znamja truda*) and the journal *Our Path* (*Naš put'*), 1917–1919.
3. Participation in Free Philosophical Association (Vol'fila), various journals, and the scythian Press, 1919–1924.

The scythians counted among their adherents some of the most prominent literary personalities of the period. Although several writers drifted in and out of the group, two figures remained dominant throughout—Ivanov-Razumnik and Andrej Belyj. Ivanov-Razumnik was the centripetal force who brought the individualistic, diverse scythians together.[1] His house in Carskoe Selo (now Puškin, outside of Leningrad) was the center of scythian activities. He served as editor and ideological spokesman for the various scythian publications and helped found Vol'fila. Belyj (1880–1934), the most idiosyncratic member of the group, was particularly close with Ivanov-Razumnik in the years 1916–22.[2] According to the writer Nina Berberova, Belyj regarded Ivanov-Razumnik as a father figure and accepted his scythian views.[3] Belyj was staying with Ivanov-Razumnik at the time of the February Revolution, working as co-editor of the second scythian Miscellany. He was the major contributor to scythian publications—fiction, poetry, and criticism—and one of the main figures in Vol'fila.

Although Aleksandr Blok did not contribute to the two miscellanies, he did participate in later scythian publications and in Vol'fila. Other scythians saw Blok's work—particularly the poem "The Twelve" (Dvenadcat') and "The Scythians" (Skify)—as embodying their scythian ideas. Blok's diaries, notebooks, and correspondence in this period show warm regard for Ivanov-Razumnik and interest in his theories combined with occasional annoyance at being drawn to projects and meetings.

A common, but mistaken line of criticism depicts the scythians as primarily a group of peasant poets. Although the peasant group was well represented in the miscellanies and in *Znamja truda*, most were not concerned with a scythian ideology and lost their interest in scythianism by the twenties.

Nikolaj Kljuev (1887–1937) published poetry in the miscellanies and in *Znamja truda* which used folk and religious imagery to express admiration for the Revolution. Kljuev, however, quickly lost his enthusiasm for scythian revolt when the Revolution failed to produce a peasant paradise. He did not participate significantly in further scythian activities although he remained friendly with Ivanov-Razumnik.

Sergej Esenin (1895–1925), one of the most popular peasant poets of the time, was close to Ivanov-Razumnik in the early revolutionary period (Rozanov 1926, 16). His poetry in the scythian publications shows the influence of Ivanov-Razumnik's view of the revolution. Complaining, however, of the scythians' insufficient attention to literary technique, Esenin began moving away from them to the imaginist group by early 1918.[4]

Other minor peasant poets whose association with scythianism covered the same time span include Aleksej Ganin (1890–1923), Petr Orešin (1887–1943), and Aleksandr Širjaevec (pseud. for A. Abramov, 1887–1924).

Two other figures involved in scythian activities were Konstantin Èrberg (pseud. for Sjunnerberg, 1871–1942) and Evgenij Lundberg (1887–1965). Èrberg published poetry and esthetic criticism which linked artistic creativity to a desire for absolute freedom. Lundberg, a journalist and literary critic, is one of the best sources on the scythians. The first volume of his memoirs, *A Writer's Notes* (Zapiski pisatelja) provides a unique picture of the scythian group in 1918. Lundberg founded the scythian press in Berlin in 1919, which he managed until his return to Russia in 1924.[5]

The Scythian Miscellanies

The scythian group originated in 1916 with plans for a journal. Many of the participants were close personal friends and had already published together: almost all had contributed to the populist-oriented journal *Testaments* (Zavety, 1912–1914), of which Ivanov-Razumnik had been a literary editor. Ivanov-Razumnik first used the term "scyth" as a pseudonym in Zavety (1912: 6, 46–68). The first *Scythian Miscellany* appeared in the spring of 1917. The material in it, except for Ivanov-Razumnik's introduction and afterword, had been gathered before the February, 1917 Revolution.

In the publicistic introduction ("Vmesto predislovija") Ivanov-Razumnik scarcely differentiates between the scythian as a real member of his group and the scythian as a goal—a new individual formed by cultural revolution. He describes his scythians as modern counterparts to the fierce nomadic tribes which left Central Asia in the 8–7th centures B.C. and succeeded in establishing an empire between the Don and Dnepr rivers. The analogy between past and present is drawn by projecting onto the ancient scythian the qualities valued in the modern one.

The scythian is first and foremost a maximalist: he possesses an "eternal revolutionism against any order, the searching of an untamed and untamable soul" (Ivanov-Razumnik 1917, X). This maximalism manifests itself more in spiritual and intellectual independence than in political action. The scythian does not fear any target, any prejudice or any god (VII). Although rejecting the metaphysical schemes of others, he retains his own vision of Justice, Truth, and Beauty (VIII).[6]

According to Ivanov-Razumnik, scythian maximalism is not opposed to artistic harmony (Hellenism). All the scythian writers agreed that the process of artistic creativity and cultural renewal, in fact, demands "eternal readiness to revolt". The true enemy is *meščanstvo*— petty philistinism:

> It is he, the worldwide *meščanin* [philistine], who destroyed universal Christianity with platitudinous morality; he is the one who is now destroying ... art in estheticism, science in scholastics, life in stagnation, revolution in petty reformism.
>
> (XI)

In "Trial by Fire" (Ispytanie ognem), written in 1914–15, but first published in the scythian miscellany, Ivanov-Razumnik linked *meščanstvo* with support for Russia's participation in World War I. Dissatisfaction with World War I appears in fictionalized form in the

140

miscellany in Mixail Prišvin's short work "Last Judgment" (Strašnyj sud), which brings out the hypocrisies of the supposed war backers.[7]

Although Ivanov-Razumnik welcomed the February Revolution as a potential manifestation of the scythian spirit, he remained cautious about the provisional government's attitude toward the war. In an afterword to "Trial by Fire", written in 1917, he warned against continued socialist support of the war. The future, he urged, belonged to the heretic minority, whose victory would come not through numbers, but through the inner strength of their ideas (Ivanov-Razumnik 1917a, 307–309. See also Ivanov-Razumnik 1918). Ivanov-Razumnik constantly linked the scythians with Aleksandr Herzen's form of populist socialism by drawing parallels between the revolutionary movement in Herzen's time and in the present.[8] A previously unpublished article of Herzen's, "Once Again in Paris" (Opjat' v Pariže) appeared in the first miscellany. Ivanov-Razumnik obviously found his own fears about a decline in "eternal revolutionism" echoed in Herzen's description of the watering-down of the French revolution of February, 1848.

Scythian ties with the Left Socialist-Revolutionary Party (Left S-R's) are consistently overemphasized by Soviet and emigré critics and played down by the scythians themselves, who stressed their independence of any political dogma and their interest in esthetic and moral over political issues.[9] Scythian publications, however, invariably appeared under Left S-R auspices. One of the editors of the miscellanies, S. D. Mstislavskij, was an active Left S-R, part of their delegation at the Brest negotiations. The first miscellany contains tributes by Mstislavskij and by the populist Vera Figner in memory of A. I. Ivančin-Pisarev, another noted populist who, until his death in June, 1916, also worked on the miscellanies.

Although the critical articles in the first miscellany differ in point of view and scope, they are united by a certain scythian maximalism— dissatisfaction with the present, resistance to intellectual complacency and stagnation, and a desire for boldness and daring in the future. These attitudes appear in Lev Šestov's "Music and Apparitions" (Muzyka i prizraki) and in Arsenij Avraamov's "In the Labyrinth of Esthetics" (V debrjax éstetiki).

Belyj's article "Aaron's Rod" (Žezl Aarona) attacks the present state of the word. His approach is a paradigm of scythian attitudes toward art in revolution. Belyj and the other scythians typically sought a reunification of divided entities—the mind and heart within the individual, the intelligentsia and peasantry within Russia, and East and West on the universal plane. They rejected overemphasis on only one-half of what should form a complete whole. Belyj describes the word itself as having lost an original, mythic wholeness and having degenerated into abstraction and sterile dogmatism. According to Belyj, current literary schools err by one-sidedness in their approach to the word. The formalists incorrectly find meaning only in phonetics and other formal aspects of a poem; poetic methods become ends in themselves. The other side strays equally in placing form within content, leading them back to the old tendentious type of literature (Skify I, 174). Using an organic analogy common to the scythians, Belyj compares the true word—a combination of form and content, sound and thought, spirit and nature—to a tree whose life is perceived in the movement of the whole, from crown to underground roots.

The scythians as a group praised peasant over proletarian poets. In "Aaron's Rod" Belyj looks to the peasant poets, particularly Kljuev, to give birth to a new, live word since they were furthest from abstraction and closer to the organic roots of meaning (Skify I, 189). The process—in typically scythian manner—involves quiet gestation followed by abrupt change—the "scabs" of old, dessicated meanings must be violently removed before the new word can be born. Any attempt to bring forth the new word prematurely only results in an "abortion" such as futurism (Skify I, 209).

Ultimately, the newborn word becomes alive in each individual who imparts a spiritual content to it, and inversely, each person becomes a "tree of life" through the creative, spiritual act of speech (Skify I, 205–207).

Belyj's novel *Kotik Letaev*, printed in two installments in the miscellanies, treats fictionally many of the same topics as "Aaron's Rod". The growing awareness of the world by the young child Kotik parallels the adult need to expand consciousness, to develop one's inner self to the point where it can reach out toward greater cosmic understanding. The child's perception of words is a central part of his development. In trying to get at the essence of words, he experiences their primitive, mythic sense. He also delves at the roots of words and at the significance of their sound in order to recreate for himself their basic meaning. The child, however, cannot attain the ultimate goal—the birth of a new word—he only traverses the first steps of consciousness—"*mig, komnata, ulica, proisšestvie, vremja goda, Rossija, istorija, mir*" (Skify II, 103).

Spiritual rebellion is also a theme in the other fictional work in the first miscellany, the prologue to a novel *The Possessed Ones* (Oglašen-nye), written by Ol'ga Forš (under the pseudonym A. Terek). Gurij, the hero of this unfinished novel, appears in the prologue as a formerly zealous novice who is now gnawed by doubts and rellious feeling. In the course of the novel he was to leave the Church and find his own path to revolution, like the scythians, through art (Tamarčenko 1966, 96–108).

In the first volume, the peasant poets are modestly represented. The four poems by Esenin entitled "Goluben'" and five by Kljuev—"Zemlja i železo" describe a rural Russia as yet untouched by revolution. Their praise for a calm, rural Russian homeland and their love for its unspoiled nature provide a standard for measuring their later revolutionary expectations. Esenin's longer poem "Marfa Posadnica", offers the fifteenth century Novgorod heroine as a model for modern day rural democratic independence and rejects Moscow, the authoritarian, urban, centralized power.

Material in the second scythian Miscellany, which appeared at the end of 1917 (although dated 1918), reflects the influence of the February Revolution. The critical articles—publicistic rather than theoretical—devote their attention mainly to the peasant poets. Both Ivanov-Razumnik and Belyj see in the peasant poetry the embodiment of their own understanding of the revolution. This standard is then used to castigate opponents of the revolution. In "Poets and Revolution" (Poėty i revoljucija) Ivanov-Razumnik labels the peasant (*narodnyj*) poets, in particular Kljuev, Esenin, and Orešin, as the only valuable poetic voices heard during the revolution because only they spoke with the force of genuine feeling. The city poets, with the exception of Majakovskij, failed to meet the challenge of World War I and the Revolution. (Ivanov-Razumnik 1918a, 3.) In "Two Russias" (Dve Rossii) Ivanov-Razumnik attributes to the *narodnyj* poets his own frequently repeated formula for the progression of the revolution—from political to social freedom toward international freedom and the ultimate goal—spiritual freedom. Opponents of the Revolution are compared to Old Testament believers seeking refuge in outmoded, moribund beliefs. The Revolution's supporters such as the *narodnyj* poets, understand that after the Golgotha of revolution lies "future resurrection in strength and glory" (Skify II, 218).

143

Belyj's introduction to Kljuev's poem "Song of the Sunbearer" (Pesn' solncenosca) compares the Revolution to the infant Jesus, born in humble surroundings, i.e., backward Russia, unrecognized by the cultural world. Kljuev, whom Belyj identifies with the voice of the *narod* or nation, like the legendary shepherds, foresees and welcomes the holy infant. The *narodnyj* voices blend with those of the magi, the wise men of the West, i.e., enlightened intellectuals, in praising the new revelation.

The revolutionary peasant poetry in this volume is not commensurate in literary worth with the praise bestowed on it. Esenin's three revolutionary poems are weak; for example, the poem "Tovarišč", about a worker's son, lacks vivid characters, imagery or style. More lively imagery can be found in "Otčar" where the Revolution is personified in the legendary peasant hero Otčar. Kljuev's language in "Song of the Sunbearer" and in "February" (Fevral') is less rich than usual in imagery and peasant expressions.

More subtlety and originality can be found in the pre-revolutionary poetry in the miscellany—Kljuev's fourteen poems "Hut Songs" (Izbjanye pesni). Esenin's fifteen poems "Under the Paternal Roof" (Pod otčim krovom) and Orešin's "Dulejka" and "Ded-krasnobaj". As the titles suggest, these poems describe an essentially immutable rural Russia whose native essence is dear to the poets. Esenin's imagery brings the cosmos and the peasants' native earth together into fertile union: "Otelivščeesja nebo / ližet krasnogo telka" (Skify II, 166). In Kljuev's poems, village life and wisdom are seen as part of unfolding eternity:

I Deva-blagodat'
kak tixij len sprjadaet dni,
čtob večnoe sotkat'

(Skify II, 117)

Both cycles are enveloped by a dream-like atmosphere from which the poet does not want to be awakened. Orešin describes a suffering, burdened peasantry, but also does not reject the rural life:

Celujte každyj kom zemli neraspylennoj,
Molites' v oblaka i ržatyj černozem
Pod mesjacem sedym v molitve tixozvonnoj
Dvuxžil'nuju soxu vsemirno vospoem!

(Skify II, 33)

144

Other scythians such as Blok, Belyj, Ivanov-Razumnik, Lundberg or Érberg could never share the same satisfaction with the exclusively rural life which emerges in these poems. They saw in the peasant life spiritual values which they praised, but preferred to incorporate them into a revitalized urban society. Such differences contributed to the eventual withdrawal of the peasant poets from the scythian group.

Fictional works in the second miscellany included the second half of Belyj's *Kotik Letaev* and the story "The Islanders" (Ostrovitjane) by Evgenij Zamjatin. Written in 1917 during Zamjatin's stay in England, the story shows a scythian distaste for the stagnant, stolid life of the British bourgeoisie. The ultimate stage in *meščanstvo* is the "Zavet prinuditel'nogo spasenija", a minute code of daily living by which the respected Vicar Dooley (D'juli) hopes to ward off any incipient spontaneity in his town. Through the character Kemble and his passion for a burlesque dancer, Zamjatin suggests that the life force can never be fully petrified and will always burst forth despite attempts at suppression.[10]

The prose writer Aleksej Remizov, a friend of Ivanov-Razumnik, contributed to both miscellanies. He expressed his antagonism to the Revolution in "Lay of the Ruin of the Russian Land" (Slovo o pogibeli Russkoj zemli) in the second volume. Using the style and language of an ancient Russian lay, Remizov mourned the passing of orthodox, patriarchal Russia and treated the Revolution as a judgment for past sins.[11]

Znamja truda and Naš put'

The careful composition of literary miscellanies was suited to more stable times than the tempestuous ones following the February and October Revolutions. Informal, open meetings provided a more immediate platform for writers to read their latest works and to discuss the most recent theories of art and revolution. In his *Writer's Notes* Lundberg describes a typical scythian evening at Ivanov-Razumnik's house in January, 1918. Zamjatin gave his views of England while Olga Forš enjoyed his anecdotes. "Esenin, rich in talent, almost a boy, plays with verse, plays with the sharpness of conviction." Ivanov-Razumnik presented his theories on eternal revolution and on the cyclical nature of national uprisings. "In the evenings at Ivanov-Razumnik's, literature is not merely presented, it is created, especially during the long winter nights when one of the guests remains tête-à-tête with the host." (Lundberg 1922, 117).

Abandoning plans for a third miscellany, the scythians began publishing in the Petrograd daily newspaper *Znamja truda*, which became the official organ of the Left S-R's after they split from the S-R's in November, 1917. Poems by Blok, Belyj, Ėrberg, Esenin, Kljuev, Orešin, Širjaevec et al. and essays by Ivanov-Razumnik, Ėrberg, Lundberg, and Avraamov appeared regularly. With Ivanov-Razumnik serving as literary editor, the editorial office became another scythian meeting place. Blok notes meeting various scythians there (Blok 1965, 383–443).

The scythians supplemented the newspaper with a journal *Naš put'*, sponsored by the central committee of the Left S-R's. Most of the literary works had been published previously in *Znamja truda*. Two issues appeared in spring, 1918. The Bolsheviks closed the newspaper and journal in July, 1918 after having accused the Left S-R's of attempting an uprising in early July.

The scythians also organized public poetry readings. Ivanov-Razumnik gave the opening address before a May, 1918 gathering at which verse by Blok, Kljuev, Esenin and Ėrberg was recited (ZB 1918: 45, 14.5). In June, Belyj, Esenin, Orešin, Lundberg, and A. Lur'e participated in a literary musical evening.

Although many groups sprang up in the revolutionary period, each enthusiastically proclaiming its own brand of art in revolution, the scythians were an anomaly—they were among the few pre-revolutionary intelligentsia who welcomed the Bolshevik Revolution. Many of their former acquaintances repudiated the Revolution and its supporters. Lundberg wrote, "The Merežkovskijs spread the first dirty rumors about us [the scythians]. Here they didn't shake someone's hand, there they met like enemies" (Lundberg 1922, 120–121). Zinaida Gippius particularly disliked Ivanov-Razumnik; in her memoirs she referred to him as a "dark personality" and "deserter, half Left S-R, already half Bolshevik partisan" (Gippius 1925, 57, 62).

On the other hand, the scythians' anti-Marxist idealism and their preference for the peasantry over the proletariat, separated them from established pro-Revolutionary groups such as the futurists and from the new proletarian groups.

Scythian diatribes in the *Znamja truda* period were directed more against the intelligentsia than against any other group. This preoccupation with their own self-image is typical of the intelligentsia in general (see Raeff 1966) and of the scythians in particular. The scythians had been actively involved in the lively debates on the future of the intelligentsia in the years of disappointment and stagnation which followed the 1905 Revolution.[12] In 1918 they renewed their earlier critique. They underscored the connection between the two periods by reprinting in *Znamja truda* several of Blok's critical essays on the intelligentsia from 1908 such as "Narod and Culture" (Narod i kultura), "The Elemental and the Cultural" (Stixija i kul'tura), and "Flame" (Plamen').

Blok's essay "Intelligentsia and Revolution" is typical of the scythians' post-October attitude. The criticisms were at the same time hortatory. Blok's essay and Lundberg's articles find the same faults in the intelligentsia—sudden concern for their own comfort, property and for formal legal procedures (ZT 1918: 110, 17.1 (under the pseud. Sven); ZT 1918: 137, 7.2; ZT 1918: 180, 14.4; Blok 1961). Blok appeals to the intelligentsia to forget these petty bourgeois concerns and to become true *intelligenty*. Blok, like the other scythians, refuses to define the intelligentsia through Marxian concepts of class, economics or politics. It is a "special kind of unity which exists, however, in reality and by the will of history entered into a very notable relationship with the *narod*, the elemental, namely that of struggle. The intelligentsia, like Russia, continually changes its external appearances, but also remains itself in something essential".[13] The essence is nonmaterial. "Skills, knowledge, methods, habits, talents are nomadic and winged property. We are homeless, without family, without rank, poor—what do we have to lose?" (Blok 1961, 18).

The scythians had hoped that the Revolution would bring together intelligentsia and *narod* to create a new individual whose qualities were, in fact, more typical of the intelligentsia than *narod*—self-reliant creativity, innate morality, individualism combined with a sense of community and spiritual maximalism. Intelligentsia rejection of the scythians' call was, therefore, a crushing blow to scythian expectations.

Ivanov-Razumnik compared the reluctant intelligentsia to the generation of Israelites who cried out against a premature departure to Egypt (ZT 1918: 114, 9.1). He insisted that only what Blok described in "The Twelve" as "*svjatuju Rus', kondovuju, izbjanuju, tolstozadnuju*" would disappear. Russia's eternal "Hellenic" values would be carefully transferred to the new world (Ivanov-Razumnik 1920, 14).

147

The scythians considered the triumph of revolutionary socialism in Russia dependent on its universal acceptance. Although present-day Soviet critics are fond of referring to them as naive Messianists, their call for worldwide revolution was not so different from Bolshevik rhetoric at the time. The possibility of Allied intervention after the signing of the Brest-Litovsk treaty was seen as a threat not only to international revolution but to the Russian Revolution itself.

Faced with this immediate danger, the scythians often directed their appeals and invectives in the *Znamja truda* period against external as well as against internal enemies. Although critics stress the scythians' eastern orientation, in fact, their attention was turned more toward the West. Their ambiguous, even inconsistent attitude toward the West—a mixture of disdain and admiration—already evident in their pre-Revolutionary writings, follows in the nineteenth century Russian intellectual tradition (see Hoffman 1975, Chap. 5). In the past, *intelligenty* like Aleksandr Herzen, who became disenchanted with the West, still considered Russia's revolutionary fate tied to Europe's (see Herzen 1963, 201). The scythians not only retained this belief; they wanted to show that the Russian pupil would now lead the former master.

Scythian views can best be seen in Blok's poem "The Scythians", first published in *Znamja truda* in February, 1918, and in interpretations of it by other group members. Blok's poem neither rejects the West (i.e., Europe) entirely nor identifies Russia completely with the East. The first stanza dramatically proclaims, "Da, skify-my! Da, aziaty-my, / s raskosymi i žadnymi očami!" In the next stanza, however, Blok calls Russians "poslušnye xolopy. / Deržali ščit mež dvux vraždebnyx ras / Mongolov i Evropy!" (Blok 1960, 360). Russians are not themselves Asiatics, but intermediaries between East and West—hitherto for the benefit of Europe. Russia would not sever its ties with Europe, upon which it looks "both with hate and with love". At this point Russia's Asiatic qualities are temporarily forgotten. Her love, as in Dostoevskij's famous Puškin speech, is based on a superior understanding of Europe:

My pomnim vsë — parižskix ulic ad,
   I venec'janskie proxlady,
Limonnyx rošč dalekij aromat,
   I Kel'na dymnye gromady ...

(Blok 1960, 361)

148

The common ground should be reason for reconciliation.

Pridite k nam! Ot užasov vojny
   Pridite v mirnye ob''jat'ja!
Poka ne pozdno — staryj meč v nožny,
   Tovarišči! My stanem — brat'ja!

(Blok 1960, 361)

The friendly appeal is followed immediately by a threat:

A esli net — nam nečego terjat',
I nam dostupno verolomstvo!

Only when repulsed would Russia act "Eastern" and show the West her "Asiatic mug". Europe would then fall prey to the real enemy, the genuine East:

Ne sdvinemsja, kogda svirepyj gunn
   V karmanax trupov budet šarit',
Žeč' goroda, i v cerkov' gnat' tabun ...

(Blok 1960, 362)

The East is associated with meaningless, savage destruction. The scythians threaten to act "Eastern" only as a terrible alternative. Blok's diary (Jan. 11, 1918) shows that he connected the threat with disappointment over Europe's failure to meet its revolutionary obligation: "[...] if you [Europe] destroy our revolution, that means that you already are *no longer Aryans*. And we shall open widely the gates to the East" (Blok 1963, 317). The poem ends with the more desired outcome:

V poslednij raz — opomnis', staryj mir!
   Na bratskij pir truda i mira,
V poslednij raz na svetlyj bratskij pir
   Szyvaet varvarskaja lira!

(Blok 1960, 362)

Lundberg called Blok's poem deeply unselfish in contrast to the manly practicality of Puškin's "To the Slanderers of Russia" (Lundberg 1922, 139). In the essay "Trial by Storm and Tempest" (Ispytanie v groze i bure) Ivanov-Razumnik praised Blok for going beyond the political and religious concerns of his poetic predecessors to a new international, spiritual level. He explained that Russian spiritual

149

maximalism or scythianism had the mission of purifying Europe as well as Russia of *meščanstvo*.

Significantly, the scythians believed in Europe's ability to survive the apocalyptic times awaiting her. They took issue with Dostoevskij's reference in *Brothers Karamazov* to Europe as the most dear cemetery. According to Ivanov-Razumnik, "it [Europe] is genuinely alive, dear, our own" (Ivanov-Razumnik 1920, 37). Lundberg commented, "Those very buildings and the hands which created them died, but not the element of construction" (Lundberg 1922, 194).

Scythian calls for European participation in a common revolutionary effort continued in the twenties, although by that time prospects had dimmed. Belyj, in particular, wrote several articles contrasting Russia with the West to the latter's detriment ("Kul'tura v sovremennoj Rossii", NRK 1922: 1, 2–6; "O 'Rossii' v Rossii i o 'Rossii' v Berline", Beseda 1923: 1, 211–235; see also Belyj 1967, 296–310). By the time he returned to Russia from Berlin in 1923, he seemed doubtful about Europe's ability to achieve regeneration through revolution (Belyj 1924).

The scythians used the terms "Eastern" and "Western" in an additional sense. They viewed Russia as a microcosm of the world—divided between a "Western" highly educated, rational and individualistic intelligentsia and an "Eastern" barbaric, i.e., instinctive and uncultured but sensitive and communal *narod*. Revolution would be the first stage in reuniting these two sides to create a new individual and renewed Russian culture which could then influence universal culture. Belyj's pre-Revolutionary novels *Petersburg* and *The Silver Dove* deal on different levels with the complex process of achieving such a synthesis through revolutionary cataclysms.

In the years before 1917, several scythians, notably Blok and Belyj, seemed more fearful than optimistic about the effects of the *narod*'s barbarism on Russia. After 1917, however, they praised highly the scythian or 'barbaric' potential in the *narod*, which, they felt, was combined with a sincere desire for deep spiritual transformation. They frequently compared the Russian revolutionary *narod* to the barbarian masses in the Roman period who accepted a revolutionary new doctrine—Christianity—and overthrew a moribund religion and empire (Ivanov-Razumnik 1920a; Blok 1961, 60–91).

The peasant poets, like the other scythians, did not support the Russian orthodox Church. Rather, they seemed to share Ivanov-

Razumnik's feeling that revolutionary socialism was replacing Christianity as a moral, spiritual force. Esenin began his most famous poem of the period "Inonija" (which first appeared in *Znamja truda* and in *Naš put'* No. 2) by proclaiming himself the replacement for previous Biblical authority:

Tak govorit po Biblii / Prorok Esenin Sergej: ...
Telo, Xristovo telo / Vyplevyvaju izo rta. /
Ne xoču vosprijat' spasenija / Čerez muki ego i krest:
Ja inoe postig učenie / Probodajuščix večnost' zvezd.

(Esenin 1966, 33)

In "Sel'skij časoslov" Esenin calls upon old Rus' to perish and heralds the birth of a new holy infant named Izramistil.

The peasant poets, however, present a different vision of the new socialist paradise than the other scythians do. They see the Revolution as a victory for the Russian land in a literal sense. The resulting abundance belongs as much to a mythical Russian past as to a hoped for future. In "Red Song" Kljuev called the legendary town of Kitež "our native, longed for paradise" in which the land would bear free bread for the peasant. Esenin, however, rejects Kitež as a symbol tied only to the past and declares: "Obeščaju vam grad Inoniju, / Gde živet božestvo živyx!" (Esenin 1966, 35). It too is dominated by images of rural fertility:

I vspašu ja černye ščeki / Niv tvoix novoj soxoj;
Zolotoj proletit sorokoj / Urožaj nad tvoej stranoj.
. . . .
Novye vyrastut sosny / Na ladonjax tvoix polej.
I, kak belki, želtye vesny / Budut prygat' po suč'jam dnej.

(Esenin 1966, 39)

The peasants generally ignored the industrialized city; when mentioned, it appears as a place of suffering:

Gorod-d'javol kopytami bil / Ustrašaja nas kamennym zevom ...
Gnev povel nas na tjurmy, dvorcy, / Gde na pravdu okovy
kovalis' ...[14]

In "Inonija" Esenin warns America, the symbol of industrialization, to keep away from Russia:

Ne otjagivaj čugunnoj radugoj / Niv i granitom-rek.
Tol'ko vod'ju svobodnoj Ladogi / Prosverlit bytie čelovek.

(Esenin 1966, 37)

Although Belyj, Blok, and Ivanov-Razumnik often stated their preference for the rural over the urban, they did not want to eliminate the city or technology from the ideal future. Both before and during the scythian period, they called on man to overcome the harmful effects of technology and to use it to develop man's spiritual state (see Ivanov-Razumnik 1912 and Belyj 1910 / "Gorod", "Radužnyj gorod"/). Rural Russia to them represented the reserve of spiritual strength in the nation from whence the transformation could come. Ivanov-Razumnik expressed these views in an article about Majakovskij and the futurists—"Misterija ili Buff" written from 1918–1919. He credited futurists for valuing the Machine (sic) as the path for the liberation of mankind, but faulted them for not seeing beyond the paradise of material abundance described at the end of Majakovskij's play *Mystery Bouffe*. Ivanov-Razumnik reiterated his praise of the peasant poets' spirituality, but he clearly did not go along with their rejection of the city. Like Belyj, he called for a solution which combined the two worlds: "[...] one must be able to adapt to both: beyond the hell of the City to see the paradise of the city, beyond the paradise of the Country to see the hell of the country" (Ėrberg 1921, 70).

City and country were also symbols—the halves of a lost unity in contemporary civilization—the city associated with alienation and cold rationalism and the country with instinctive creative forces (Belyj 1910a /"Lug zelenyj"/; Blok 1962, 66–82 /"Bezvremen'e"/). For Belyj, East and West were other symbols of this contemporary crisis. According to Belyj, individual disharmony between reason and feeling, mind and heart was projected as a split between East and West, between Russia and Germany, between subconscious and supraconscious. He urged a return to vital unity by overcoming meaningless barriers—between East and West, between heart and head (Ėpoxa 1918, 202). The typically scythian method is creative rebellion—an explosion breaking out of the confines of ordinary consciousness.[15] The new, unified world culture would be built syncretically out of the elements of the past. The unifier is designated as Solov'ev's Sophia, the Spirit of the World. She represents a living unity, a mixture of

152

Eastern myth and Western abstract thought. Russia herself, according to Belyj, could be the Sophia: "We, as those obligated to unite East and West, we, scythians, must carefully absorb all this [the international characteristics mentioned in Blok's 'The Scythians'] and place it not in a dead museum, but in a live museum of our heart, our Russian consciousness" (Blok 1922, 28).[16]

Vol'fila Period

The closing of *Znamja truda* and *Naš put'* in July, 1918 was only one of a series of events which continued to frustrate the scythians' lofty expectations. A new Left S-R-sponsored journal *Znamja* appeared twice in early 1918 and was also forced to cease publication; a new *Znamja* was started a year later.

The scythians also encountered difficulties publishing in *Alkonost*, a private Symbolist oriented press started in June, 1918 by S. Aljanskij. In 1919 M. Lisovskij, Petersburg Commissar on Press Matters, halted publication of six Alkonost books including Belyj's *Krizis kultury*, Ėrberg's *Cel' tvorčestva*, and the journal *Zapiski mečtatelej*. Only Gor'kij's intervention kept these publications alive. Blok's distress over these obstacles can be seen in a note he prepared to commemorate Alkonost's first anniversary (Černov 1964, 532). Lisovskij also interfered with works by Ėrberg and Ivanov-Razumnik published by *Kolos*, a cooperative socialist publishing house (see Vitjazev 1921 on problems encountered by private publishing houses in this period). The scythians were more successful in publishing abroad in this period. Lundberg's scythian Press operated in Berlin until his return to the Soviet Union in 1924.

Because of their publishing problems, the scythians considered starting a scythian academy in the fall of 1918. They associated the term "Academy" with "the first sources of European culture, when sciences, arts, society were still connected in the wholeness and completeness of the ancient world view" (first notice on the creation of Free Philosophical Academy in Gagen-Torn 1975, 444). Initial problems included objections to the title Academy and the arrest of Ivanov-Razumnik and others in February, 1919 for supposed connections with an alleged Left S-R plot (Ivanov-Razumnik 1965, 18 ff.).[17]

Vol'fila, The Free Philosophical Association, finally opened in November, 1919 with the presentation of Blok's speech "The Collapse

153

of Humanism" (Krušenie gumanizma). The charter declares their goal as "the investigation and solution of problems of cultural creation in the socialistic and philosophical spirit; also the goal of spreading among the national masses a socialistic and deepened philosophical approach to these questions" (Blok 1928, 157).

The Association held large open meetings on Sunday afternoons devoted to lectures, panel discussions or debates. Topics included ancient philosophy (Plato), religion (comparisons between Judaism and Christianity), nineteenth century Russian thinkers (Herzen, Lavrov, Leont'ev, Danilevskij, Tolstoj, Dostoevskij, and Vl. Solov'ev), and the problems of contemporary culture ("Proletarian culture", "Crisis of Culture", and "Time and Space in Philosophy and History"). Vol'fila also offered specialized courses such as Ivanov-Razumnik's "Philosophy of Culture", Belyj's "Culture of Thought", Štejnberg's "Basic Problems of Philosophy" and Érberg's "Philosophy of Creativity".[18]

Vol'fila was part of the intellectual ferment which flourished in Petrograd in the early twenties despite extraordinary physical hardships caused by the Civil War.[19] Belyj enthusiastically described Vol'fila activities (Belyj 1967, 296–310) and his reports are corroborated by other sources. The anti-Bolshevik philosopher Losskij describes his guest appearance before a full house at a Vol'fila meeting—in the front rows sat the *intelligenty*; in the back were the sailors and Red Army men who were too late to find seats (Losskij 1968, 208).

Scythian emphasis in 1919–24 on theoretical cultural questions can be attributed to various factors. On the one hand, the Revolution appeared to promise a new widespread cultural blossoming. Since the government encouraged diversity in literary theory, each group eagerly entered the speculative fray with hopes that their vision would prove most correct.

On the other hand, despite successes such as Vol'fila, problems with censorship and bureaucracy led to greater scythian frustration and disappointment in the concrete present—hence the focus on a more theoretical future. Belyj labeled the period 1919–22 as a "crisis in revolutionary expectations" with 1919 as the most difficult year: "sharp disappointment in the nearness of a revolution of the Spirit" (Nivat 1974, 47–48). Blok's mental depression in the years before his death in 1921 was connected with his disillusionment in the Revolution. To the scythians, his death marked a turning point in their own growing estrangement from the Bolshevik Revolution (see Ivanov-Razumnik, in Blok 1922, 60–63).

Scythian interest in cultural theory was also very personal. Their generation had experienced a crisis in the humanistic culture on which they had been nourished, a crisis which they linked directly to the major upheavals of their time—World War I and the Revolution. They endeavored both to explain the failure of humanism and to delineate the rising new culture.

The definition of culture was basic to this task. Belyj emphasized its vitality in numerous articles: "Culture is not in what *has been formed*, but in *forming*, not in form but in the creative process of molding a multitude of forms (NRK 1922: I, 3–4, and Belyj 1923, 161–188). In "The Collapse of Humanism", Blok stressed the dynamic, harmonious aspects of culture.

The scythians opposed civilization—the accumulation of mechanical, material phenomena—to culture. Blok identifies civilization with the styles, artifacts and institutions which remain when the cultural spirit dies (Blok 1961, 101, 111). In flower from the fourteenth to mid-eighteenth century, humanistic culture turned into civilization in the nineteenth century.

Like many other critics influenced by currents of romanticism, the scythians attributed the decline in humanistic culture to a mechanistic world view which became prevalent after the Industrial Revolution. Man lost his vital organic unity with nature. Instead, nature and the arts were turned into objects. Each field of science and art became so narrowly specialized that the sense of belonging to a unified whole was lost (Blok 1961, 103 ff.; Belyj 1920, 12).

Both Belyj and A. Z. Štejnberg saw the fashionable decadence in twentieth century art as part of the humanistic crisis. Art, Štejnberg explained, reveals the highest realm of consciousness since it creates unity out of the discontinuity of time. But contemporary consciousness had lost the ability to create unity. A split existed between subject and observed object with no unifying link between the two (Štejnberg, in Ėrberg 1921, 24). The gap created by the withdrawal of live content from a creative work was filled by an excess of empty form; Štejnberg thereby explained the contemporary emphasis (also noted by Belyj) on stylization, imitativeness, primitivism or supposed simplicity arrived at by contrived efforts (Ibidem, 32).

Despite its degeneracy, humanist civilization fought for its survival

155

and came into conflict with the new, rising culture. According to the scythians, the tension between the two could be resolved only by revolution, which would provide the force necessary to shatter stagnant, outmoded forms. Scythian emphasis was not, as in the more publicistic *Znamja truda* period on revolution as a complete break with the past but on revolution as part of an ongoing process of organic change which Belyj calls involution: "the embodiment of soul [the creative idea] in conditions of organic life" (Belyj 1917, 13). The birth metaphor implies a relationship between old and new—the latter exists within the old in an invisible, embryonic state and is nurtured by it until the new bursts out of its protective covering. Belyj claimed that the term "revolution" did not apply to economic or political changes; such developments were only the natural consequences of evolution. Belyj felt that the ultimate revolution—the attainment of genuine, unconditional freedom—still lay hidden in the future (Ibidem, 19–20).

Èrberg also viewed revolution in artistic, organic terms. In a post-Revolutionary essay he repeats his earlier claim (Èrberg 1913) that art, by definition, is revolutionary, inspired by a desire for unconditional freedom, by the need to revolt against the constraining laws of nature. The artist must constantly rebel against dogmas which have stagnated into obligatory norms.

But rebellion is not a complete break. Èrberg describes cultural change with the image of a nodular stalk. Each new nodule or cultural epoch is firmly joined to the past one. By seeing revolution as an ongoing phenomenon, Èrberg, like the other scythians, was able to value both present and past iconoclasts (Èrberg 1921, 1–18).

Štejnberg differed from most scythians in his ultimate view of history, but he shared with them similar ideas on revolution as an organic means of transition from past to future. He compares cultural growth in a society to the growth of a tree. The visible part—the top—keeps branching out, but the hidden roots secretly maintain the unity of the whole. When a culture or tree has grown and branched out, i.e., become so diffuse that it can no longer survive, the leaves dry up, fall to the ground, and provide fertilizer and seeds for new trees (Èrberg 1921, 25). In this image Štejnberg suggests a continuity which bridges seeming gaps: although one culture seems to end abruptly, the sprouts of a new culture derive from the seeds of the old. The cycle of growth and withering of cultures will repeat itself until the

very process of decay disintegrates and man achieves the final goal—
the overcoming of history and of time itself.

The scythians predicted that the cultural revolution would produce
a new type, a "man-artist", unlike the isolated figures of the past
(Blok 1961, 25; 126). According to Belyj, humanism had idolized the
individual personality (ličnost') as a being in opposition to the collective. The new I (Ja) is complete only as part of the collective.
Heroic anarchy will be replaced by synarchy, "You in Me and I in
You" (Èpopeja 1922: 1, 14). Each person would become a creative
being, but the transformation of the masses into heroes would not be
easy. Belyj compared the new heroes to Christ; each faced a tragic
fate and each had to prepare himself to receive the new creative word
or Logos within himself.

Belyj reiterated the favored scythian pattern of a syncretic combination of opposites. The new artistic person would unite the Dionysian
elements of ecstasy and fire with the Apollonian elements of thought
and lyricism. This union at the same time represents the marriage of
the intelligentsia (the Apollonian intellect) with the narod (Dionysian
heart) (Ibidem, 15).

Blok represented to the other scythians a model for the future
heroic artistic individual whose work would embody collective aspirations. In the Vol'fila meeting dedicated to Blok's memory, Belyj
focused on Blok's role as the organ of self-consciousness of the Russian
nation. Blok embodied the special Russian features:

Vot èta vsečelovečnost' i čelovečnost', vot èta ideologija — delaet
Aleksandra Aleksandroviča vo-pervyx Skifom, vo vsex smyslax
slova, kak maksimalista, kak togo, kto dovodit svoj xod mysli —
ne v abstraktnyx sxemax, no v žiznennyx pereživanijax — do konca.
Èto osobenno ego svjazuet s sud'bami russkogo naroda, s sud'bami
naroda, prizvannogo primirit' Vostok i Zapad, sozdat' uslovija
dejstvitel'nogo bratstva narodov (Blok 1922, 27).

Predictions about a new individual and a new role for art abounded
in the tumultuous literary world of the twenties. The scythian model,
however, possessed distinctions which would eventually cause conflict
with Communist culture. For example, although both Trockij and
the scythians predicted a new man whose reason and feeling were in
harmony, each actually envisioned different halves of the equation
predominating. Trockij, in Literature and Revolution, portrayed a

157

society in which man gained greater and greater control over his sub-conscious processes and over nature itself. The end result would be a controlled, primarily rational individual living in a functional, artificial universe. The scythians' new individual has more Slavophile over-tones—he would combine reason and feeling into a higher, organic whole. Man would not so much control nature as be in accord with it.

Literary debates inevitably touched on the role of the proletariat on the path toward a new collective culture. The Proletkul't urged the proletariat to develop its own culture as a way of organizing its experience and expanding its influence. Trockij, on the other hand, dismissed proletarian art as an unnecessary stage on the way to the more important goal of socialist culture. The futurists vigorously op-posed concepts of art exclusively by or for the proletariat. They emphasized the need for talent and hard technical work but stressed that the new professional artists, unlike bourgeois talents, would create for the collective, not for personal glory (see Jangfeldt 1976).

The scythians welcomed proletarian involvement in cultural ac-tivities; workers and sailors were among those attending Vol'fila functions. Belyj gave lectures to the Proletkul't and reported enthusi-astically on their receptivity (ZM 1919: 1, 121). But the scythians all denied not only the possibility of a proletarian culture but also the existence of any culture as the property of one class. Culture to them always implied a broader outlook. Èrberg rejected efforts to label art bourgeois or proletarian: "I think the only measure applicable to art is the greater or lesser degree of its revolutionism" (Èrberg 1921, 1).

Ivanov-Razumnik argued that culture was national and hence beyond class. For example, Puškin's and Tolstoj's works never represented only the nobility since their inspiration came from deep *narodnyj* roots. He felt that the proletariat could be leaders in destroy-ing old bourgeois forms (civilization as the scythians understood it) and in building new ones. But the creative content which would turn these forms into living culture had to come from the entire *narod*, of which the proletariat was only a part. The new culture would be neither proletarian nor bourgeois, but *narodnyj*, representing the entire nation (Znamja 1921: 2, 24–26).

Belyj also argued with the Marxist view of the proletariat's cultural role. He pointed out that according to the logic of Marxist mech-anistic theory, the proletariat could produce only the final class culture of the old world since they were a part of this bourgeois world of necessity and their actions were determined by it. Belyj himself suggested a more creative role for the proletariat. As the most dynamic group they were best able to lead the way to a new realm of freedom which existed up to now only in embryonic form, toward a culture which would be "neither bourgeois nor aristocratic nor proletariat, but human" (Znamja 1921: 2, 23). In this new realm, labor would no longer be an enslaving burden but an act of human creativity.

Discouragement about developments toward a scythian culture grew stronger in the twenties. Any further organized scythian efforts ended in 1924 with the forcible closing of the Petersburg Vol'fila. Individual scythians found it almost impossible to get published. In 1925 the censor informed Ivanov-Razumnik's publisher, "You'd be well advised not to submit anything by Ivanov-Razumnik—irrespective of its contents, we shan't pass it anyway" (Ivanov-Razumnik 1965, 1973). Belyj also encountered difficulties at this time after Trockij's unfavorable remarks in 1923 and criticism from RAPP, the proletarian writers organization.

Belyj expressed his disappointment in Bolshevik society along with his hopes for the distant future. In the introduction to the first volume of *Zapiski mečtatelej*, Belyj uses the metaphor of a forest to describe his ideal human collective. This commune should strive for the harmonious unity of all parts, but not for regimental equality. Forcing human identicality would be like changing a natural, living forest into a fence where all pieces are equal and alike, but are also rigidly stuck into the earth. A fence offers the equality of slaves rather than a fraternal commune. A fence is barren; a forest is a fertile community.

The forest gives off moisture which condenses in clouds and waters the area. This cloud, "the product of the spiritual culture of dreamers" defines the community as a whole since it is the part visible from a distance. Belyj concluded with a plea not to turn all the groves into fences since the climate of the whole country could be changed (ZM 1919: 1, 6).

In other articles he also chastised the Bolsheviks for trying to impose a collective culture from above and for trying to build rigid institutions instead of promoting unconstrained cultural flowering (NRK 1922: 3–4, 2; ZM 1919: 1, 6).

Scythian discontent was directed not only at the new government but also at the new generation of writers. Art could accomplish all its revolutionary goals only if the artist himself imbued his art with

159

a live word issuing from his very soul. An artist content to practice his craft in a mechanical, technical way defaulted on both the immediate and distant goals of art—i.e., such art could neither benefit contemporary Russia nor lead to spiritual transformation. Blok criticized the Acmeist poets because "in their poetry (and consequently, in themselves) they are silent about the most important, the only worthwhile [thing]: soul" (Blok 1961, 183). Scythian objections to the Formalist approach to literature can be seen in the report of a Petersburg Vol'fila meeting in 1923 when the works of OPOJAZ, the Formalist group, were discussed (NRK 1923: 1, 23). The scythians were also unenthusiastic about the various writing workshops which sprang up after the Revolution. Blok, for example, considered that a poet needs general culture and knowledge, but it is impossible to teach the writing of verse (Pavlovič 1964, 481).

Ivanov-Razumnik's dissatisfaction with the contemporary literary scene appeared in an article "A Glance and Something" (Vzgljad i nečto), which was published under a pseudonym. Written to commemorate the 100th anniversary of the appearance of Griboedov's play *Woe from Wit*, the article was signed Ippolit Uduš'ev, after a character in the play. The name is also a pun on the Russian verb *udušat'*—to suffocate.

In the article Ivanov-Razumnik denigrates current emphasis on techniques and formalist efforts to tear literature away from other fields of culture. True literature, he affirms, involves a "burning of the soul" (Ivanov-Razumnik 1925, 160).

In his remarks, literature becomes a medium for protest against the general social situation, and the present is fitted into the long range context of Russia's troubled social history. Modern writers' concern with technique becomes a sign of the epoch, part of the petty, external understanding of the Revolution. Although Ivanov-Razumnik labeled contemporary literature a decline based on old forms, he remained optimistic about the long range possibility for spiritual transformation: "It [the Russian *narod*] perhaps is only beginning to live ... The new seeds, sown by the Revolution, will come up perhaps in tens or hundreds of years, was it not always that way?" (Ibidem, 181).

The scythians did not live to see their hopes realized in the USSR. But their theories on how art and revolution could transform the individual, the Russian nation, and the world remain provocative, and their revolutionary poetry best conveys the exuberance of a time when the Revolution of the Spirit seemed imminent.

1. Ivanov-Razumnik is the pen name for Razumnik Vasil'evič Ivanov (1878–1946). Brief biographical and bibliographical information on him is available in *Literaturnaja Ènciklopedija*, Vol. IV, 1930, 410–413, and in Ivanov-Razumnik 1953. The latter is available in English as *The memoirs of Ivanov-Razumnik* (transl. P. S. Squire), London 1965. Further references to the memoirs will be included in the text as Ivanov-Razumnik 1965.
2. See Nivat 1974, 45–82; Cvetaeva 1953, 206–352; Gippius 1925, 7 70; Xodasevič 1939, 61–99; and Stepun 1968, 160–186.
3. Personal interview with Nina Berberova in October, 1971.
4. Esenin's coldness to scythianism was also related to a developing anatagonism to his former mentor Kljuev. See his letter in Esenin 1968, 79.
5. References to volume I of *Zapiski pisatelja* come from the Berlin, 1922 edition, since some material about the scythians was eliminated from the 1930 Leningrad edition. Volume II was published in Leningrad in 1930.
6. Ivanov-Razumnik's portrayal of the ideal scythian resembles very strongly the definition of the ideal *intelligent* which he had developed earlier in his *Istorija obščestvennoj mysli*.
7. Mixail Prišvin (1873–1954) did not get involved in the ideology of scythianism. He is known in Soviet literary history primarily for his prose works, which display his interest in nature. He remained in touch with Ivanov-Razumnik, even during the time when the latter was a political outcast. See Lowe 1974, 498.
8. The process of comparison makes an interesting study: as Ivanov-Razumnik's own opinion of the 1917 revolutions changed, he either altered the meaning of the parallels or drew on later periods when Herzen modified some of his former positions.
9. Cf. notes by Blok on "Dvenadcat'", in Blok 1960, 474–475, and Belyj on "Xristos voskres", in Belyj 1966, 557. Ivanov-Razumnik consistently denied that he ever belonged to the left S-R party (see Ivanov Razumnik 1965, 90).
10. Zamjatin did not remain active in the scythian activities. In an article "Skify-li?", *Mysl'*, 1918: 1, written under the pseudonym Mix. Platonov, he criticized Ivanov-Razumnik for not emphasizing sufficiently the elitist, uncompromising, and eternally rebellious nature of the true revolutionary. For a good biography of Zamjatin which includes a discussion of his relationship to the scythians, see Shane 1968.
11. Remizov left Russia for Berlin in 1921 and in 1923 settled in Paris. After Ivanov-Razumnik left the USSR in 1946, he renewed contact with Remizov. See Lowe 1974, 495–501.
12. See S. Hoffman 1975, 73 ff. for a further discussion of these views in the pre-revolutionary period.
13. Blok, "Intelligencija i revoljucija", ZT 1918: 122, 1.2. Later reprinted as the introduction to the 1918 collection of Blok's essays *Rossija i intelligencija*.

14. "Iz podvalov, iz temnyx uglov", in Kljuev 1969, 471. See also Orešin's poem "Gorod" in Orešin 1918.
15. This way of thinking is also typical of Rudolf Steiner's anthroposophy, which greatly influenced Belyj at this time.
16. See also Belyj's poem "Xristos voskres", first published in *Znamja Truda*, for a poetic rendering of these themes.
17. A. Z. Štejnberg, Vol'fila's "scholar-secretary", describes his incarceration then with Blok in Blok 1922, 35–53.
18. See the "chronicle" in NRK 1921: 1, 23, and 1922: 1, 32. Some Vol'fila reports were printed in *Znamja*; others appeared in two collections edited by Èrberg (Èrberg 1921 and 1922).
19. See, for example, Ol'ga Forš 1964, which describes in fictional form the literary life in the *Dom iskusstv*.

References

Belyj, A.
1910   *Arabeski*, Moskva.
1910a   *Lug zelenyj*, Moskva.
1917   *Revoljucija i kul'tura*, Peterburg.
1920   *Krizis kul'tury*, Peterburg.
1923   "Problema kul'tury", *Strugi. Literaturnyj al'manax*, No. 7.
1924   *Odna iz obitelej carstva tenej*, reprint Letchworth 1971.
1966   *Stixotvorenija i poèmy*, Moskva–Leningrad.
1967   "Pis'mo Andreja Belogo", *Vozdušnye puti*, No. 5.
Blok, A.
1922   *Pamjati Bloka*, Peterburg.
1928   *Dnevnik 1917–1921*, Leningrad.
1960   *Sobranie sočinenij v vos'mi tomax*, t. III, Moskva–Leningrad.
1961   *Ibidem*, t. VI.
1962   *Ibidem*, t. V.
1963   *Ibidem*, t. VII.
1964   *Blokovskij sbornik*, Tartu.
1965   *Zapisnye knižki*, Moskva.
1975   *Blokovskij sbornik*, Tartu.
Cvetaeva, M.
1953   "Plennyj dux", *Proza*, New York.
Černov, I.
1964   "Blok i knigoizdatel'stvo Alkonost", in: Blok 1964.
Èrberg, K.
1921   (Ed.) *Iskusstvo staroe i novoe*, Peterburg.
1922   (Ed.) *Iskusstvo i narod*, Peterburg.
Esenin, S.
1966   *Sobranie sočinenij v pjati tomax*, t. II, Moskva.
1968   *Ibidem*, t. V.

Forš, O.
1964 *Sumasšedšij korabl'*, Washington.
Gagen-Torn, N.
1975 "Vospominanija ob Aleksandre Bloke", in: Blok 1975.
Gippius, Z.
1925 "Moj lunnyj drug. O Bloke", *Živye lica*, Praha.
Herzen, A.
1963 *From the other shore and the Russian people and socialism*, Cleveland.
Hoffman, S.
1975 "Scythianism: a cultural vision in revolutionary Russia". Unpubl.
       diss., Columbia.
Ivanov-Razumnik, R.
1917 "Vmesto predislovija", *Skify*: I, Peterburg.
1917a "Socializm i revoljucija", *Ibidem*.
1918 *God revoljucii*, S. Peterburg.
1918a "Poèty i revoljucija", *Skify*: II, Peterburg.
1920 *Ispytanie v groze i bure*, Berlin.
1920a *Rossija i Inonija*, Berlin.
1925 "Vzgljad i nečto. Otryvok", *Sovremennaja literatura*, Petrograd.
1953 *Tjur'my i ssylki*, New York.
1965 *The memoirs of Ivanov-Razumnik*, New York.
Jangfeldt, B.
1976 *Majakovskij and futurism 1917–1921*, Stockholm.
Kljuev, N.
1969 *Sočinenija*, t. 1, München.
Losskij, N.
1968 *Vospominanija, žizn' i filosofija*, München.
Lowe, D.
1974 "Unpublished letters from Pilniak and Ivanov-Razumnik to Remi-
       zov", *Russian Literature Triquarterly*, No. 8.
Lundberg, E.
1922 *Zapiski pisatelja*, I, Berlin.
Nivat, G.
1974 "A. Belyj. Lettre autobiographique à Ivanov-Razumnik", *Cahiers du
       monde russe et soviétique*, Vol. XV, 1–2, Paris–La Haye.
Orešin, P.
1918 *Krasnyj zvon*, Petrograd.
Pavlovič, N.
1964 "Vospominanija ob Aleksandre Bloke", in: Blok 1964.
Raeff, M.
1964 [Preface to] *Russian intellectual history*. An anthology ed. by M.
       Raeff, New York.
Rozanov, I.
1926 *Esenin o sebe i drugix*, Moskva.
Shane, A.
1968 *The life and works of Evgenij Zamjatin*, Berkeley.

Stepun, F.
1968   "Pamjati Andreja Belogo", *Vstreči*, New York.
Tamarčenko, A.
1966   *Ol'ga Forš*, Moskva–Leningrad.
Vitjazev (Sedenko), P.
1921   *Častnye izdatel'stva v sovetskoj Rossii*, Praha.
Xodasevič, V.
1939   "Andrej Belyj", *Nekropol'*, Brussels.

Nils Åke Nilsson

Mandel'štam and the Revolution

Modern research has fully established that Osip Mandel'štam, contrary to the common view of his contemporary critics, was, as Steven Broyde has said, "immensely involved in his age". "His poetry", Broyde goes on, "represents a continuing commentary on it, an attempt to comprehend and record his reactions to an era which was changing, if not disintegrating before his eyes" (Broyde 1975: 3).

This is true already of the first collection, *Stone*, but applies, of course, even more to the poems of the following period. With the outbreak of The First World War the cultural model demonstrated in *Stone* and the poetics connected with it began to falter. It may still seem rather surprising—and this is a fact which has seldom been directly emphasized—that Mandel'štam was the first of the great Russian poets of his time to react to the October revolution. He printed the first poem on the revolution just a few weeks after the Bolshevik take-over and one month before, for instance, Aleksej Remizov's "Lay of the Destruction of the Land of Russia" ("Slovo o pogibeli russkoj zemli"), often quoted as one of the first poetic reactions, and long before the well-known poems by Blok, Esenin, Pasternak, Majakovskij and Xlebnikov.

This paper will examine two of Mandel'štam's poems written immediately after the October revolution and will do so from a special point of view connected with our project. Since the poet did not take part in the revolution himself, he learned about many events—which eventually roused his poetic imagination—through oral information or, as modern man usually does, through the newspapers. In the first months after the October revolution—as long as there existed a non-Bolshevik press—the newspapers were a very important source of information to the inhabitants of especially such cities as Petrograd or Moscow. As Hackel (1975: 54) says: "Undoubtedly, the contemporary press was one of the many sources for the *realia* which unobtrusively infuse "The Twelve", and speak of that unique January of 1918." As

165

we are going to show, this holds true also for Mandel'štam. Some of his poems from this period are, in fact, difficult to understand without the background provided by the contemporary press.

The "Kerenskij Poem"

On November 15, 1917 *The Will of the People* (*Volja naroda*) published on its first page an untitled poem by Osip Mandel'štam:

> Когда октябрьский нам готовил временщик
> Ярмо насилия и злобы,
> И ощетинился убийца-броневик
> И пулеметчик узколобый,
>
> Керенского распять потребовал солдат,
> И злая чернь рукоплескала:
> Нам сердце на штыки позволил взять Пилат,
> Чтоб сердце биться перестало!
>
> И укоризненно мелькает эта тень,
> Где зданий красная подкова;
> Как будто слышу я в октябрьский тусклый день:
> Вязать его, щенка Петрова!
>
> Среди гражданских бурь и яростных личин,
> Тончайшим гневом пламенея,
> Ты шел бестрепетно, свободный гражданин,
> Куда вела тебя Психея.
>
> И если для других восторженный народ
> Венки свивает золотые —
> Благословить тебя в глубокий ад сойдет
> Стопою легкою Россия.

There have been few comments on this poem. It is perhaps not difficult to see why. This is Mandel'štam's first reaction to the Bolshevik revolution, the first in a series of poems reflecting and commenting on the new political changes in Russia. The poem represents a simple model which, no doubt, has similarities with other poetry written at this time. It is open and straightforward, it mentions actual names directly ("Kerenskij") or indirectly ("oktjabr'skij vremenščik"; the expression "vremenščik" was used in *The Will of the People* with the

166

same reference some days before Mandel'štam's poem was published), it has an emotional, agitated tone. It is not merely a general, spontaneous reaction to the October events, however. It clearly has a specific aim: an homage to the ousted minister-president Kerenskij. There was a special reason which so far has eluded discovery. The contemporary newspaper will provide the necessary context.

Let us remember the historical situation. The ministers of the provisional government were arrested immediately after the Bolshevik take-over. Those who represented non-bourgeois parties were, however, very soon released while the others were kept in the Peter and Paul fortress for some weeks. *The Will of the People* noted the difference in a comment under the heading "The Martyrs of Freedom" ("Mučeniki svobody", 1917: 15.11). But Kerenskij, the most wanted of them all, escaped. During several weeks he hid out in a dacha in the woods not far from Gatchina. There was a warrant for his arrest and the press reported that almost every day somebody was arrested in Petrograd under suspicion of being a disguised Kerenskij. He could nevertheless receive visitors in his hiding-place and even write an open letter to the Russian people which was printed in *The Cause of the People* (*Delo naroda*; Kerenskij 1965: 452). As late as end of March 1918 a big raid took place at the Nikolaevskij station because of rumours that Kerenskij was on his way to Moscow in an ordinary train (NS 1918: 26.3.). By that time he was already in Moscow, living secretly in a private apartment in the Arbat district and discussing politics with representatives of the Socialist Revolutionaries (the right wing) and of the new coalition group "Union for the Regeneration of Russia", before leaving by train (with a false passport) to Murmansk and further to London.

The Russian intelligentsia followed with a feeling of uneasiness this man hunt. To many Kerenskij, no doubt, incorporated the Russian liberal ideals of the 19th century. And whatever they thought of him as a leader of Russia, they were of the opinion that removal from office should not subject him to humiliation by the press or general persecution. But to express such a view openly was not so easy. The bourgeois press had been closed down by a decree immediately after the Bolshevik coup. Among the remaining non-Bolshevik newspapers some were critical towards the new regime, it is true. This did not necessarily mean, however, that they felt like standing up for the ousted minister-president.

A few newspapers actually did. One was, as we have seen, *The Cause of the People*, another was *The Will of the People*. On November 4, ten days after the Bolsheviks had seized power, an article entitled "A New Golgatha" ("Novaja Golgofa") appeared on the first page of *The Will of the People*. It strongly opposed the way Kerenskij was treated by the new government. The use of biblical parallels—signalized already by the title—gives the article a special note which tells us that this was a highly personal matter.

The Socialist Revolutionaries were after all Kerenskij's party. After its split he was close to the moderate wing which published both *The Cause of the People* and *The Will of the People*. E. N. Breškovskaja, one of the editors of *The Will of the People* and known as "the Grandmother of the Russian revolution", was his personal friend. One of Kerenskij's first measures as Minister of Justice in the Provisional Government was to release her from an exile in Siberia. This explains why especially *The Will of the People* stood up so strongly in defense of Kerenskij and why the article published here had such an emotional tone.

Part of the article is worth quoting in full:

Перед нами снова Голгофа. Мы снова видим, как толпа, подстрекаемая иудами и фарисеями революции, хочет распять и быть может уже распяла того, кто все свои силы, всю жизнь отдавал на служение народу, на его благо, на борьбу за свободу и революцию.

Мы говорим о А. Ф. Керенском.

Его травят ... Толпа тех самых солдат и рабочих, за права которых он десятки лет стойко боролся, рискуя всем, ищет его и кричит: "Распни, распни его." Военно-революционный комитет отдает приказы об его аресте и благословляет толпу на самосуд над А. Ф. Керенским ...

В этот момент мы считаем своим долгом поднять голос протеста и возмущения против этой травли того, кому русская революция и родина всего более обязаны, кто чист, велик и благороден, кто все свои силы отдал на служение революции ...

Живой — он принадлежит всему народу, которому отдал все. Мертвый — он принадлежит вечности и история повторит вслед за нами что он был святыней русской революции и остался ею ...

Certain parts of the article are clearly utilized in Mandel'štam's poem. The article speeks, for instance, about "a crowd ... of soldiers and workers" searching for Kerenskij and crying: "crucify him, crucify him". The second stanza of the poem opens with "Kerenskogo raspjat' potreboval soldat". The parallel with Christ's Passion is here further stressed by a reference to Pilate: "Nam serdce na štyki pozvolil vzjat' Pilat, / Čtob serdce bit'sja perestalo".

The third stanza brings in another parallel. Here appears an example of Mandel'štam's well-known use of literary subtexts. As Omry Ronen has observed, the line "vjazat' ego, ščenka Petrova" is a ciphered citation from Puškin's *Boris Godunov* ("Vjazat' Borisova ščenka") (Ronen 1973: 374). It is the scene at the "lobnoe mesto" in Moscow, in which the nobleman Puškin (one of the poet's ancestors) by a demagogical speech succeeds in inducing the people to recognize Dmitrij as their true lord and master. Incited by the speech, a mužik exclaims:

Народ, народ! в Кремль! в Царские палаты!
Ступай! вязать Борисова щенка!

The quotation apparently wants to say that also today the fickle masses are ready, under the influence of demagogical speeches, to turn against their former leaders. Steven Broyde comments that the change to "Peter's whelp" in Mandel'štam's poem implies that Kerenskij is "a continuer of a line begun by Peter, the true Russian tradition" (Broyde 1975: 30). This calls for some modification, however. To the intelligentsia Kerenskij was certainly a representative of "a true Russian tradition", which means a Western line that aspired to bring Russia closer to Western Europe. The point is, however, that the exclamation here comes from the mob, to which the true Russian tradition was instead an anti-Western line of national revolutions in the style of Stenka Razin. The Bolsheviks were at first seen as continuers of just such a tradition. "The Russia of Razin and Lenin" was a common slogan in those days (Men'šutin & Sinjavskij 1964: 177).

Uncertainty as to what actually had happened to Kerenskij is expressed in several places in the article, most emphatically at the end with its contrast between "alive" and "dead". The last sentence has almost the ring of an obituary: "Dead he belongs to eternity and history will repeat after us that he was and remained a sanctuary of the Russian revolution". The last stanza of Mandel'štam's poem also assumes a similar solemn note. We observe that this change of tone brings a new subtext. The image of "going down to hell", to follow the dead leader, reads as an echo from classical poetry. In the span of four stanzas the poem consequently succeeds in evoking three different parallels: Christ, Boris Godunov, leaders from classical times.

It seems plausible to assume that Mandel'štam's poem was written after the poet had read the article in *The Will of the People*, that is between November 5 and November 15. It may have been the result of a spontaneous reaction or it may have been written on the request of the editors who actually launched a campaign for Kerenskij. Five days after the article "A New Golgatha" an open letter was published to Kerenskij's wife (9.11), urging her to keep hoping ("ne padajte duxom"). Another article, as we will see, would soon follow.

The defense of Kerenskij in *The Will of the People* was an exception. Most newspapers kept silent. Others, especially the evening papers, made a few malicious remarks about Kerenskij as a person, supplying bits of gossip to the effect that he was hardly the kind of saint the intelligentsia was trying to make of him. Rather unexpectedly *New Life* joined the choir.

This newspaper, under the direction of Maksim Gor'kij, had taken a critical attitude towards the Bolsheviks already before the October revolution. They continued do so after October—Gor'kij's *Untimely thoughts* (*Nesvoevremennye mysli*) is well-known proof. Kerenskij's fate did not arouse any feelings of sympathy here, however. On November 11 1917 *New Life* published an article entitled "In the Winter Palace" ("V Zimnem dvorce") written by the journalist and writer Larisa Rejsner. A few weeks after the storming of the Winter Palace she paid a visit to the now deserted building which once had accomodated the chancellery of Kerenskij.

Walking through the empty halls she first noted the petty bourgeois taste with which the apartments of the last czar had been furnished ("Vsemu étomu trudno poverit' v žilišče postroennom dlja polubogov"). She then reached the rooms recently occupied by Kerenskij and his staff. During his stay he did not change or remove anything, it is true, but

все затерто, закурено, зашаркано, оглушено пишущими машинками и закапано чернилами. В 10 покоях, выходящих на площадь — водворился караул. Его меняли чуть на каждый день (наш премьер никому не доверял свою особу) — и каждый новый отряд хозяйничал по своему. Грязные тюфяки на полу, продырявленные картины, бутылки и бутылки и все это не где-нибудь, но вокруг самой 'особы', на ее глазах и с ее ведома.

If Kerenskij was lenient toward his staff and his guard he showed, according to Rejsner, the same nonchalance and insensibility toward the historic and artistic milieu where he had established his office:

О частной жизни Керенского во дворце и безчисленных признаках бестактности в отношении к интимной собственности Романовых мы не станем здесь говорить. Бог с ним. Все это дурно пахнет. Но вот мелочь, пустяк, а какой характерный. У Николая II был собственный биллиард. При отъезде в Тобольск шары слоновой кости, как личное имущество были уложены и приготовлены к отправке. Министр приказал их вернуть, и, как говорят сторожа, "собственноручно изволили забавляться".

И так во всем, начиная с уборной и кончая библиотекой. Мы бы хотели знать, зачем вообще нужно было вселяться в Зимний дворец? Зачем нужно было есть и спать по-царски, попирать ногами изящество, роскошь и богатство, которыми имеет право распоряжаться только народ, который принадлежит будущему, как музей Александра III, как Эрмитаж и Третьяковская галлерея.

After all, Rejsner concluded, Kerenskij should have realized that by settling in the Winter Palace he exposed its treasures to an obvious risk. Had he not placed his chancellery there, the revolting masses would never have caused any damage to it.

While Rejsner's reportage, no doubt, renders the atmosphere of the deserted palace a few weeks after the revolution, it follows at the same time a standard model, well known from many revolutions: the fallen leader (or king or czar) must be exposed as not only human but as a too human being. His vanity, his corruption, his exploitation of the possibilities his position offers him ("to eat and sleep like a czar") should, of course, be stressed. His leniency toward filth and disorder around him ("bottles and bottles") is equally important to mention in order to destroy any image of "purity"—every soldier or peasant could now see that he was no better than they.

That the article followed a common pattern was pointed out four days later in a sharp answer in *The Will of the People*. It was entitled "To the Slanderers" ("Klevetnikam") and signed by N. Čaadaev. The fall of a great politician or statesman is always accompanied by gossip and malicious joy in the evening press and less serious journals, the article began. There is hardly need for any comment in such cases. But when an important and serious newspaper follows the lead, this calls for attention.

After having stated that he is ready to bear the full responsibility for his words, the author takes up the accusations against Kerenskij and repudiates them point by point. First of all, Kerenskij did not choose the Winter Palace as a place for his chancellery out of some conceited wish to embellish his personal image, the rooms were simply alloted to him by the authorities. He did not "amuse himself" with the billiard table belonging to Nikolaj II, the cover was never even removed during his stay in the Winter Palace. He certainly did not "eat and sleep like a czar". He got the same food as other officials of his chancellery and like them, he paid for it—and these meals were far from luxurious. And, of course, he did not sleep in the beds of the czarist family. As for the bottles, the pierced pictures and the general filth, the author—who must have been a member of Kerenskij's own staff—guarantees that up to the moment when the Bolsheviks took over the palace everything was kept in the best order—leaving the readers to draw their own conclusions as to who was obviously responsible.

The answer ends with a challenge to *New Life* to present facts instead of slander:

Мы не удивляемся, что всякие Ларисы Рейснер могут заниматься сплетнями и клеветой, едва ли достойными даже уличной прессы, но как может печатать их "серьезная" "Новая жизнь"? Неужели ей не стыдно? Или лавры "Нов. Руси" и "Живого слова" не дают покоя "Новой жизни"?

Г. Рейснер и "Новая жизнь"! Мы ждем вашего ответа!

But there followed no answer, either from Larisa Rejsner or from the newspaper itself.

172

A Dying City

The following is a four-stanza poem by Mandel'štam in which every
stanza ends with an identical last line, like a refrain: "Your brother,
Petropolis, is dying" ("Tvoj brat, Petropol', umiraet").

На страшной высоте блуждающий огонь.
Но разве так звезда мерцает?
Прозрачная звезда, блуждающий огонь,
Твой брат, Петрополь, умирает,

На страшной высоте земные сны горят,
Зеленая звезда мерцает.
О если ты звезда — воды и неба брат,
Твой брат, Петрополь, умирает.

Чудовищный корабль на страшной высоте
Несется, крылья расправляет —
Зеленая звезда, в прекрасной нищете
Твой брат, Петрополь, умирает.

Прозрачная весна над черною Невой
Сломалась, воск бессмертья тает,
О если ты, звезда — Петрополь, город твой,
Твой брат, Петрополь, умирает.

Seen as a comment on the October revolution this poem is quite
different from the Kerenskij poem and represents another poetical
model. It has a lyrical tone which may remind us of Blok. A topical
call for help to Petrograd is here transformed into a poem with a
special poetic dynamism, due to the recurrent "refrains" and some
traditional but effective key words ("star", "ship", "dream", "green").
These keywords, as it were, move freely around in a sweeping lyrical
flow. They are never stopped and given a fixed meaning but constantly
keep on moving (as, for instance, in Blok's *Snežnaja maska*). Because
of this the poem is as much a suggestive sound gesture as a com-
municative message.

The poem, published in *The Evening Star* (VZ 1918: 6.3), is clearly
connected with two poems from 1916 ("Mne xolodno", "V Petropole
prozračnom my umrem"). All depict a Petrograd under the name of

"Petropol'", and might therefore be called Mandel'štam's "Petropol' poems" as a subdivision within his many poems dedicated to Petersburg/Petrograd). The season—spring—is the same in all of them and all are pervaded by an atmosphere of coldness, darkness and death. The realistic picture is not the essential thing, however; behind it emerges a historical perspective of doom and downfall (the poem "The Levite" with its picture of the destruction of Jerusalem is connected with the Petropol' poems, see N. Mandel'štam 1972: 121).

"Mandel'štam felt early the end of Peterburg and the whole Peterburgian period of Russian history", says Nadežda Mandel'štam (N. Mandel'štam 1972: 114). She dates the beginning of this theme in his poetry with the two Petropol' poems from 1916 (N. Mandel'štam 1972: 212). They were printed before the October revolution, it is true, but eschatological ideas had become widespread in Russia (as in Europe) long before that date, Dostoevskij's vision of Petersburg as "just a dream" again became topical (cf. Mandel'štam's book of prose *The Noise of Time*: "Ves' strojnyj miraž Peterburga byl tol'ko son, blistatel'nyj pokrov, nakinutyj nad bezdnoj", combining Dostoevskij and Tjutčev). Annenskij's well-known poem "Peterburg", printed in *Apollon* 1910, forebodes in many respects Mandel'štam's Petropol' poems. Also here is a spring which cannot change the general feeling of gloom and hopelessness:

Даже в мае, когда разлиты
Белой ночи над волнами тени,
Там не чары весенней мечты,
Там отрава бесплодных хотений.

(Annenskij 1959: 199)

The Petropol' poems have further certain key-words in common. One of them is "green" ("zelenyj"). It is the conventional color of spring and hope. In Mandel'štam's poetry, however, it is something more. As Levin and Segal have pointed out, green is one of the few constant, positive colors in Mandel'štam's color scheme ("Èto cvet Sredizemnogo mor'ja, cvet Italii i, nakonec, cvet žizni", Segal 1975: 68). Thus positively charged it appears in the first Petropol' poem:

Мне холодно. Прозрачная весна
В зеленый пух Петрополь одевает,
Но, как медуза, невская волна
Мне отвращенье легкое внушает.

The sentence about the transparent spring which dresses Petropol'
in green down implying warmth and hope, is enclosed by two senten-
ces, suggesting the opposite: coldness and nausea. The "no", beginning the third line marks the contrast between the two spheres. It
is also a contrast between two colors: the positive green and the negative black, implied in "nevskaja volna". In the poem from 1918 the
same contrast reappears ("Prozračnaja vesna nad černoju Nevoj"),
but here the black color is stated and the green is implied. The black
and yellow colorism had its special tradition in poems on Petersburg
in Russian Symbolist and post-Symbolists poetry, as has been pointed
out by Taranovsky (Taranovsky 1974: 147).

In the poem "On a Frightful Height" green appears in unusual connections. It is not "green down", it is not part of man's world any
more. It is seen at a distance, the color of stars and dreams. This
creates a feeling of anxiety and alarm; the first three stanzas repeat
over and over again: "on a frightful height".

Another key-word of the Petropol' poems is "transparent" ("prozračnyj"). The spring is transparent, the stars are transparent and so
is the city itself. "Transparent" is, of course, a proper word to describe
on a realistic level the nakedness of an early spring. It could also
indicate a transparency which makes it possible to see through the
outward forms of an object and discover something behind. A
"transparent" Petrograd lets a "Petropolis" shine through, opening
a historical perspective, linking the fate of the city with that of ancient
cities. "Prozračnyj" may further evoke a similar word, "prizračnyj".
In the sense of "nereal'nyj" it was part of the Petersburg myth, as
founded by Puškin and Dostoevskij. In 1917, just before the October
revolution, a newspaper took up the concept in an article, full of
eschatological (and slavophile) ideas. The title of the article was
characteristic for this particular moment: "The Decline of Petersburg"
("Zakat Peterburga"):

> Мне кажется, что в поэтическом венце порожденном столицей,
> есть одна связующая нить, одна вечно-повторяющаяся идея.
> Это — идея призрачности Петербурга, как будто для нее не
> было корней в русской истории ...
>
> (UR 1917: 8.10)

But "prozračnyj" has also an obvious reference to death: "Petropol'" suggests another word "nekropol" (St. Peterburg was already

in the 1830's dubbed "Nécropolis" by Petr Čaadaev in his "Philosophical letters", then because of its spiritual sterility; see Hackel 1975: 29). It is a city no longer ruled by "Stern Athene, the goddess of the sea", but by Persephone, the goddess of the underworld, as one of the poems from 1916 tells us. It is spring and time has come for her to return to earth as the goddess of sunshine and abundance. However—and this is the special point of the poem—in this early, naked, barren spring it seems as if the goddess of death rather than the goddess of life has come to rule Petrograd.

There is, however, a difference between the two Petropol' poems of 1916 and the one from 1918. The former poems speak of death but in the future tense, and those who are going to die are a rhetorical "we" ("V Petropole prozračnom my umrem"). In the 1918 poem appears the present tense ("umiraet") and it is the city which is dying. While the earlier poems express general eschatological ideas, the latter poem points to something much more concrete. The image of "a dying Petrograd" was an obvious and grim reality in the months following the October revolution—this was something every inhabitant could see with his own eyes. The process had started earlier, as the quoted article entitled "The Decline of Petersburg" indicated. Six months later appeared another article entitled "A Dying City" ("Umirajuščij gorod"). It was published in the Moscow newspaper *Fatherland* (*Rodina* 1918: 19.4) in the form of a letter from Petrograd. It gives a rough and naked picture (much more pessimistic than the picture given a few weeks earlier in *The Evening Lights*, see p. 10) of how life was in Petrograd in those days and how people experienced the changes. It seems to serve as an interesting parallel to Mandel'-štam's poem "On a Frightful Height".

"Petrograd is dying" ("Petrograd umiraet"), thus opens the letter. Such a conclusion seems justified, says the author, merely in view of the fact that it is no longer the capital of Russia and that the new government as a consequence has moved to Moscow. But this is, in fact, a change for the better. After the departure of "sovremennye vlastiteli" the population of Petrograd "can only give a sigh of relief: life is becoming more peaceful".

One could also point to the deserted street of the city after 7 p.m., to the closing of the tramway traffic after 9 p.m., to the complete darkness of the street at night. But there is another darkness which is more threatening:

176

Нет, мертвая печать лежит не только на внешнем обличии города, — дух смерти витает над всей ее общественной и деловой жизнью. Пустуют театры, стремительно падает тираж всех без исключения газет; лекции, привлекавшие раньше тысячи слушателей, теперь еле-еле собирают сотни, а то даже и десятки. Пусто в рабочих клубах, еще недавно оживленных; не дымятся трубы большинства фабрик и заводов; рабочие митинги, если и происходят, то исключительно по вопросам, связанным с желудочными интересами, как то: вопросам о разсчетах, уплате за 6 недель, об эвакуации, продовольствии и т. д. И оживление заметно только в очередях продовольственных лавок и интерес возбуждается лишь тогда, когда речь заходит о получении того или иного продукта, запасов которых с каждым днем становится в городе все меньше и меньше.

The peace treaty with Germany deprived Petrograd of its living soul, its mission as a center of the political, public and cultural life in a united Russia. It ceased to be the window towards Europe it was intended to be by its founder and was now converted into just an outpost exposed to the economical and political influence of Germany:

Нет Петрограда и как общепризнанного центра национальной революции, ибо от этой революции осталось одно только печальное воспоминание, и широкий поток ее разбился на ряд мелких грязненьких ручейков анархо-коммунистических движений — областных, губернских, городских, уездных и даже волостных ...

Петроград умирает и умирает в нем всякая общественная жизнь. И на тех немногих ее проявлениях, которые еще маячат на тусклом фоне сумеречной Петроградской жизни, явственно сказывается эта обреченность, эта безкрасочность существования некогда великого, а теперь внушающего только чувства глубокой боли и сожаление народа.

The grim picture given by this report corresponds with official statements from this time. On May 11 *Izvestija* printed a telegram sent by Lenin and his Food Commissar to all provincial Soviets asking for help to Petrograd: "Petrograd is in an unprecedentedly catastrophical condition. There is no bread. The population is being given the remaining potato flour and crusts. The Red capital is on the verge of perishing from famine. Counterrevolution is raising its head, directing the dissatisfaction of the hungry masses against the Soviet Government. In the name of the Soviet Socialist Republic, I demand immediate help for Petrograd" (Chamberlin 1965: 416).

This background certainly aids our understanding of Mandel'štam's Petropol' poem from 1918 (although it was published before the article appeared). It is also worth noting that the report, quoted above, contains one word which we are inclined to call a typical Mandel'-štamian one during this period: "sumerečnij" ("na tusklom fone sumerečnoj Petrogradskoj žizni"). We recognize it from the beginning of the poem. "The Twilight of Freedom", which appeared in ZT in May 1918: "Proslavim, brat'ja, sumerki svobody—/ Velikij sumerečnyj god".

References

Annenskij, I.
1959 *Stixotvorenija i tragedii.* Leningrad.
Broyde, S.
1975 *Osip Mandel'štam and his Age.* Cambridge, Mass.
Chamberlin, W. H.
1965 *The Russian Revolution 1917–1921.* Vol. I. London.
Hackel, S.
1975 *The Poet and the Revolution.* Oxford.
Kerenskij, A.
1965 *Russia and History's Turning Point.* New York.
Mandel'štam, N.
1972 *Vtoraja kniga.* Paris.
Men'šutin, A. & Sinjavskij, A.
1964 *Poėzija pervyx let revoljucii 1917–1920.* Moskva.
Ronen, O.
1973 "Leksičeskij povtor, podtekst i smysl v poėtike Osipa Mandel'štama", *Slavic Poetics: Essays in Honor of Kiril Taranovsky.* The Hague.
Segal, D.
1975 "Fragment semantičeskoj poėtiki O. Ė. Mandel'štama", *Russian Literature,* 10/11.
Taranovsky, K.
1974 "The Jewish Theme in the Poetry of Osip Mandel'štam", *Russian Literature,* 7/8.

Lars Kleberg

"People's Theater" and the Revolution

On the History of a Concept Before and After 1917

1.

The notion "the people's theater" was formulated in Europe near the end of the 19th century. Many involved with both the theoretical and practical aspects of the theater reasoned that a new relationship between the "people" and the "theater" was vitally necessary to both: the theater, the socially most effective of the arts, was to resolve the economical and political antagonisms that divided the people. And only this great task, on the other hand, could lead the theater out of an isolation that had given rise to constantly recurring aesthetic and ideological crises.

The idea of the people's theater was advanced at somewhat different points in time—and naturally in nationally conditioned variations—in a number of different countries, including Germany, France, Russia and Scandinavia. The chronological differences in the spread of the notion from the 1890s to WWI derive from the fact that certain external prerequisites must be present for this universally European idea to take root:

1. The traditional popular theater tradition in rural areas must definitely be dead or dying.
2. Industrialism must have produced an urban working class which, although severed from rural culture, has not yet absorbed urban bourgeois culture (let alone had time to create a proletarian culture of its own).
3. The moving picture must have made its appearance as a potential and in the near future real rival of the theater in the cities.
4. The earlier bourgeois theater must have split into commercialized boulevard theater and artistically independent but isolated modernist experimental theater.

179

5. The means of production of the artistic theater must have reached a level of development at which a new and larger audience is necessary if the theatrically possible is also to become economically feasible.
6. The Labor Movement must have developed as a potential organizer of a new mass audience.

The first man in Russia to speak of "the people's theater" was the playwright Aleksandr Ostrovskij, who on the eve of the abolition of the Court's theater monopoly in 1882 attempted to persuade the City Fathers of Moscow to establish a national or municipal theater as a counterweight to the predictable explosion of commercial melodrama and vaudeville theaters. The question was raised prematurely, however, for the conditions outlined above did not exist in Russia until the turn of the century. At that time, on the initiative of liberal educators, a number of amateur or semiprofessional theatrical societies were organized in connection with the newly established People's Houses (*narodnye doma*). In 1902 there were already 102 such theatrical groups, which had increased to 361 in 1905 and approximately 420 in 1909 (Xajčenko 1975, 96). The level of artistic ambition in these societies was as a rule modest, the repertory in most cases being restricted to popular farces, didactic plays advocating temperance and adapted versions of Gogol's and Ostrovskij's comedies. Occasionally, however, classical drama on a larger scale was attempted. The object of this theatrical activity was a form of cultural philanthropy, that is, liberal educators and temperance societies attempted to make the culture of bourgeois society available to the masses by letting them see and even produce their own theater under expert supervision. This popular theatrical movement was dependent upon the tsarist regime in two respects. First, it was connected economically to the official temperance committees (*popečitel'stva o narodnoj trezvosti*); the authorities were of the opinion that the theater would divert the masses from drunkenness and perhaps even more from politics, trade-union struggle and other "mischief". Secondly, the repertory of the popular scenes was subject to extremely severe control beyond the usual theater censorship; for example, plays by Gor'kij that could be performed for MXAT's prosperous audiences were unthinkable at the People's Houses, where workers could buy tickets for five kopecks or were sometimes even admitted free of charge.

The popular theatrical movement, which despite its limitations was the basis of a broad interest in the theater in Russia before 1917, was in the beginning uninfluenced by the West European people's theater ideology to be discussed here. As was mentioned by way of introduction, this was an ideology developed above all by the artistic intelligentsia. The theory *postulated* that the people yearned for the theater but was itself to a large extent a product of the opposite situation, namely that the theater needed the people. The breakthrough of the concept of the people's theater in Russia, which occurred in the years after 1905, had less to do with the rapid spread of the existing popular stages than with Symbolism and the intelligentsia's self-criticism after the abortive revolution.

2.

Among the first titles to be printed by Narkompros' newly established publishing house in Petrograd in 1918 was Richard Wagner's pamphlet *Art and Revolution*, with a new foreword by Lunačarskij. Like the Communist Manifesto of "our brilliant teachers" Marx and Engels, declared the People's Commissar, this brochure by "the no less brilliant Richard Wagner" was a product of the German Revolution of 1848. Its topicality, however, was undiminished, and Lunačarskij recommended it "for the edification of both artists and the victorious workers' democracy" (Lunačarskij 1918).

Wagner's brochure had already been published in Russian in 1906. Only in that context, the Russian debate of the time on the people's theater, does it become possible to understand how the Bolsheviks' minister of culture could in 1918 place the German opera reformer side by side with the fathers of Marxism.

The theater's reputation as the socially most effective of all the arts derives from two notions. The first is the idea of the theater as an "art of the moment" in which stage and auditorium, art and reality confront each other face to face on either side of the footlights. The second is that the audience is regarded as being somehow representative of the social collective as a whole. Even if the notion that the theater speaks through its audience to the entire "society", "nation" or "people" must be said to be a myth or false concept, this does not prevent the myth from being a reality. On the contrary, it played an important role in the development of the 19th and 20th century theater in Europe generally and especially in Russia *as a myth*, as an ideological fact.

The "myth of the representativeness of the audience", as I have called it in another context (Kleberg 1977, 60 ff.), is of romantic origin. It was canonized by the young Richard Wagner in his pamphlets *Art and Revolution* and *The Work of Art of the Future*, both published in 1849 and immediately inspired by the revolutionary wave in Germany.

As the prototype of an art that broke down class barriers and created a genuine democratic collectivity Wagner the revolutionary pointed to the theater in ancient Athens. In his opinion, the development of the theater since Greek antiquity was nothing but a long history of decadence and prostitution. At no time since the days of Greek democracy (which he greatly idealized) had art performed such a social function or been a matter of such urgency to the entire people.

The Greek tragedy, Wagner maintained, had in an unparalleled manner both manifested and confirmed the community of the entire collective:

> /.../ dieses Volk strömte von der Staatsversammlung, vom Gerichtsmarkte, vom Lande, von den Schiffen, aus dem Kriegslager, aus fernsten Gegenden zusammen, erfüllte zu Dreissigtausend das Amphitheater, um die tiefsinnigste aller Tragödien, den Prometheus, aufführen zu sehen, um sich vor dem gewaltigsten Kunstwerke zu sammeln, sich selbst zu erfassen, seine eigene Tätigkeit zu begreifen, mit seinem Wesen, seiner Genossenschaft, seinem Gotte sich in die innigste Einheit zu verschmelzen, um so in edelster, tiefster Ruhe das wieder zu sein, was es vor wenigen Stunden in rastlosester Aufregung und gesondertster Individualität ebenfalls gewesen war.

> (Wagner 1887: 3, 11)

The task of the new theatrical art in the new society envisioned by Wagner was not to imitate the external characteristics of the Greek tragedy. It was instead to restore the social utility and necessity of art and the theater. This utility the young Wagner perceived to lie in an extatic, cathartic experience of community that would ultimately erase the boundaries between creative artist and passive spectator. A similar vision of the Dionysian cult theater, in which the barrier between stage and auditorium is dissolved, is fully developed and presented as the ideal for the art of the future in Nietzsche's *Geburt der Tragödie*:

Singend und tanzend äussert sich der Mensch als Mitglied einer höheren Gemeinsamkeit: /.../ als Gott fühlt er sich, er selbst wandelt jetzt so verzückt und erhoben, wie er die Götter im Traume wandeln sah. Der Mensch ist nicht mehr Künstler, er ist Kunstwerk geworden /.../.

(Nietzsche 1906: 1, 56)

Nietzsche's book appeared in Russian translation in 1903, when it had the effect of a veritable "bomb" in Symbolist circles (Belyj 1922, 134). Wagner's brochure *Art and Revolution*, which was first translated in 1906, was no less influential.

The Symbolist poet Vjačeslav Ivanov's grand vision of the collective, reconciling and liberating ritual (*sobornoe dejstvo*) was no purely aesthetic matter, but a religious and ultimately social utopia in the spirit of Wagner and Nietzsche. In 1906 Ivanov described the cult theater as the model for a real people's theater which would involve the people as co-participants:

Театры хоровых трагедий, комедий и мистерий должны стать очагами творческого, или пророчественного, самоопределения народа; и только тогда будет окончательно разрешена проблема слияния актеров и зрителей в одно оргийное тело, когда при живом и творческом посредстве хора, драма станет не извне предложенным зрелищем, а внутренним делом народной общины /.../.

И только тогда, прибавим, осуществится действительная политическая свобода, когда хоровой голос таких общин будет подлинным референдумом истинной воли народа.

(Ivanov 1909, 218)

Ivanov was by no means the only theorist to believe in a new cultic people's theater. The contributors to *Teatr. Kniga o novom teatre* (1908) included, beside the Symbolists Brjusov and Sologub, the "God-building" Bolshevik and admirer of Nietzsche Anatolij Lunačarskij.

The beautiful Utopia envisaged by Ivanov and others thus proposed that the theater as a cult ceremony would abolish the dualistic disintegration of the world into body and soul, matter and spirit, a disintegration of which the division between spectator and actor or auditorium and stage was but one manifestation. Andrej Belyj, however, one of Ivanov's Symbolist colleagues, doubted the feasibility of the vision. Suppose, he said, that we—the lady with Jugend dress, the stock market speculator, the worker and the Privy Councillor—all dress up in white robes and enter the "temple" to fuse with one another in the cultic dance. "I am convinced", wrote Belyj, "that our prayers are not going to coincide". As long as society was marked by class antagonisms and lacked a common faith that could unite all citizens it was absurd to speak of a cultic theater. He concluded sarcastically: "The 'temple' will remain the Mariinskij Theater, and rhetoric will remain rhetoric" (*Teatr* 1908, 272).

Andrej Belyj's skepticism towards the cultic people's theater may seem justified. The fact remains that the external prerequisits for the appearance of the idea of a people's theater outlined above were present in Russia after 1905. The "crisis of the theater" was discussed right and left, and calls for a theater of the people continued to be heard. *Teatr. Kniga o novom teatre*, which despite certain dissenting voices became something of a manifesto for the cultic people's theater, was soon countered by Marxist critics in *Krizis teatra*. They attacked the cultic theater's mystical vision of a community extending over all class barriers and complained that the naturalistic, socially critical repertory had been pushed aside even at Stanislavskij's MXAT. The realistic and politically progressive theater which they proposed as a solution to the crisis nevertheless patently derived from Wagner's vision of the great, democratic drama and from the myth of the representative audience.

In 1910 Romain Rolland's book *Théâtre du peuple* (1903) was published in Russian translation by "Znanie", a firm close to the Bolsheviks. The foreword was signed "L." (Lunačarskij?). Rolland, who referred openly to Wagner, regarded the re-establishment of a living connection between the theater and the people as the only remedy for the theater's ideological, aesthetic (and presumably also economic) "crisis". The lost social utility of the theater could be recovered in two ways. One was by presenting before mass audiences grand, inspiring historical and political chronicle plays in which the people could reexperience their own fate. The other consisted in reviving the mass festivals from the days of the French Revolution, in which the ceremony itself gave all the participants a feeling of union and community and the boundary between actors and spectators were erased. Rather than go back to the Greek Dionysus cult for his prototype Rolland contented himself with the French Revolution, but the similarities with the idea of the cultic people's theater in Russia were otherwise striking.

Rolland's program for the great uniting mass drama or mass festival was—like that of Wagner, his source of inspiration—ideologically extremely contradictory. The notion of a theater that manifests and confirms the unity of the people can result either in revolutionary agitational mass dramas or in festivals of class consensus such as Gémier's "republican celebrations" in France of the 1920s and 1930s. The point, of course, was how one chose to define "the people", whether as the working classes or the entire nation, high and low, regardless of class relationships. But it was not this ambiguity in Rolland's program to which "L." objected in the foreword to the "Znanie" edition. Rather, he criticized Rolland's negative appraisal of the value of the cultural heritage for the working class and his tendency to replace the traditional theater with mass festivals—farsighted criticism, as it was precisely in these areas that Rolland would acquire radical followers after the October Revolution.

Under tsarism both the Symbolist-inspired cultic theater and Romain Rolland's "théâtre du peuple" remained utopias. While Ivanov's theories concerned only a very small elite, Rolland's ideas were disseminated to some extent among the more radical popular theatrical societies. But the censorship if nothing else effectively obstructed any plans for a political people's theater involving pageants and mass festivals. As Nina Gourfinkel, one of the few scholars who have dealt with the problem of people's theater in Russia, points out, the greater the obstacles, the more exalted the ideology tended to become:

De même que la plupart des idées révolutionnaires russes, l'idée d'un théâtre pour le peuple resta, durant toute la période qui précéda la revolution, une théorie toute abstraite; privée de la saine experience des faits réels, elle devenait, dans l'esprit de ses adeptes, toujours plus grandiose et, partant, plus irréalisable.

(Gourfinkel 1930, 101)

3

One of the most important consequences of the February Revolution for the Russian theater was that the hated censorship was abolished. The practical result of this in the established private theaters was above all a boom of "daring", more or less risqué comedies and dramas dealing with Rasputin. There was no breakthrough at all for any politically oriented repertory. The effects of the new freedom were different in the popular theaters connected with the People's Houses, in workers' clubs, etc. These so called public (*obščedostupnye*) theaters were, as was noted above, subject to very rigorous control beyond the usual theater censorship. True, during the Revolution of 1905 the censorship had in practice ceased to function for a time, and many groups took advantage of the situation to play works by Suxovo-Kobylin, Gor'kij, Tolstoj and West European naturalists that had been forbidden earlier, but during the subsequent period of reaction the tsarist regime increased its vigilance toward authors and subjects suspected of being "criminal". It was only with great difficulty and in almost conspirational conditions, for example, that certain amateur or semiprofessional theaters managed to present Hauptmann's *The Weavers*, Gogol's *The Inspector General* and Gor'kij's plays in the years preceding WWI (Xajčenko 1975, 214). For all the small popular theaters—i.e. those with cultural ambitions as distinct from those which only aspired to provide entertainment and therefore even plunged into the new "risqué" vogue—the Revolution immediately signified much more liberty of action and improved possibilities both to disseminate the cultural heritage and present a politically conscious repertory.

An inquiry in the daily *Novaja Žizn'* 25.5.1917 entitled "The Tasks of the People's Theater" provides an interesting view of the situation. The editors began rhetorically:

> Театр для народа — вот лозунг нашего времени. Могучий, окрыленный свободным, чуждым всяких давлений извне и изнутри порывом к творчеству, новый театр — этот фокус всех художественных устремлений, эта великая, светлая и бодрящая трибуна должен стать достойным великой нации, должен быть ярким выразителем его стремлений, верований и прозрений.
>
> Подлинно демократический театр должен неизбежно стать

глубоко идейным театром, в нем нет места легкому развесе-
лому времяпрепровождению, столь необходимому буржуа
после "делового" дневного безделия.

One might expect that this would be followed by declarations that the
utopian projects of the people's theater had finally been placed on the
agenda. But the four participants in the inquiry—Aleksandr Benois,
the playwright and popular theater organizer E. Karpov, Lunačarskij
and one I. Gol'denberg—all answered with concrete, practical sugges-
tions that mainly concerned questions of repertory.

Both Benois and Karpov emphasized that in the democratic conditions now prevailing no restrictions should be made in the repertory
of the popular theaters. Neither conscious political control nor
condescending enlightenist ambitions were acceptable: "the people
are not children—they can assimilate everything just as well as educated persons" (Karpov). Only Lunačarskij called for a conscious
political line in the matter of repertory, listing the works presented by
Social Democrat influenced popular theaters in Western Europe: Ver-
haeren in Belgium, Rolland in France, Gottfried Keller in Switzerland,
etc.

The most remarkable point in the inquiry was the unanimous opinion of the four men that the existing popular stages could provide
the basis of a real people's theater in Petrograd. And Petrograd, for
those who wanted to translate into reality the many prerevolutionary
phrases postulating that "the people need the theater and the theater
needs the people", was certainly where the people were. Karpov en-
numerated more than a dozen functioning popular theaters in the
city, including the outdoor stages, and Gol'denberg reported that
these together could attract as many as one million spectators a
month.

There was one shining exception to the generally low artistic level
and material shabbiness of the existing popular theaters, namely the
Obščedostupnyj teatr at the Ligovskij narodnyj dom, a People's House
in one of Petrograd's working-class districts started and subsidized
by Countess Panina. This theater had been led since its beginning in
1903 by P. Gajdeburov and N. Skarskaja, who despite the special
censorship for popular theaters soon brought it up to a high professional level. Characteristically enough, this was the only popular
theater to be influenced by prerevolutionary cultic people's theater

ideology; this circumstance was furthered by both the professionalism of the theater and the personal relationships of its leaders—Skarskaja was the sister of the actress Vera Komissarževskaja, the legendary "priestess" of the symbolist theater.

Gajdeburov's Mobile Public Theater (so named because touring was an important part of its work) was aesthetically a mixture of stylized realism and "contemplative" symbolism. Its greatest success was a production of Bjørnstjerne Bjørnsson's *Beyond Our Power*, which was presented regularly during the course of many years, but the repertory embraced such varied works as Gogol's *Ženit'ba* and pseudo-symbolist montages called "masses". The ambitious cultural and philanthropic activity of the theater was based on a belief in the purifying and healing mission of art in society that was not far removed from the Wagnerian theater utopia. Gajdeburov's theater greeted the February Revolution and liberation from the tsarist dictatorship in the following rhapsodical manner:

> Открылись тюрьмы, раскрылись души и приняли в себя свет всенародного единения. Каждый гражданин, озаренный этим светом, каждая группа граждан, объединенных общностью труда, идейных или духовных интересов, каждая организация несут ему в дар лучшее своей души, своего разумения. Группа актеров, писателей, художников, музыкантов и других работников сцены, объединенных деятельностью Общедоступного и передвижного театра, в сознании великой ответственности, возложенной на служителей Искусства, как и на всех участников всенародного подвига, — установления на земле царства Высшей Правды, — выражает уверенность, что впредь, как и ныне, все партии и весь народ останутся верными чувствам гуманности, терпимости, взаимного доверия и не омрачат новую жизнь старыми средствами политической борьбы и местью невозвратному прошлому.

> (Rafalovič 1933, 64)

Rather than such pathetic declarations, however, it was its efforts to bring the stage to the people that made the Mobile Public Theater a pioneer of the new theatrical types that flourished after the October Revolution, during the Civil War. It did not content itself with playing to proletarian audiences in Countess Panina's People's House and touring the provinces. In May 1917 Gajdeburov's company presented, for presumably the first time, *street theater* in Petrograd, in connection with the Art Union's propaganda for the so called "Freedom Loan" (war bonds). And shortly before the October Revolution the theater toured the front and played Gogol' and Ostrovskij for the soldiers; at the same time the first attempts were made to conduct audience polls in the form of questionnaires and interviews.

4.

The period between February and October 1917 was of course too short for anything new in the cultural field to take form, at least anything that derived immediately from the February Revolution. Possible novelties during this brief time were instead the result of initiatives begun during the final phase of the tsarist regime, while new ideas born during the short months of the bourgeois revolution were not realized until after the Bolshevik takeover, during or even after the Civil War.

The idea of reprinting Richard Wagner's manifesto *Art and Revolution* may have arisen between the revolutions of 1917, but the fact is that it became the first significant publication on theatrical theory to appear in Soviet Russia. In a sense it set the tone of the theater debate during the first years of the Revolution. Already in 1919 the time had become ripe for a new edition of the second important manifesto of the people's theater, Romain Rolland's book, which carried a foreword by no less a figure than Vjačeslav Ivanov, then working at Narkompros' theater section (TEO).

The incomparably most influential book on the theater to appear during this period, however, was the Proletkul't leader Keržencev's *Tvorčeskij teatr*, an apology of the proletarian theater that was published in four more editions by 1923 and translated into German as early as 1922.

Keržencev's project for "creative theater" was by its mixture of formal eclecticism and idealistic proletarian ideology a typical product of the early Proletkul't movement. The "creative theater" derived directly from the people's theater program that began with Wagner and continued through Rolland and others strongly emphasizing that part of it which envisaged mass festivals that would transform passive spectators into active participants. The October Revolution, contended Keržencev, for the first time provided the necessary social conditions

189

for realizing this program. True, the theater in bourgeois societies had in recent decades been changed by various important theatrical reformers who had rejected commercialism and created great artistic productions:

> но они тем не менее сохраняли фатальное разделение между сценой и зрительной залой, между теми, кто творит и действует, и теми, кому остается лишь смотреть и апплодировать.
>
> (Keržencev 1919, 21)

The theater was a prisoner of its dualism; it had become a place where a few performed creative work and others merely relaxed or amused themselves, lacking "the slightest possibility to display their theatrical instinct or scenic creativity" (ibid., 22).

The established popular theater movement, which presented "good theater for the people", was dismissed by Keržencev as a philanthropic affair which could in no way liberate the theater from its bourgeois dualism. What was needed was a theatrical revolution, and it was only the socialist revolution in Russia that made the utopia possible:

> Новаторы театра реформировали его вместо того, чтобы революционизировать.
>
> Только переживаемая нами переходная к социализму эпоха сможет преобразовать театр на новых началах.
>
> (ibid., 24)

The precondition for the realization of the "creative theater" was the erasure of the boundary between manual and intellectual labor and between the artist and his audience—a change the Proletkul't ideologists believed lay just around the corner.

Keržencev sought the concrete prototypes of the revolutionary society's mass festivals in various quarters, drawing upon his own experience of mass historical chronicle plays, so called pageants, in England and the United States, Rolland's descriptions of French and Swiss popular festivals and memorial festivals devoted to the French Revolution. Theoretically as well Keržencev's program was a conglomerate of earlier ideas. The influence of the various utopian conceptions of the Russian "cultic" people's theater is obvious. The term *tvorčeskij* itself was one of Ivanov's catchwords, as is evident from his statements of 1906 quoted above.

Keržencev maintained, however, that the October Revolution had

190

given a totally new meaning to all the forms of theater which he admitted to have gathered together from different ages and societies. The socialistic society would abolish the difference between artist and audience, but this goal would be attained through the development of a purely *proletarian* culture rather than by activating a vaguely conceived "people". Once "the people" had been exchanged for "the proletariat", however, Keržencev was prepared to accept both the "cultic" mass drama and the "Wagnerian" notion of the great, unifying work of art, not to mention the concept of the audience as representative of the entire collective (which was now no longer the "people" but the working class).

In the fourth edition of his book (1920)—upon which the German edition was based—Keržencev was able to state with a degree of justified satisfaction that "much of what only two years ago seemed utopia is now becoming reality" (Keržencev 1922, 111).

At the First All-Russian Congress for Worker and Peasant Theater held in Moscow 17–26 November 1919 reports from across the country indicated that the theater and above all revolutionary mass festivals had become a central element in the public life of the new state. Mass dramas, which were often organized under the supervision of the local Proletkul't, followed the guidelines outlined by Keržencev. The repertory was dominated by summary pageants depicting revolutionary history from Spartacus' revolt in Rome to the Civil war in Russia and allegorical accounts of the October Revolution.

The singing of the "International" by all present was the obligatory ending of all mass dramas. Often the actors and the audience joined together in a parade or some such demonstration, but more active participation on the part of the audience—for example, collective improvisations—was still a future goal.

5.

A great many non-Communist cultural figures had found employment at TEO's Petrograd and Moscow offices, including writers such as Blok, Belyj and Remizov, philosophers and scholars like Georgij Čulkov and the "Scythian" Ivanov-Razumnik, Gustav Špet and V. V. Gippius (*Sovetskij teatr* 1968, 76 ff.). It seems an oversimplification, however, to conclude therefore that TEO functioned chiefly as a kind of warm shelter for these and many other non-conforming intellectuals

(Fitzpatrick 1970, 137 f., 162 f.). Vjačeslav Ivanov, at any rate, is an example of a great intellectual innovator who played a considerable role in the theater debate after the Revolution. It was anything but a coincidence that TEO published a new translation of Romain Rolland's book in 1919 with a foreword by Ivanov.

Ivanov represented TEO in a number of important connections; like Keržencev he was a member of both TEO and the administration of Centroteatr. At the First All-Russian Congress on Adult Education (*vneškol'noe obrazovanie*) in early May 1919 Ivanov presented his ideas on "the organization of the creative forces of the popular collective in the area of artistic activity". Ivanov's subject was as ten years earlier the folk theater as an expression of

> преодоления новою, целостною, органическою культурою культуры вчерашнего дня, характеризующейся чертами классовой и индивидуальной обособленности, личного и группового разделения, уединения и разномыслия /.../.
>
> (Ivanov 1919)

The October Revolution had made this cultural metamorphosis possible. One is struck, however, by the way in which Ivanov—in sharp contrast to Keržencev—regarded the Revolution as promising to abolish all social antagonisms within the people as a collective; the proletariat was conspicuous in its total absence from his propositions. The forms of theater Ivanov suggested were markedly like those in *Tvorčeskij teatr*—song festivals with theatrical elements; the development of mass festivals into grand dramas involving the active participation of all; open-air theater presenting monumental, allegorical scenes from the past. The difference was that while Keržencev had an abstract Proletariat as the basis of his theatrical revolution, Ivanov still had an abstract People.

When Ivanov published his theses in TEO's *Vestnik teatra* in May 1919 the days of the people's theater as a slogan in Soviet cultural policy were already numbered. During the subsequent few years it was replaced by in turns "worker and peasant theater", "proletarian" and "socialistic" theater. This development appears clearly in the pages of *Vestnik teatra*, which was the main area for the debate on theater policy during the transition period between War Communism and NÈP 1919–1921.

VT No. 2, dated 6–7 February 1919, published the first convocation to the First Congress of Worker and Peasant Theater, which was to take place in late February but was postponed several times due to the critical military situation and finally was held 17–26 November.

The opening of the proclamation is interesting with respect to its vocabulary:

Театр — народная радость и народное дело.

Совокупно всем сходом творится и переживается театральное действие. Сообща веселятся и печалятся все собравшиеся на зрелище, — сообща задумываются над тем, какова жизнь, и над тем как жить и как строить жизнь.

Театр — сила, соединяющая людей в общении восторга и разумения, ликования и скорби, решимости и надежды.

Театр — сила, организующая народную душу, выковывающая и выражающая народную мысль и волю народную.

Театр — самовоспитание народное.

Whereas *narodnyj* (people's, popular) is repeated almost as in an incantation, neither "proletarian" nor "worker and peasant" (which was the name of the congress convoked by the manifesto!) occurs in the introductory text.

There is good reason to believe that the convocation of the congress was written by V. V. Tixonovič, the newly appointed leader of TEOs section for worker and peasant theater. Tixonovič had been an organizer of popular amateur theater before the Revolution, had edited the journal *Narodnyj teatr*, which was published with the support of the cooperative movement in 1918 (three issues, 1, 2, and 3–4 appeared), and had also written a practical guide for workers in the popular theater (Tixonovič 1918). Tixonovič's most important contribution had been to provide recommendations for raising the theoretical and artistic level of the popular theaters that had been granted full political freedom after the February Revolution, and his task in TEO was presumably to help integrate the rather spontaneous and disorderly movement into the cultural policy of the new Soviet state.

The passage quoted above echoes distinctly Wagner's and Rolland's rhetoric. The popular theater movement was no longer to be a mere recreational occupation for amateurs, but would be raised to a morally and socially significant institution. At the same time, the notion of "the people" remained completely unspecified.

Soon, however, Tixonovič made such a necessary clarification, in a long article in *VT* (Tixonovič 1919), where he discussed the various transformations that had occurred in the notion of people's theater from the earliest philanthropical theaters to the popular theater of the day, which he maintained was represented by the working people's own theatrical activity. Or perhaps one should say the popular theater of yesterday, for now Tixonovič himself recognized only the term "worker and peasant theater" to designate the earlier popular theaters that continued to function under Soviet rule. The purely proletarian theater advocated by representatives of Proletkul't, especially Keržencev and P. Kogan, he regarded as a subdivision of this activity. In the very long run, noted Tixonovič, concurrently with the emergence of socialist society, the pure class theater of the proletariat could be developed ultimately to produce a theater that was really of the entire people (*vsenarodnyj teatr*).

The Proletkul't ideologists, of course, could not but protest against this long-term, gradual perspective, especially as their organization at this particular time was involved in an intense struggle to gain rapid and total control of various sections of Narkompros. Kogan's bitter attacks at the Congress for Adult Education in May 1919 on those advocating anything less than pure proletarian theater must be seen in this context. Kogan dismissed the idea of a people's theater as reactionary, stressing instead the leading role of the proletariat, especially in relation to the peasants:

> Независимо от того лежит ли в основе его мистическая идея народа (народная душа потустороннего происхождения) или научная идея народа (народный уклад, определяемый географическими, историческими и другими подобными условиями), представление о народном театре чуждо пролетариату. Источником его театрального пафоса может быть: идея интернационализма, идея трудового общественного товарищества, идея классовой борьбы /.../.

(Kogan 1919)

Evidently, Kogan's criticism was directed both against Ivanov and the continuators of the tradition of the pre-revolutionary popular stages, represented by Tixonovič—the main opponents to Proletkul't's secterian ideology within TEO.

The antagonisms culminated at the postponed First Congress for Worker and Peasant Theater in November 1919. A series of stormy ballots strained Lunačarskij's ability to slap together compromises to the utmost and even beyond, as he was forced to allow the congress to adopt two program resolutions, the one that of the majority, the other that of the in reality defeated Proletkul't minority. The point of dissent was whether workers and peasants were to be given equal status in the notion "worker and peasant theater" or the proletarian element was to be accorded superiority. This might seem to be a rather exaggerated demand in a country whose population consisted of 80 % peasants and only 2 % industrial workers, but Proletkul't, aware that the question was strategically decisive, waged a life-and-death struggle and suffered what was perhaps its first (at least public) political defeat.

Keržencev, spokesman of the minority, made an evaluation of the Congress soon afterwards in *Proletarskaja kul'tura* (Keržencev 1920). He pointed out the "opportunism" of the congress and its organizers and stressed that the majority, which defeated the Proletkul't members and their followers repeatedly, were "representatives of cooperative organizations, trade unions, and delegates from the provinces", i.e. presumably cadres from the prerevolutionary popular theater movement. Nevertheless, the author of *Tvorčeskij teatr* could not help noting with satisfaction that the *practical* resolutions—concerning not the interrelation between worker and peasant culture but the future of the popular theater movement in Russia—in many respects followed the programme propagated by himself and Proletkul't.

Nina Gourfinkel's observation that 'the weaker the practice, the more lofty the ideology', seems to be very apt. When popular theatrical life in Soviet Russia, as the First Congress of Worker and Peasant Theater showed, started developing and the contact between theater workers and the audiences seemed to be reestablished, the time for the great utopian programmes came to an end. The output of pure ideology decreased, but theatrical life flourished, within the existing institutions as well as in new forms. Of course, the discussions about the new theater and its social functions did not end. But other and more concrete issues than "people's theater" were now on the agenda: the reorganization of the old theaters, the search for a new repertory, the role of the new audience.

References

Belyj, A.
1922 "Vospominanija o Bloke", *Épopeja* 1, Berlin.
Bradbury, D. & McCormick, J.
1978 *People's Theatre*, London.
Fitzpatrick, S.
1970 *The Commissariat of Enlightenment*, Cambridge.
Gourfinkel, N.
1930 *Théâtre russe contemporain*, Paris.
Ivanov, V.
1909 *Po zvezdam*, Sankt Peterburg.
1919 "K voprosu ob organizacii tvorčeskix sil narodnogo kollektiva v oblasti xudožestvennogo dejstva", *Vestnik Teatra* 1919: 20, p. 4.
Keržencev, P.
1919 *Tvorčeskij teatr*, 3. izd., Moskva.
1920 "Bor'ba za socialističeskij teatr", *Proletarskaja kul'tura* 1920: 13–14, p. 77–80.
1922 *Das schöpferische Theater*, Hamburg.
Kleberg, L.
1977 *Teatern som handling. Sovjetrysk avantgardeestetik 1917–1927* (= Stockholm Slavic Papers, 1), Stockholm.
Kogan, P.
1919 "Puti proletarskogo teatra", *Vestnik Teatra* 1919: 27, p. 2.
Krizis teatra. Sbornik statej, Moskva 1908.
Lunačarskij, A.
1918 "Vstuplenie", in: Vagner, R., *Iskusstvo i revoljucija*, Petrograd, p. 3.
Narodnyj teatr, 1918: 1–4, Moskva.
Nietzsche, F.
1906 *Werke. Taschenausgabe*, 1–10, Leipzig.
Pervyj vserossijskij s"ezd po raboče-krest'janskomu teatru 17–26 nojabrja 1919, Moskva 1920.
Piotrovskij, A.
1926 "K teorii samodejatel'nogo teatra", in: *Problemy sociologii iskusstva*, Leningrad, p. 120–129.
Rafalovič, V. (ed.)
1933 *Istorija sovetskogo teatra*, 1, Leningrad.
Rollan [= Rolland], R.
1910 *Narodnyj teatr*, Sankt Peterburg.
1919 *Narodnyj teatr*, Petrograd–Moskva.
Sovetskij teatr. Dokumenty i materialy. Russkij sovetskij teatr 1917–1921, Leningrad 1968.
Teatr. Kniga o novom teatre. Sbornik statej, Sankt Peterburg 1908.
Tixonovič, V.
1918 *Narodnyj teatr*, I–VI, Moskva.
1919 "Na novyx putjax", *Vestnik Teatra* 1919: 11, p. 2–3; 1919: 12, p. 3–4.

Wagner, R.
1887 *Gesammelte Schriften und Dichtungen*, 1–10, 2. Auflage, Leipzig.
1906 *Iskusstvo i revoljucija*, Sankt Peterburg.
1918 *Iskusstvo i revoljucija*, Petrograd.
Williams, R. C.
1977 *Artists in Revolution. Portraits of the Russian Avant-garde 1905–1925*,
    Bloomington.
Xajčenko, G.
1975 *Russkij narodnyj teatr konca XIX–načala XX veka*, Moskva.
"Zadači narodnogo teatra. Anketa", *Novaja Žizn'* 1917: 31 (25.5), p. 5.

Kate Betz

As the Tycoons Die:
Class-struggle and Censorship in the Russian Cinema 1917-1921

Film and Revolution

The February Revolution triggered a wave of great hopes and expectations among the Russian film workers. At the outbreak of the First World War the Russian film industry was mainly controlled by a "troika" of enterprises—the Pathé, the Thiemann & Reinhardt and the Xanžonkov studios. Now the leading positions were taken by the companies Xaritonov and Ermol'ev, which based their strength not only on skilful executive power but also on talented, professional directors like Čardynin and Protazanov and on the immense popularity of the two superstars of the time—Vera Xolodnaja and Ivan Mozžuxin (Bratoljubov 1976, 31).

Even though the market structure remained intact, the very atmosphere brought about by the events in early March 1917 called for a thorough break with previous routines. The censorship had been abolished; wild illusions and hopes for the future were voiced. The time had arrived to create great cinematic masterpieces worthy of and true to the newly won "freedom".

> Никогда еще так радостно, так искренне и так светло не праздновалась Пасха в целом мире, как она будет праздноваться в свободной отныне России! (...)
>
> Каждый из нас должен заглянуть внутрь себя, проанализировать себя и решить вопрос — достоен ли он самого драгоценного в мире дара — и при малейшем сомнении в этом — немедленно же приняться за самоперевоспитание.
>
> Этот процесс самоанализа охватил сейчас всех граждан России. (...)
>
> Но Свобода должна коснуться также и кинематографии, как таковой.

Кинематография, отныне не стесненная никакими администативными и цензурными рамками, должна проявить себя достойной носительницей Свободы.

(CF 1917: 11/12, 47)

S. V. Lur'e, editor of the film magazine *Cine-Fono*, continued to appeal to all film artists to join forces and protect the film from those elements who up till now had debased it. He concluded with the following remarks:

Комитет союза кинодеятелей, обсудив на заседании 12 марта 1917 года вопрос о постановке картин, имеющих явное стремление к спекуляции на мрачные явления низвергнутого режима, не имеющих художественной ценности и способствующих лишь к разжиганию страстей, единогласно признал постановку таких картин явлением неприемлимым и недопустимым.

(CF 1917: 11/12, 48)

However, the belief that the situation would change overnight soon proved to be wishful thinking:

Правда, первые дни после Революции показали, что вынесение резолюции это одно, а проведение ее в жизнь — это другое.
Несмотря на постановление комитета кинематография буквально наводнилась пошлыми постановками, обсуждаемыми резолюцией, типа.

(CF 1917: 11/12, 48)

Before 1917 there existed only one film organization—that of the theatre-owners and distributors. Trade unions were completely unknown in the film industry. Clinging to the revolutionary band-wagon in February "… many had hoped that the revolution would finally reconcile the studio owners with the creative workers, put an end to competition and stop the clashes between theatres and distributors. The cinema mechanics were expected to put aside their demands for vacation and an eight-hour working day. There were dreams about enough raw film to be able to produce true, uncensored works of free cinematographic genius" (Rosolovskaja 1937, 44).

The film industry interpreted the concept of "free cinematographic genius" in its own special way. Responding very rapidly to the new signals launched by the latest political events, new productions were planned in accordance with the present "free, revolutionary" spirit. Old films were given a hasty face-lift to match the political state of the market and were re-issued with new, sensational subtitles. The journals proudly announced the premieres of "exciting" films like "From Gloom of Tsarism to the Radiance of Freedom" (Iz mraka carizma k sijan'ju svobody), "Let Us Renounce the Old World" (Otrečemsja ot starogo mira) etc. There was a steady flow of anti-Romanov films, frequently based on the Rasputin scandals; "Dark Powers—Grigorij Rasputin and his Associates" (Temnye sily—Grigorij Rasputin i ego spodvižniki), "The Secret of the Romanovs" (Tajna doma Romanovyx) and "In the Tenacious Clutches of the Double-Headed Eagle" (V cepkix lapax dvuglavogo orla). Oldtime "pornographic hits" as "Keys to Happiness" (Ključi sčast'ja) were put on the screen again, this time sensationally "unclipped" (Lebedev 1965, 82).

Apart from the newsreels and some of the semi-documentary films produced by the Skobelev Committee (whose production will be discussed later on) the great bulk of films now flooding the market did not aim at filling any distinct agitational purposes. At least not in the sense that they provided any outspoken comments on the current social problems facing Russian society. What the much praised "revolutionary freedom" connoted to the film entrepreneurs was above all the abolition of censorship. Due to their great financial stake in the future development of the Russian cinema, the film enterprises naturally wanted to keep their sphere of interest free from the previous control. In view of these economic considerations and the dependence of the industry on a paying mass audience, the February Revolution did not result in an upswing of suppressed politically oriented themes.

Instead, releasing films on the Rasputin affair was a natural consequence of the success formula elaborated by the entrepreneurs. Here was a combination of two taboo themes (religious ethics and the Tsar's family) both of which were likely to attract audiences and would have been impossible to screen during the previous political and church censorships. (For an account of the concept of "freedom" and censorship in conjunction with the Russian theatre, see Nils Åke Nilsson's article in this volume.)

Furthermore, the studios again turned to fictional material; detective stories, murder dramas and scenes from the life of upper bourgeois circles flourished. Audiences were invited to share solid salon melodramas set in luxurious, plushy, overstuffed environments, where passions were acted out in a theatrical manner. Adventures and "crimes passionnels" ensured reliable box-office revenues.

However, the rivalry and social gaps that existed within the film industry were not to be eliminated easily. The film workers were becoming aware of their situation, demanding their own unions and a rapid improvement of present material conditions. In this context it might be appropriate to say a few words about the role of the unions before and immediately after the February Revolution.

Before 1917 the unions had been relatively unimportant in Russian labour history. The industry as such was also still young. Under Tsardom (at least until the turn of the century) trade union organization had been illegal and was consequently suppressed. Only the most politically-minded workers, those prepared to pay for their conviction with prison and exile, were willing to join them in these circumstances. The union movement, reborn in a sense after February 1917, was pushed forward by the more educated workers, favourable at first to the Mensheviks and SR, but later won over to the Bolsheviks in varying proportions (Brinton 1975, 6–7).

The Name of the Game: Co-Existence

The studio owners answered the film workers in their own way by advancing the idea of a non-political "classless union, which according to their plans should reflect and defend the public interests of the Russian cinema" (Bratoljubov 1976, 32). On March 3, the "All-Russian Society of Cinema-Theatre Owners" called its members to a meeting in the "Ars" cinema in Moscow. Some 350 delegates attended. The chairman of the Society, P. S. Antik, endorsed the Provisional Government in a salutatory telegram to the Moscow commissar Čelnokov. On the initiative of Antik a "Provisional Executive Committee" was formed in which people from all groups present— studio owners, distributors, theatre and laboratory owners, professionals and workers—were to be represented. The Committee was granted the right "to function as representative of all groups of cinema officials and issue standards regulating professional relations;

norms which should be compulsory for all cinema officials" (CF 1917: 11/12, 49).

As was the case in most Russian industries, the "dual power" was also reflected within the film industry. The meeting held at the "Ars" cinema on March 3 was no exception. In one camp were the theatre and studio owners and distributors headed by Antik, who quite openly supported the Provisional Government. In the other camp were the artists (the directors, screenwriters and actors), the administrative personnel and the studio workers, who leaned toward the Soviet of Workers' Deputies. Antik demanded one strong organization which would unite workers, artists (xudožestvennaja intelligencija) and employers. The workers and the artists themselves, however, who were not present in any great numbers at the meeting, advocated the idea of several independent unions, one for each professional group (Rosolovskaja 1937, 47).

In the general chaos following the February Revolution very few people actually brought their cameras out to shoot what was taking place. Several days elapsed before anything was filmed at all. The outcome of the meeting on March 3 was an announcement to the Soviet of Workers' Deputies: of all footage taken and assembled of the historical events no individual films would be released or circulated. Instead it was decided to:

> (...) выпустить одну общую ленту под названием "Великие Дни Российской Революции 28 февраля по 4 марта 1917 г.". Снято Союзом Отечественной Кинематографии, весь доход от эксплуатации ленты предоставлен Совету Рабочих Депутатов для помощи политическим заключенным, освобожденным Революцией, и их семьям.
>
> 2. В виду большого исторического значения негативы этой ленты передаются Комитетом Уполномоченных Союза Отечественной Кинематографии в собственность Государства через Совет Рабочих Депутатов.

(CF 1917: 11/12, 50)

Since the "Provisional Executive Committee" was formed from a comparatively small group of people attending the "Ars" cinema on March 3, another meeting was set for March 6 at the same place. This time the invitation was extended to all workers attached to the film industry. More than 2 000 people from all branches of the

Moscow film world appeared. Trade union newspaper representatives, directors, actors, cameramen, designers and studio workers turned March 6 into a mass meeting which was to play a crucial and decisive role in the coming surge of class-struggle confronting the motion picture industry.

The big turnout may have surprised Antik and his group, but the strategy adopted during the meeting was on their part nevertheless well rehearsed. With the strong backing of Antik and several others a I. A. Kistjakovskij was elected chairman of the meeting. A barrister at the Xanžonkov studio by profession and a Kadet by political affiliation, he was considered well qualified to smooth out eventual clashes and to make the right kind of appeal to the influential groups of liberals in the audience (Rosolovskaja 1937, 48). The stenographic account of the March 6 session published in CF provides a detailed and very interesting description of the unfolding events. After his vague and non-committal opening remarks Kistjakovskij turned to the assembly, hopeful that it would assist him in his own modest attempt to make the meeting a successful one that would arrive at results pleasing to all.

Then Antik took the floor. Happy to greet the delegates "in a free country" he expressed his joy at seeing that so many were concerned about the future of the cinema, that they were interested not only in the film as an art but also in the economic prospects of the industry and "the common task we can accomplish". He continued:

> Судьбы этого дела, которые вершили при прежнем полицейском режиме, полицейские административные власти, в смысле допуска картин, распространения их, открытия и закрытия театров — все это может теперь перейти к нам.
>
> (CF 1917: 11/12, 50)

This suggested nothing but the mere transfer of censorship—a police function of the former regime—to the film industry, i.e. the enterprises themselves. Vengerov, also a studio owner, added further arguments to Antik's plea for strengthening the motion picture business. The latest events, he said, had clearly indicated that when people had obtained certain political and economical rights, they were also fully capable of forming a committee with room enough for two groups whose interests might not coincide totally. Though there existed antagonisms and conflicts on some issues there was also consensus on others. For instance, did not all the delegates present agree upon the necessity of freedom of speech? Of course, Vengerov continued, on this matter we are clearly united as on many others, and it is of vital importance to the country and to the growth of the cinema that we stand united and protect our common interests.

> Необходимо объединиться и выбрать комитет, в который бы вошли представители капитала и рабочих и который будет решать все вопросы, касающиеся кинематографии по существу.

> (CF 1917: 11/12, 52)

Thus, Vengerov also advocated one union for all groups connected with the film industry—an organization which would protect *all* interests, economic and political, of *all* its members.

> Наш долг не вносить раздоров и объединиться для защиты от мощного германского кулака, объединиться в союз.

> (CF 1917: 11/12, 52)

The director Bonč-Tomaševskij adopted similar views, referring to the "co-existence" of the Executive Committee of the State Duma and the Soviet of Workers' Deputies as a viable working arrangement of capital and labour. The film industry would do well to follow this policy. He even gave further emphasis to his remarks by concluding thus:

> Но в то время, когда вся Россия собирается в одно целое, когда Россия напрягает последние усилия, чтобы свергнуть проклятый, ненавистный строй и организовать демократическую Россию, призывать к разъединению преступно (аплодисменты).

> (CF 1917: 11/12, 53)

When the rostrum was finally free, two workers who had not entered their names on the speakers' list approached the chairman and asked to address the audience. The worker Zel'st took the floor, turning to his comrade workers:

> Мы представляем собою совершенно обособленную группу со своими особыми интересами. Я предлагаю собраться тут внизу, и мы отдельно выберем своих делегатов в Совет рабо-

чих депутатов и в Совет Российской Социалдемократической партии. Наши интересы обособленные. Мы не можем объединиться ни с представителями капитала ни с артистами. (...) Мы должны, товарищи, отдельно организоваться.

(CF 1917: 11/12, 55)

Zel'st's colleague Savel'ev retracted his request to speak—the message was clear enough. Zel'st then urged all the workers to leave the meeting immediately. He was interrupted by Lur'e, the editor of *Cine-Fono*, who tried to persuade everyone to remain seated and take part in the balloting. The director Čardynin, who feared that the intelligentsia would be isolated if they lost the support of the workers and completely smashed by the enterprises, appealed to the workers' self-interest, urging them to stay and not pay any attention to the agitators. In the ensuing general chaos, chairman Kistjakovskij called for order and announced an intermission during which members of the intelligentsia dashed to the workers to convince them to vote in the common interests of both groups. Some of the workers did stay.

The final outcome of the meeting on March 6 was the establishment of a "Provisional Committee" of 24 members representing various fields in the film industry. The places on the Committee were divided among the different occupational groups as follows: manufacturers and distributors 8 seats (among them were Kistjakovskij, Xanžonkov and Ermol'ev); theatre owners 4 seats (this group was headed by Antik); artists 4 seats; a group of well-known directors—Perestiani, Čardynin, Gardin and Bonč-Tomaševskij, together with office- and professional personnel 4 seats (here we find again the editor of *Cine-Fono*, Lur'e); artistic workers 2 seats (one cameraman and one actor); studio-workers 2 (sic!) seats (CF 1917: 11/12, 62).

During the first weeks of its existence the "Provisional Committee" of the new body called the "Union of Patriotic Cinematography" did accomplish one project of importance. It managed to compile the material shot by various cameramen of the events in Moscow during the February Revolution. The film was released under the title of "Velikie dni Revoljucii v Moskve". It opened solemnly at the "Ars" cinema on March 26 in the presence of high officials of the Provisional Government, (friendly) members of the diplomatic corps and representatives of the Soviet of Workers' Deputies. The omnipresent Antik greeted the guests, and there were beautiful speeches about the "sunny freedom" now awaiting the Russian cinema. "Then the orchestra played the 'Marseillaise', which everyone heard through standing. The film started. It recalled again for everyone those joyous moments in February; it seemed the applause would never cease, and when the screen lights went out, nobody wanted to leave the theatre" (CF 1917: 11/12, 64).

Behind the slogan of one "classless union", however, the theatre and studio owners closed ranks even more in defense of their own interests. Working-conditions were not improved.

The Workers are Leaving the Factory

In view of the deadlock the film workers decided to act and form their own unions. The "Provisional Committee", the idea of the "Union of unions" finally collapsed.

The trade union movement and the Factory Committees now appearing all over Russia as vehicles for workers' control (see Brinton 1975, Pankratova 1976, Brügmann 1972), also significantly affected the workers in the film industry. The disorganization created by the war and the resistance of the employing class, a hostility which, as we shall see, the employers later expressed by sabotaging or deserting their enterprises, clearly made it imperative for the workers to minimize and if possible eliminate unnecessary struggles between various professional groups. There was now a definite need to co-ordinate the activity of the unions on a vast scale. The point at issue was the drafting of immediate tasks and demands.

During March–July 1917 the film workers formed ten professional organizations not only in Petrograd and Moscow but also in Kazan, Minsk, Omsk and Odessa (Rosolovskaja 1937, 52). The film artists, the mechanics and the office employees were the first groups to form their own unions in Moscow after the meeting on March 6. Two main demands were voiced; the inviolability of active union leaders and seniority rights and a 50 % pay increase. These demands were presented to the employers, who by now had established an organization of their own the "United Society of Film Producers"—OKO (Ob"edinennoe kinoizdatel'skoe obščestvo). OKO rejected the claims. Strikes broke out. The employers immediately called in strike-breakers and in some cases tried to run the theatres themselves. The public was urged to boycott the theatres controlled by the striking workers.

206

Totally some 25 theatres went on strike. Though often quite fierce, the strikes remained mostly local and did not immediately affect the film industry as a whole. In the larger cities, depending on the number of theatres, no more than 10–20 people struck at any one time and they seldom included office workers, artists or well-paid specialists (Bratoljubov 1976, 34).

Even if the strikes did not occur on a large scale they did have a strong psychological impact on the workers. Union membership increased rapidly and new departments were set up to organize workers from the rental agencies and laboratories.

The "xudožestvennaja intelligencija" i.e. the "creative workers" in the film industry, adopted a clear strategy of their own. Screenwriters, directors, actors and photographers formed their special organization, the "Union of Workers of the Fictional Cinema"—SRXK (Sojuz rabotnikov xudožestvennoj kinematografii) setting up their base in a café called "Desjataja muza" in Kamergerskij pereulok. Most of the professional discussions and meetings in the café, which incidentally earned a reputation as one of the leading gambling-dens in Moscow, circled around practical matters. Routines were worked out to settle the widespread practice of duplicating scenarios. It was decided that the production of pornographic—and other films "lacking in artistic taste"—was to be denounced. The latter action, however, proved to be somewhat ambiguous. Many of the members continued to follow a policy of total pragmatism, writing pornographic scenarios that were sometimes released under various pseudonyms. On the whole the members of the "Desjataja muza" catered to their own interests, which also frequently meant support for the endeavours and platform of OKO.

On the eve of the Kornilov revolt the Second All-Russian Conference of Cinema was held at the "Ars" cinema. The conference was called by OKO and opened on August 22. However, due to political developments and a threatening railway strike, many delegates were unable to attend the gathering, which was declared to be preparatory (it was decided that the "real" conference should be held before December 1). The August congress was a last attempt, as far as OKO was concerned, to "unite" the various occupational groups in the film industry. The congress set out to discuss the urgent material problems of the cinema, juridical issues and the question of the cultural–educational significance of cinematography to the country (Rosolovskaja 1937, 63).

The October events, however, rapidly terminated the results of these discussions. It is interesting to note though, that Antik in his contribution to the debate pleaded for the reintroduction of censorship (Rosolovskaja 1937, 64). Censorship was indeed restored about half a year later by the Bolsheviks. We will return to this important issue and its consequences below.

Immediately following the October Revolution there were more problems in store for OKO. There were almost daily reports of theatres being taken over and run by the local Soviets. OKO quickly responded with a declaration, appealing to rental offices and the public, to boycott all theatres "seized" by the Soviets.

The situation changed from day to day. Soviet organizations had obtained control of theatres in Petrograd, the Urals and in Xar'kov. In the midst of all the confusion OKO was struck an even greater blow, namely an announced visit by Lunačarskij, who was to speak at the Sovnarkom on the nationalization of the Russian film enterprises. In great distress, the entrepreneurs turned to their allies in SRXK and asked them to form a special delegation which was to demand that Lunačarskij define more accurately what the government actually had in mind regarding the future of the film industry. According to OKO, the appeal was to be "broad-cast", through the press in an attempt to arouse the "human sentiments" of the public.

Союз работников художественной кинематографии, ввиду слухов о предстоящей будто бы национализации кинопромышленности, решил отправить специальную делегацию к приехавшему в Москву т. Луначарскому с целью выяснитх его отношение к этому вопросу, а также и возможную судьбу всех киноработников. В настоящее время собираются подписи сочувствующих под протестом против немедленного осуществления проекта о национализации в то время, когда государство занято более серьезными задачами и недостаточно разработан и освещен этот важный для всей кинопромышленности вопрос.

(Kinogazeta, 1918: 13, in Bratoljubov 1976, 37)

During March–October 1917 even the government-operated Skobelev Committee was afflicted by political riots and strikes. About 250 workers and office employees struck for wage increases, the right to exercise their influence on all managerial functions and in addition to achieve full control over hiring and firing. The conflict was not settled until after the October Revolution, when the Committee was finally nationalized.

The Skobelev Committee and its activities are interesting inasmuch as the organization was the only governmental film enterprise established in 1915 during the tsarist regime.

Originally a philanthropic society, the Committee formed a military film department during the war. It produced and then distributed and projected patriotic films with the aid of mobile screen units mounted on trucks. Incidentally this strategy was in a way a tsarist parallel to the later brigades during the Civil War. The Committee was furthermore granted a monopoly, which it retained until December 1916, of all newsreel filming at the front. Following the February Revolution the Skobelev Committee remained in business and managed to sustain its production. The Provisional Government's handling of the Committee was typical of its general attitude to the cinema. During March–October 1917 the Committee was transferred from one ministry to another, all of which declined to deal efficiently with its activities.

The situation in the country—economic ruin, galloping inflation, the scarcity of consumers' goods—was also clearly reflected in the film industry. There was a constant shortage of raw film stock and equipment of all kinds. The commercial side of the industry received increased emphasis. Rapid transactions and profiteering speculation boomed. The Skobolev Committee was no exception. The new "Department of Social Newsreels of the Skobelev Instructional Committee" released its films at a speedy rate. Quantity often took precedence over quality. The foremost objective was fast, commercial exploitation at the theatres. Consequently many newsreels suffered from bad laboratory processing. However, in the "Free Russia" series, the Department of Newsreels boasted of having caputered "the most recent events of the week". Audiences were shown "Funeral of the Cossacks—Victims of the 3rd–5th of July" (Poxorony kazakov—žertv 3–5 ijulja), "War and Marine Minister Kerenskij's Visit to Kiev" (Prebyvanie voennogo i morskogo ministra Kerenskogo v Kieve) and the like (Lebedev 1965, 83). The Skobelev Committee waved a banner of pseudo-social committment—"instructional" and "educational" became the catchwords of its production.

However, there were testimonies of other kinds of educational and toilsome efforts put in by people travelling in the villages, trying to show and explain the new device, the "velikij nemoj", to the peasants.

In the paper *Ermak* a teacher wrote about his experiences, which involved some unexpected problems. With great difficulties and personal sacrifices he had managed to buy a projector on credit. Having obtained the necessary permit from the district police officer, he set out to sell tickets at the price of 20 and 30 kopeks. Soldiers and children were admitted free. The announcement had been put up three days in advance:

Прочитав объявление, местный усениновский настоятель Павел Смороденников в свою очередь расклеил рядом с моими объявлениями свои, писанные мелким почерком, на целых листах объявления.

В объявлениях было воззвание к православным христианам не ходить и не смотреть живые картины, что это и грех и стыд и проч. Была им в церкви на эту тему сказана 11-го сентября и проповедь — не ходить и не смотреть картины. Начало сеанса у меня было назначено в 3 часа дня. Но в 3 часа ровно зазвонили в большой колокол ко всенощной, хотя и не было в понедельник 12-го никакого праздника. Устроено было чтение в церкви, чего никогда тоже не было. Пришлось мне отложить сеанс до окончания всенощной. И только в 7 часов вечера кинематограф был пущен в ход. Несмотря на поздний час, на тесноту и на неприспособленность помещения, публика была 200 человек. Дышать было нечем. Картины смотрелись с большим интересом. Нельзя передать всего восторга, переживаний зрителей — крестьян. Демонстрировались картины и в других местах.

(Reprinted from *Ermak* in CF 1917: 9/10, 58)

After the October Revolution the social struggles within the film industry assumed a different character. The private enterprises and their press, mainly the magazines *Vestnik Kinematografii*, *Cine-Fono*, *Kinogazeta* and *Proêktor* still maintained a hostile attitude towards the Bolsheviks. The newly established Cinema Committees in Petrograd and Moscow considered it a matter of vital importance to fight the influx of enterprise-produced films on the market. The battleground was thus transferred to the films themselves. However, as

Soviet film production was still operating on a very low scale, in the beginning of 1918, Narkompros considered it a matter of some urgency to launch a major overhauling of the existing films being circulated in the country. We will now try to examine some of the intentions and criteria behind this ideological control. To this end it might be useful first to briefly survey the major "genres" and contents of the films made by the private enterprises.

An Important Footnote Missing

One of the dangers threatening any study of the very first years of Soviet film production is that it can easily be caught in the official mythology that has grown up around the subject. That is, one risks becoming entangled in the very legend one is trying to destroy.

Another danger lies in retrospective identification with certain individuals, tendencies or phenomena on the cultural scene. Hopefully, these traps will be avoided below.

Many accounts of Soviet film history tend to neglect one area. Several film historians, not only Soviet ones, have contributed to the myth that the films made by state organizations during the Civil War were the only films produced during that period. There is a general tendency to regard the films made by private enterprises in those years as simply leftovers from a pre-revolutionary buffet, most of them then being lumped together and disposed of as having no significance or influence on the development of the real Soviet cinema. However, there existed a private film industry, and it was not about to give up its positions easily. Technically silent, the film was not silent in the metaphorical sense (see Nils Åke Nilsson on the silence of art in 1918). Nor could it afford to be. Like any other capitalistic industry, the private film enterprises had to produce and preferably show a profit.

In the early spring of 1917, the Xanžonkov studio announced a screenplay contest, thus inviting authors to write directly for the film, incidentally a policy that was later to be adopted and used by the Soviet cinema authorities.

Tempting money prizes were offered as bait to attract writers to the new medium. Entries in the contest were subject to the following general rules:

1. Представляемые на соискание премий произведения должны состоять не менее, как из 4 актов, считая приблизительно по 20 картин в каждом акте.
2. Должны быть оригинальные и нигде раньше непечатавшиеся.
3. Место действия должно быть в пределах Российской Империи, а время действия — современная эпоха.

(CF 1917: 9/10, 55)

There was indeed a pressing need for new films. The film booming and the rise of giant enterprises like Xapsaev, Transatlantik and Biofilm (the last two of which distributed only imported films), entailed an increased monopolization that profoundly affected the Russian market. In addition, the cinema network expanded rapidly throughout the country, numbering some 4 000 theatres by the end of 1917 (Bratoljubov 1976, 31). Each company had to provide the theatres with a steady flow of box-office successes in order to keep pace with the devastating competition.

Instead of Reality: From Exorcism to Apotheosis

What then did the private enterprises offer Russian audiences at this time? What kind of film formed the heritage that the Soviet cinema—which did not start from scratch in some sort of vacuum—was later to build on? Among the films produced by private firms in 1917–1921 there are some easily discernible groups, that tend to cluster around certain common motifs. In order to make them more easily manageable I will term them "genres", though I am quite aware that the concept used in this context may very well be debatable.

One theme that occupied many directors was the mysticism attached to the idea of Satan. In fact, so many films were made on that subject that the film magazine *Kinogazeta* ironically remarked: "If the devil didn't exist he would have to be invented ... Film-makers won't take a step without him ... Every firm has some sort of devil in its soul" (KG 1918: 15, 7).

Very often these films were connected with the tradition in Russian literature that depicted the devil as a demon, as an equal of Christ. The history of mankind is seen merely as an eternal struggle between religious forces—the commanding power of Christ or Antichrist. In

212

the typical plot the devil takes on a human shape and, releasing all evil forces, seduces some innocent soul. This theme was demonstrated in varying ways in films like "Descendant of the Devil" (Potomok d'javola), "Satan Triumphant" (Satana likujuščij), "Schérzò of the Devil" (Skerco d'javola) etc. One of the very few, partially preserved films belonging to this "genre" is "Satan Married Them" (Venčal ix satana) released in Petrograd in December 1917. Based on a "boulevard novel" and part of the "Russian Golden Series" the film provides us with a good insight into the "decadent" atmosphere usually cultivated in this group of films. Shot almost entirely in studio, the story takes place in an overstuffed aristocratic milieu. The cast is the usual set of melodrama characters—the aristocratic lady and her husband, the lady's young male friend, whom she later marries, and the maid in whom she confides. Through some additional characters, among others a female fortune-teller, we are led into a richly ornamented devil-mass. Cross-cutting between various symbols establishes the framework of a ceremony, which the devil then performs.

In this "genre" there was rarely any room for expressive shades or nuances. The sinister reality was constructed on the antagonism between Good and Evil, Innocence and Guilt. The root of all evil was always within the individual, not in a social context. Man was the tangible victim of evil "forces" that often had sexual connotations. Despite lack of an obvious social context these films, however, sometimes in an allegorical sense pointed to the connection between Antichrist and the threats of the revolution.

Closely related to the "Satan-genre" was a group of films issued as a series under the title of "The God-Seekers" (Iščuščie boga). These productions, which centered around the life of various religious sects, stressed the mystical and erotic elements even more. Films like "Beguny" and "White Doves" (Belye golubi), both of which are partially preserved, are still very far removed from the lives of ordinary individuals. The leading characters, now monks and nuns or aristocrats, act out their passions and desires in the often amazingly elaborate settings of old churches, monasteries and at court. These films display a whole rang of occult and sinister symbols, all of which serve to emphasize the nature of the rites and the orgies and exorcism. Here, man is even more doomed, the individual is clearly heading for disaster unless superior forces decide otherwise.

The private studios also had a clear predilection for the historical past, which easily lent itself to the kind of romantic, pompous stage designs which were much in demand among many directors at the time. Triggered by the revolutionary events in February 1917, a series of films like "Peter and Aleksej" (Petr i Aleksej), "The Secret of the Death of Peter III" (Tajna smerti Petra III) and "The Favourite of Catherine II" (Favorit Ekateriny II) were rapidly released on the market. Equally prominent was the interest in the works of classical Russian writers. Tolstoj, Čexov, Puškin, Gogol', Lermontov etc. were all brought to the screen and in order to celebrate the centenary of Turgenev's birth a screenplay contest was announced by Narkompros, inviting private firms to collaborate with the cinema committees in Petrograd and Moscow (KT 1918: 2, 15).

However, sensing the tightening political climate, many enterprises (under the pretext that they had to prepare for their summer shooting) gradually moved south in early 1918. They brought most of their facilities—both skilled manpower and cameras—along with them and with an eye on developments in Moscow prepared for the final take-off.

One of the first studios to move to the Crimea was Xanžonkov's. Here, against the fashionable, "exotic" background of Yalta he initiated a series of romantic melodramas, a trend soon to be taken up by others.

Already in 1917 Xanžonkov produced "In the Land of Love" (V strane ljubvi) which is partially preserved. The film is interesting from several viewpoints. It depicts realistically a segment of contemporary life, though still a privileged one. In contrast to the "genres" described above, human passions are quite earth-bound and secularized here. The frequent use of exterior shots is also striking. We leave dusty studios and enter the sunny streets of Yalta where most of the action takes place. The changing fortunes of some of the couples are presented through an advanced and very effective parallel-editing technique.

"Aziadė", a sheik-melodrama, was produced by the Abramovič company in 1918 and shot on location partly in the southern areas of Russia, possibly the Crimea, and partly (the harem-scenes) at GUM(!) in Moscow. The film is interesting in that from a stylistical point of view it provides a striking parallel to "Quo Vadis?" and "Cabiria", which were made in Italy in 1912 and 1913. With its extensive cast and elaborate sets "Aziadė" was a commercial success and must have been considered a "super production" and a remarkable feat by entrepreneurs at the time. In retrospect, however, we can see that the plot itself (which was based on a ballet), and the directing and acting, showed little or no cinematic originality.

Already approaching the eve of their destruction the private enterprises refused to let their swan song be infected by the listless moods outside the theatre. Still nursing the carefully created images of a handful selected actors and actresses, the studios introduced the clear-cut film star apotheosis. Following the tradition of the "divine" Asta Nielsen and rivalling the Polish star Pola Negri, Vera Xolodnaja appeared in her own film biography "Thorny Path to Glory" (Ternistyj slavy put'). In a film with the very allegorical title "Though Tomorrow We Die—Today We Live" (Pust' zavtra smert'—segodnja my živem) and in "Behind the Screen" (Kulisy ėkrana) featuring Ivan Mozžuxin and Natalija Lisenko, some of the "secrets" of the private lives of the stars were "revealed". The mere existence of this genre underlines the fact that the cult and worship of film stars was not at all an alien phenomenon among Russian audiences at this time. The Russian film industry carefully cultivated its own idols, much as Hollywood would later create the legend of, for instance, Valentino. Some of the film magazines also contributed by promoting the concept of "film gods" and "goddesses" among their readers and presumptive movie-goers. KT published a series of articles devoted to the subject "In the Service of the Tenth Muse" informatively subtitled—"what every-one wishing to work in the movies ought to know" (KT 1918: 4, 14).

The magazine quite seriously scans every professional branch of the motion picture industry and confidently informs aspiring stars of the necessary prerequisites. The articles are interesting as examples of the prevailing "popular culture" and as contributions to the myths attached to the film industry. The reader who dreamed of becoming the "movie king" of 1918 had merely to consider the following recipe:

Вам, конечно, в день отправления на испытание, уже хочется знать: будете ли кино-королем? Я вам советую проделать такой опыт: когда вы будете уже совсем одеты, постарайтесь вообразить себя уже достигнувшими своей цели и следите за своим внутреннем "я": если душа ваша в этот момент увидит что-то светлое, безконечно прекрасное, какой-то лучезарный образ, словом, если "распустится цветок вашей души", смело идите — вы будете кино-королем, тем скорее, чем ярче, чем могущественнее, чем лучезарнее было видние души вашей. Но если вы увидите кучку кредиток все равно керенок или старых бумажек, золота или серебра или вдруг, чего доброго, покажется вам стол, уставленный жирными явствами и питиями, то идти на испытанье вы можете, но кино-королем вы не будете никогда: потому что проработав статистом, или, как в ателье принято называть "сотрудником" год, изобразив для экрана десяток раз народ или благородного прохожего вы в конце-концов поступите помощником бухгалтера на колбасную фабрику, где и достигнете полного благополучия.

(KT 1918: 4, 14)

But once you haved proved that you possess the inner qualities needed to serve the "Great Silent" you need not worry any further, KT continues. Even if one studio should happen to overlook your talent some other one is bound to discover it. Talent and a small measure of patience are all that is necessary to launch you on the path of glory. Just remember to leave the Tenth Muse your address, concludes KT prosaically.

Reality Arranged: Censorship Restored

The new tasks facing the cinema immediately following the October Revolution became even more urgent during the Civil War years.

What possible use could be made of it, how should it be employed in order to achieve maximum efficiency in agitation and propaganda work? The October Revolution certainly failed to produce any rapid metamorphosis in the film industry resulting in a new, distinctly Soviet film art. Suffering from the energy crisis still prevailing in the country, the Soviet film industry was also in desperate need of film stock and other basic material and furthermore saw itself deprived of many skilled film professionals, who had gone into exile. The constant shortage of equipment and an insufficient supply of raw film stock meant that hardly any new feature-length films were made by state organizations during the Civil War. In their efforts to cope with the urgent need for films, however, the Soviet authorities had another asset that with a little trimming could be put to immediate use, namely the supply of pre-revolutionary Russian and foreign films formerly concealed by the private enterprises in anticipation of

216

"brighter", political prospects. Also, in early 1918, the entire film supply of the former Skobelev Committee had been turned over to the Soviet Government.

Considering the contents of the majority of these films outlined above, it is not hard to realize that they were scarcely fitted to contribute ideologically to any agitational work anticipated by the Bolsheviks. On the other hand, waiting for a sufficient supply of useful Soviet films to materialize did not appear to be a very constructive alternative either.

Thus it was decided as soon as the necessary censoring had been accomplished, these films would be circulated with a party lecturer (Boltjanskij 1959, 84). Through a decree issued in June 1918 (Proėktor 1918: 1/2, July) the Moscow Cinema Committee in conjunction with Narkompros set about a general overhauling of all films being circulated in the country. To ensure the fullest possible measure of control, a special body, "Prosmotrovaja Kollegija", was established within the Cinema Committee. It was to view not only newly produced films but also the entire supply of old films belonging to the Cinema Committee. Narkompros stated "... regarding the public education ... it was all the more important, considering the increasing popularity of the cinema among the masses and its easy access to it, — and the fact that the entire film production up till now had been in private hands—to fight all the bad influence the cinema could possibly exercise". It was a matter of vital importance to put an end to speculation "on all sorts of sensations and the vulgar tastes of the crowd" (KB 1918: 1/2, 3).

Guiding principles were thus set up to aid the "board of censors" in their work:

Задача просмотра кинематографических лент заключается в выделении из общего количества имеющихся в обращении кино-лент тех из них, которые действительно обладают культурным значением (художественным научным или воспитательным) и в исключении из обращения лент безнравственного и, в частности, порнографического характера, а также оскорбляющих религиозное чувство или политические взгляды, или же умышленно искажающих, в каких-либо предосудительных целях, смысл художественных произведений.

(KB 1918: 1/2, 3)

217

This investigation concerned not only the films themselves, but also programmes, posters, scripts etc. After each screening a report was drawn up of the film in question, stating productional and technical data and the censors' opinion of the contents. The reports were published in October 1918 in *Kino-Bjulleten'* (Kino-Komiteta Narodnogo Kommissariata Prosveščenija).

The censors were allotted proportionally among the regions of Moscow. Their professional qualifications were no less important. In order to make sure that the film reviewer would carry out his job properly a set of requirements were issued. For instance:

1. Основательное знакомство с художественной литературой русской и иностранной, дабы они были в состоянии немедленно констатировать соответствие инсценировки — определенному художественному произведению, я — надписей — тексту автора.
2. Знакомство с художественно-литературной критикой русской и иностранной, — для установления определенного взгляда на данное художественное произведение.
3. Знакомство с Историей Искусства — в частности — с историей архитектуры и костюма, для определения соответствия инсценировки стилю данной эпохи.
4. Желательно знание современного городского и деревенского быта, русского и иностранного, для определения соответствия постановка деталям современного быта.

(KB 1918: 1/2, 4)

There was also a fifth requirement, interesting and very informative of the films being made at this time—"familiarity with the theatre is desirable to be able to direct the performance of the actors". Notwithstanding the specific contents and the visual style developed in the agit-films made during the Civil War, a conventional, theatrical way of acting stemming from the pre-revolutionary cinema still prevailed in the Soviet films for quite some time.

The task that the Cinema Committee had imposed upon itself was indeed a gigantic one. KB was intended to be published regularly, but only two issues appeared. A glance at the films listed and reviewed by the Committee reveals that several films produced as early as 1915–1916 were thoroughly examined though some films made in 1917–1918 were omitted. Ambitions may have been just a little too high—in any case it is obvious that Narkompros was not able to carry out full-scale censorship as intended.

The Bolsheviks were determined to maintain the state censorship function. After the nationalization of the Russian film industry was decreed in August 1919 the duties of the "Prosmotrovaja Kollegija" were transferred to a special commission for censorship (Boltjanskij 1959, 91).

However, the political reality facing the country—the Civil War accompanied by famine and energy crisis—soon made it imperative for Narkompros to make immediate use of the Soviet cinema in the current struggle. There was in the very beginning of 1918 an urgent need to set the Soviet film production going in order to meet the agitational tasks issued by the government. Nevertheless, the Bolsheviks' contention that the old film stock needed censorship was well-founded. Enterprise-produced films could not be abolished overnight. In fact, the following item indicates that in some villages and countryside areas pre-revolutionary films prevailed for quite some years to come:

От плохого репертуара провинциальные кино страдают не меньше, чем от налогов и бешеных цен за прокат. Во многих районах только в самое последнее время появились советские картины прошлогоднего выпуска. В некоторых районах (Сибирь) до сих пор не сходят с экрана Веры Холодные, Руничи и прочая заваль, заплесневшая на складах. ... И в тоже время — почти всюду, а не только в медвежьих углах, еще идут и идут склеенные остатки халтурных "боевиков" Дранкова и "Русской Золотой Серии".

(A.R.K. 1925: 1, 12)

In view of the character of the private films described above, to consider the intentions behind ideological control, it might be interesting to briefly survey some of the films ruled out or recommended by Narkompros. The verdict of the censors divided the films into four categories, each indicated by a certain symbol. Here, we will simply number the groups:

1. Films approved and recommended by the board.
2. Films admitted into circulation.
3. Films admitted, though not recommended, as they were of no cultural significance.

4. Films prohibited from exhibition for some reason of an artistic, ethical, religious or political nature (KB 1918: 1/2, 5).

It can generally be observed that out of the total of 174 films reviewed 18 fell into the first category, 35 into the second, 89 into the third and 32 belonged to the fourth category. Most of the films in the first group were screen versions, adaptations of novels or short stories by classical Russian writers like Tolstoj, Puškin and Gogol'. The merits of these films, according to the board of censors, consisted in their truthfulness vis-à-vis the original in question, their ability to catch the exact atmosphere of a given historical epoch, accuracy in details and often the quality of "artistic" acting, by which was meant subtle, psychological insight.

The report on "Lady into Lassie" (Baryšnja-krest'janka) adapted from Puškin provides a rather typical example:

> Инсценировка повести весьма удачно, в постановке вполне соблюдена эпоха; действие развивается планомерно, места съемки выбраны подходящие; съемка очень хорошая.
>
> (Ibid., 18)

The second and third categories contained a wide range of films representative of the private film industry. Here we find the "Satan"-films, the eternal-triangle melodrama, historical battle scenes and portraits etc. However, the criteria dividing the second and third groups in the censors' reports seem very subtle. Negative remarks that the acting was primitive or vulgar, the plot lacked in logical structure, historical reality was falsely represented etc. apply more or less equally to both categories. What actually determined the "cultural significance" of a film is not at all evident from the reports.

In the second category we find this opinion on the sheik-melodrama "Aziadė" mentioned above:

> Сюжетом является любовь шейха к бедной арабской девушке, последняя будучи по приказанию шейха похищена, отравляет его с помощью пленницы и вырывается на свободу. Поэма является инсценировкою балета того же названия. Следует признать, что балет, получив несвойственное ему драматическое воплощение, значительно теряет в своей художественной выразительности. Постановка очень удачна, как в смысле

костюмов, прекрасно передающих быт и эпоху, так и по постановке групповых сцен. Игра Мордкина и Фроман хороша.

(Ibid., 17)

"Schérzò of the Devil" (Skerco d'javola) was placed in the third category much due to its elements of "heavy" violence and its dubious moral. After a rather lengthy account of the entanglements in the plot the board of censors concluded:

Оканчивается драма апофеозом дьявола около гробов с трупами людей, погибших по его вине. Рассказ ведется от имени героини, жены дьявола, находящейся в доме умалишенных. Сюжет драмы психологически несправедлив, неправдоподобен, ибо вся серия преступлений и несчастий вытекает из легкомысленного и непредосудительного порыва. Кроме того не объяснимо с моральной точки зрения разрушение семьи, члены которой вообще весьма добродетельны. Постановка хорошая, действие протекает на фоне Крымской природы, но некоторые сцены — самоубийство, насилие — нехудожественные и нежелательны с моральной точки зрения. Может быть допущена, но не рекомендована.

(Ibid., 25)

The Black List

The fourth category is interesting in that it contains the actual "black list", films weeded out by the board of censors as definitely unsuitable for exposure to the masses for artistic, ethical, religious or political reasons. How were these criteria applied in practice? If we scan the reports of the 32 films put into the fourth group the overwhelming majority are ruled out owing to "artistic" reasons. In some cases there may be a pornographic connection, but often they are generally termed as displaying "bad taste", deplorable acting, naiveness, vulgarity, incoherent plot etc. The following judgment should suffice as an illustrative example of what was meant by lack of artistry:

"Little White Slaves" (Malen'kie belye rabyni)
Сюжет заключается в погоне представительницы "Общества покровительства женщин" за тайною торговцев "белыми рабынями". Постановка крайне нехудожественна и чрезвы-

чайно невразумительна. За ходом действия следить почти невозможно, отдельные сцены не имеют между собою никакой логической связи. Надписи просто безграмотны и не соответствуют содержанию картины. Сцены в публичном доме, в четвертой части, — решительно недопустимы. Запрещается в виду неясности сюжета, нехудожественности постановки, вульгарности и порнографии отдельных сцен.

(Ibid., 21)

Several films characterized as comedies by their originators were similarly ruled out as failing to demonstrate any "true" comic features. This together with the general coarseness and nonsense of the plot, was enough aesthetic motivation to warrant their withdrawal from public exhibition. "Oh, Don't You Believe in Advertising!" (Ax, ne ver'te vy reklame!) provides an illustrative example:

Чрезвычайно грубая пьеса, сюжет которой основан на невероятном чудодейственном воздействии патентованных средств, вследствие неправильного употребления которых возникают неожиданные эффекты. Грубость, нелепость и отсутствие подлинного комизма делают картину недопустимой.

(Ibid., 13)

There were actually only two films in the fourth category prohibited owing to ethical reasons not connected with pornography. "There You are, Kite, the Reward for Your Thievish Life" (Tak vot tebe, koršun, nagrada za žizn' vorovskuju tvoju) was ruled out because it depicted life as filled with never ending, gloomy crimes—"the drama does not contain a single bright spot and has a depressing effect on the spectator." In the report on "Paul Suffers from Hallucinations" (Pol' stradaet galljucinacijami) the censors flatly refused to admit "sick humour":

Сюжетом является психическое страдание героя, которому представляется, что он обладает способностью раздвоения; на этой почве происходит ряд комических недоразумений. В виду того, что психическая болезнь сама по себе не должна вызывать к себе юмористического отношения, а кроме того, в ходе пьесы встречается ряд совершенно непонятных мест, то картина не может считаться допустимой.

(Ibid., 14)

The rest of the films prohibited on ethical grounds contained more or less "risky" elements of pornography. Though in some cases the censors admitted conciliating traits as beautiful scenery etc. spicy details in combination with mediocre acting and a hackneyed plot automatically condemned these films. "Ladies of the Health Resort Do Not Even Fear the Devil" (Damy kurorta ne bojatsja daže čorta) got a rather typical evaluation:

> Сюжет эротического характера; фарсовые сценки не имеют внутреннего замысла и весьма рискованны: постановка интересно задумана и снята на фоне красивого пейзажа.

(Ibid., 13)

In the following rather curious passage of one report one senses that the tolerance of the censors must have been severly tried:

> Дама купает собаку вместе с собою в ванне; другая собака уносит первую из рук хозяйки; далее погоня за собаками; имеется элемент непристойности.

(Ibid., 15)

"The Jealous Dog" (Revnivaja sobaka)
In the fourth category, with a total of 32 films prohibited from public exhibition, only 6 seem to have been weeded out due to political reasons. There might even be only 5, as the report on "Feat of Arms" (Na ratnyj podvig) is very laconic and gives us no clues whatsoever as to the actual contents of the film. The report simply reads "the plot is tendentious, the staging unartistic". The title suggesting a war theme in connection with the use of the word "tendentious" and the additional fact that the film was produced by the former Skobelev Committee probably before 1917, permit the admittedly somewhat vaguely grounded assumption that there was a political judgment attached to that film. Three more films in this group of six were produced by the Skobelev Committee. In "The Career of Captain Voronov" (Kar'era kapitana Voronova) the hero is forced to take part in court martial proceedings against the brother of his fiancée. This causes a break with the girl and the hero chooses to kill himself. According to the report there was obviously an element of terrorism in the plot but taken as a whole the political story was labeled "something of a caricature". On the basis of the scanty information in the report, it

223

is hard to determine whether the censors specifically considered the film to be connected with the political reality of the time. This seems fairly obvious, though, in the case of the remaining four films.

"Power to the People" (K narodnoj vlasti) conveyed Menshevik and SR views on the importance of ensuring the fairness of the elections to the Constituent Assembly (Učreditel'noe Sobranie). The film was released in November 1917. Then, in January 1918 it was suggested to re-issue the film "with changes" but it was decided to prohibit it (Catalogue of Films of Private Production 1961, 268). The censors described the film in their report:

> Сцены агитационно-просветительного характера, приуроченные к выборам в Учредительное Собрание; для привлечения внимания зрителей к порядку и технике выборов, вставлена драматическая фабула, заключающаяся в злостном опорочении кандидата партии. Имеет чисто исторический характер: надписи приурочены к эпохе выборов в Учредительное собрание в октябре–ноябре 1917 года.

(Ibid., 8)

"When the Country is in Danger" (Kogda rodina v opasnosti) depicted various agitational methods practiced in Britain for recruiting army volunteers. The historical interest of the film was considerable, the censors concluded, but considering the present situation in the country "releasing it was deemed inopportune" (Ibid., 20).

"The Holy Devil" (Svjatoj čort) was one of many films dealing with the Rasputin affair; in fact it treated the planning and execution of the murder. The report, which contained a lengthy account of the contents of the film, sharply denounced the description given of the historical events. The principal character is an officer, whose fiancée Rasputin tries to seduce. After having failed in his attempt, Rasputin and a group of other people conspire against the officer and manage to have him arrested and put in jail. At this time, however, a plot is hatched to remove Rasputin. The conspirators' plans succeed and he is killed. At the outbreak of the February Revolution the officer is set free and he takes part in efforts to arrest the former ministers. The censors refuted every aspect of the historiography expressed in the film by pointing to inaccuracy in a number of details and a general lack of historical coherence. Further emphasis was given in the report on the matter of misrepresentation of historical facts:

В общем постановка, расчитанная на успех скандала, дает совершенно извращенное представление о жизни бывших правящих кругов, искажает историческую действительность в деле обстановки убийства Распутина и имеет целью привлечь симпатии к кругу лиц, принимавших участие в убийстве Распутина, выставляя их народными героями. ... Картина, как искажающая историческую действительность и не имеющая художественной ценности, допущена быть не может. Запрещается.

(Ibid., 25)

"Loved and Betrayed" or "Under the Clouds of Autocracy" (Ljubíl i predal ili Pod oblakami samoderžavija) from the censors' point of view probably provided the most touchy allusion to the contemporary situation in Russia. The story relates the life of an "agent", who, while betraying his own brother, enters the service of an aristocrat as a member of his guard (oxrana). Rising rapidly in his career, the agent manages to slip into court, where he soon finds himself in favour with a certain "eminent personage" who becomes his mistress. At this moment the hero falls in love with the daughter of a general, who is on the verge of putting into practice his plans to overthrow the imperial family and the government. Somehow, during the course of preparations, the general gets suspicious and the agent is arrested. Under the influence of the agent, however, the general's daughter commits "an act of terrorism" directed against the emperor. The attempted murder fails but the girl is set free by the rebelling people. Realizing that his plans have failed, the agent commits suicide.

Reacting to the "incredible twist" given to the historical ingredients in this "absurd" story the censors commented on the film:

Действие происходит в современной России — следовательно историческая нелепость сюжета очевидна. Драма является наглой спекуляцией на революционное чувство. Постановка нехудожественна и груба ...

(Ibid., 21)

In Defense of the Unartistic

What in fact did Narkompros attain by its censorship? As a starting-point for answering that question we might use an article published in the contemporary press. It provides an interesting contribution to our discussion of the censorship and its function and usefulness during the first year of building the new Soviet film production. On August 22, 1918 the Moscow Soviet of workers and Red Army Deputies' evening paper *Večernie Izvestija* carried an article entitled "In defense of the unartistic". The heading referred to the Cinema Committee's frequent criticism of films lacking in "artistic" qualities. Having established the fact that the majority of the films condemned by the censors were prohibited on pornographic or artistic grounds, the author then draws attention to the one and only film prohibited due to religious motives—"The King of the Judeans" (Car' Iudejskij). The film, which has been omitted in the KB, was released in Moscow on May 10, 1918 and only two days later the Cinema Committee of Narkompros reacted by withdrawing it from exhibition, terming it "worthless pulp" (Catalogue of Films of Private Production 1961, 303). This source also alleges that the film was to some extent based on a play by the same name (for an account of the contents and censorship of the play see Nils Åke Nilsson in this volume).

Having pointed to the main criteria behind the censors' prohibition, the critic in VI proceeds to put things straight to the readers:

> Коллегия вторглась в область, ей непринадлежащую, — ибо не дело государства — регулировать художественные запросы и вкусы общества. Да, и сомнительно, чтобы возможно было создать для этой цели достаточно авторитетный орган.
>
> (VI 1918: 30, 3)

Beneath the question as to the competence and powers of the state to exercise censorship was the more fundamental question of state art, state literature, state film etc. Was state culture possible at all? (see Nils Åke Nilsson). Further elaborating the negative aspect of state art, i.e. the censorship as carried out by Narkompros, the critic found it downright ridiculous that "socialists, Bolsheviks should make a fuss about the inviolability of philistine, religious feelings". On the issue of pornographic films he questioned the overall use of a few scattered cuts here and there. "Why throw the baby out with the bathwater?" The problem of censorship in connection with film pornography implied far deeper consequences. Where was the guarantee, he continued, "that in winnowing the grain from the chaff of culture, the heavy and untrained hands of the state, will not, in the ardour of their work, weed out something valuable?" Look at any public library:

97 percent of its books are bound to contain pornography, vulgar comedy, unartistic ingredients or other elements condemned by the censors' criteria.

In this context it is interesting to note the critic's position. If it is to stop all the possible detrimental effects of pornography on the individual, the state must not only prohibit films but all other media exposing pornographic contents as well. According to the critic, this is not only impossible but also a preposterous strategy, as it is bound to run counter to basic democratic principles.

It is terrible to think of, he concludes, "but is it really possible that in order to suppress the evil, it is necessary to prohibit the other 97 percent as well? Furthermore, all pornographic postcards, posters and magazines should then be withdrawn from circulation. Even *Večernie Izvestija* could easily be condemned as of injuring religious feelings and on far more solid grounds than—it is ridiculous even to mention it—the film 'The King of the Judeans'. The whole matter of the state as a regulator of cultural affairs, "concludes the critic," falls of its own absurdity" (VI 1918: 30, 3).

Political Control or Ideological Flop?

To the Bolsheviks and Narkompros, however, the actions taken by the state to regulate and control filmproduction were an urgent matter, considering not only the "increasing popularity and availability of the cinema among the masses" but also the fact that the film transcended all other media as a means of propaganda. The film was portable, visual and easily understood and thus much more effective than books (Lunačarskij 1965, 35).

As we have seen, 32 of the titles listed in the KB were actually prohibited. The vast majority was withdrawn due to "artistic" or "pornographic" reasons, a very small group of films was selected and prohibited on account of what we—judging from the reports—believe to be political indications. This much then, the censorship accomplished—but was that all? The fact still remains that of the 174 films listed and reviewed in the KB 142 were admitted into circulation. As has been mentioned before, that list is by no means complete, and on the whole it is difficult to establish any certain figures as to the number of films made by private firms circulated in Russia in 1918. The country was in the midst of the Civil War, and the control of production centers outside of Moscow and Petrograd passed from the Red Army to the White forces. The proportion of entrepreneurial films that actually reached the audiences is also quite hard to determine. Nonetheless, there emerges a figure of some 150 featurelength films made only in 1918 (Catalogue of Films of Private Production 1961). Taking into consideration that the Soviet film organizations did not produce one single full-length feature in that year, the supply and impact of entrepreneurial films on the market must still have been considerable.

On the whole, the censorship seems to have operated within rather strictly defined aesthetical and educational boundaries, some clues to which are provided by the professional qualifications a censor was required to possess. In practice, as we have seen, artistic and ethical criteria were those most frequently applied by the censors. Political purity seems to have been less called for in regard to the films specifically viewed and reported on. It is likely though, that further efforts in this respect were added through the party lecturers, who functioned as ideological editors pointing out and explaining weaknesses in the films as they were shown (Boltjanskij 1959, 84). The total propaganda value of this strategy must have at times been quite disasterous from the Bolshevik point of view as the speaker was often ignored or simply shouted down by the audience (Taylor 1979, 51).

Incidentally, the practice was continued with varying degrees of success throughout the 20s. Among the films selected for exhibition at workers' clubs we find as late as in 1925 Protazanov's adaptations of Puškin's "The Queen of Spades" (Pikovaja Dama) and of Tolstoj's "Father Sergius" (Otec Sergij), both of which however were furnished with precautionary notices "Pre-revolutionary film ... Showing to be accompanied by critical remarks of Marxist lecturer" (A.R.K. 1925: 2, 42).

Evaluating the application of the ethical criteria as they appear in the reports, it is hard to believe that any considerations of the public's mental hygiene ever crossed the collective mind of the Bolshevik censorship. Terming films as "bourgeois filth" or pornography were simply new labels on an old phenomenon. The puritanism of the former church censorship had been fully re-established (see Nils Åke Nilsson).

"Anti-revolutionary" was by the same token a new term for political control—i.e. state censorship was now restored. However, effective political censorship called for more delicate instruments than those used by Narkompros' board of censors. The propaganda inherent in the films in the form of subtle ideological allusions and social values not manifested on the surface level that conveyed and reproduced the myths and beliefs of the pre-revolutionary Russian society, in short the class ideology of the entrepreneurs escaped the scissors of the Bolshevik censorship. It is interesting to note the degree to which the Bolsheviks themselves were aware of this fact. As late as in 1922, Lenin himself, while stating in his by now famous conversation with Lunačarskij, that "of all the arts the cinema is for us the most important" at the same time demonstrates a remarkable ignorance—and lack of interest—as to the capacities of the fiction film to create and convey ideology. Pleading for an extended production of newsreels Lenin explains:

> Если вы будете иметь хорошую хронику, серьезные и просветительные картины, то не важно, что *для привлечения публики пойдет при этом какая-нибудь бесполезная лента, более или менее обычного типа.* Конечно, цензура все-таки нужна. Ленты контрреволюционные и безнравственные не должны иметь место.
>
> (Gak & Glagoleva 1965, 40, my italics, K. B.)

Anxious to intensify the production of weekly newsreels, Lenin overlooked the fact that the harmless, "useless" film set up as a bait to draw crowds to the theatres often remained the main attraction for the audiences, by far outstripping the Bolshevik, educational part of the program. Box-office reports up to the mid-20s even indicated that given a choice, Soviet audiences would continue to prefer imported films or films of a similar, "bourgeois" type. That trend did not turn until the season of 1927–28 (Taylor 1979, 96). Realizing the importance of the newsreel and urgently supporting its production Lunačarskij was nevertheless fully aware of the subtle, ideological dangers inherent in the entrepreneurial films. In an article entitled "Revolutionary Ideology and the Cinema" (Revoljucionnaja ideologija i kino) published in conjunction with an All-Union Conference on the Cinema in 1924, Lunačarskij pointed to the continued attraction of bourgeois films seven years after the revolution:

> Буржуазия прекрасно понимает значение кино в этом отношении и, разумеется, пользуется им в своих классовых интересах.

Однако буржуазия поступает при этом очень умно. Она чрезвычайно редко придает своим фильмам дидактический и откровенно классовый воспитательный характер. Наоборот, свой буржуазный яд она распространяет почти незаметно, органически вплетая угодные для нее тенденции и хвалу ее добродетели в разного рода кинороманы и кинокомедии.

(Gak & Glagoleva 1965, 35–36)

Consolidating Political Power

Naturally the censorship affecting the films made by private firms was not the only step the Bolsheviks took to crush the entrepreneurial film machinery. A decree issued in July 1918 by the Moscow Soviet took other measures against the financial and organizational structure of the private enterprises. A compulsory registration of all enterprises, film stock and cinema equipment was ordered, no transfers were to be allowed. Further, a limitation of electric current was declared. Also, all films produced had to be registered. In an effort to by-pass these regulations, many entrepreneurs deserted their enterprises, concealing film stock and bringing valuable apparatus along with them. Thus, as we have seen, they managed to sustain a certain proportion of their production for at least a few years.

However, the actions of the Bolsheviks gradually led to the nationalization of the Russian film industry in August 1919. There was a parallel development of the Soviet film industry starting with the establishment of the film section of Narkompros and then the Cinema Committees in Petrograd and Moscow.

The use of the film apparatus as a means of consolidating the political power of the new regime was evident to the Bolsheviks immediately following the October Revolution. Though other known instruments of propaganda as the press and the theatre were still used, new ones rapidly emerged in the form of posters and monumental art. It was soon obvious that the fundamentally visual nature of the film made it far superior to other propaganda media. By transcending barriers of language it managed to get its message across to vast segments of the illiterate population.

In this context it is interesting to note the negligible significance attached to the film by the two groups "to the left" of Lunačarskij and Narkompros in the cultural arena. Neither the avantgarde headed by the Futurists nor Proletkul't, each adopting a strategy of their own in other cultural areas, contributed in any substantial practical way to developing Soviet fictional film in the period immediately following the October Revolution.

Proletkul't, stressing its autonomy vis-à-vis the Bolshevik party and the governmental authorities, declined from the beginning to accept any responsibility and share in the most basic work among the masses, the liquidation of illiteracy, which was left to Narkompros and the Soviets (see Gorsen & Knödler-Bunte 1974 and Paech 1974). However, Proletkul't requested Lunačarskij to transfer the entire film stock of the former Skobelev Committee to them so that it could be used in educational efforts among the workers (IT 1918: 128, Jan. 26–Febr. 8). We do not know what would have materialized from this anticipated film work on the part of Proletkul't, as the film department of the Skobelev Committee was nationalized in March 1918 and its production then filtered through the Narkompros censorship, as described above. In a resolution passed at the fourth "All-town conference of cultural-creative organizations" demands were voiced to let the Petrograd Proletkul't, in conjunction with the Cinema Committee of the city, independently extend its activities into the film area (Grjaduščee 1920: 7/8, 23).

Yet, there does not seem to be any sequel to these requests or any new initiatives until 1923 and the founding of the stock company "Proletkino". By this time, however, Proletkul't itself had more or less ceased to exist.

Notwithstanding Futurist manifestos and poems, as for instance Vertov's "My" (KF 1922: 1, 11–12) and Majakovskij's "Kino i kino" (KF 1922: 4, 5), both of which expressed a strong appeal for the future of the communist cinema, the avantgarde contributed very little to the very first years of Soviet fictional film production. Even though the Futurists proclaimed that "art is production", the modernistic, abstract elements emerging in avantgarde art and literature would have had no justification in the Bolshevik concept of agitational cinema. Abstract experiments would have to be a privilege for those who preferred to dedicate themselves entirely to artistic problems.

The isolation of the revolution in Russia forced the country to fight alone both against external enemies and forces trying to overthrow the new regime from within. This put the Soviet cinema in a situation where every single film had to be socially tested. Was it efficient as a political weapon? Could it serve an immediate purpose in production or defence? Such a functional approach to the use of the cinema as an educational and agitational instrument was the foundation on which Lenin built his concept of the future role of the Soviet film.

Thus, every visual representation that tended to be complicated or filled with conflicts was abolished. There was no room for any subjective intentions or visions. The film had to be brought in line with propagandistic intentions. What was needed were tangible, figurative representations. Films that could be easily grasped and examined by the masses. Films capable of holding the attention of their audiences long enough for the agitational message to get across and strike root. The needs of the Civil War gave birth to a new type of film alongside the existing newsreel—the *agitka*. Most of the 63 *agitki* produced by Soviet film organizations in the years 1918–20 were quite short, generally not exceeding two reels or thirty minutes of projectiontime (Sovetskie xudožestvennye fil'my ... 1961, 5–26). As a rule the agit-films were not exhibited commercially at the theatres. For the most part they were shown in the streets and squares of the larger cities, at the fronts, and to audiences along the routes of the agit-trains and streamers (see Taylor in this volume). Due to the scarce supply of positive film stock it was only possible to make a limited number of prints of each film. Some *agitki* appeared in just one or two copies.

Notwithstanding the hard economic conditions affecting the productive apparatus, the agit-films nevertheless offered quite an expressive and varied canvas. Soviet film historians have tended to discern certain genres within the agit-films (Lebedev 1965, Zorkaja 1962, Drobašenko, Zak, Rizaev etc. 1969). This might very well be a matter of judgment, but apart from the unifying characteristic of frequently being visually dynamic, the agit-films did represent several narrative forms. Some were filmed versions of propaganda posters. Others had a more formal, rhetorical element built into them, illustrating for instance political slogans, "lozungi". Here the visual representation sometimes merely accompanied the rather lengthy "text". A third group reminiscent of newsreels used a documentary approach to depict theatrical mass-spectacles as "Seizure of the Winter-Palace" (Vzjatie Zimnego Dvorca). However, by far the largest part of the agit-films displayed characteristic fiction-film features. They were built on a narration formed into a dramatically structured plot conveyed to the audience by actors. Considerations of space prohibit us from embarking on a closer examination of the agit-films. Thematically very rich and worthy of a thorough investigation, they will be treated in my dissertation, where the "genre" attributes of these films as well as propaganda campaigns and intentions attached to the making of them will be discussed.

Melodramas in a Political Key

We have examined above the social clashes and the class-struggle involved in the rise of a union movement in the Russian film industry between February and October 1917. We then considered how the Bolsheviks, starting in 1918, tried to cope with the impact of the entrepreneurial films by employing certain criteria of censorship worked out by the Narkompros Cinema Committee.

In conclusion, I would like to point to just a few elements connecting private filmproduction with the emerging Soviet fiction film of 1917–1921, i.e. the agit-films displaying fiction-film features. In an article entitled "The Semantics of the Cinema", Viktor Šklovskij takes exception to Dziga Vertov and the concept of the "Kinoki"-group; the ability and desire to catch the unorganized flow of reality.

Demanding a solid structure and emphasizing the importance of a certain method in cinematography, "only a particular approach on the part of the cameraman can make an image tangible", Šklovskij then turns against the Vertov-group's belief that their refusal to use actors abolished the curse of art. This is an illusion, as "the very choice of elements to be shot is already an act of will". Thus the very essence of the film makes it gravitate towards "sjužet", "as a means of organizing cinematic words and phrases" (ARK 1925: 8, 5).

Not only did the great bulk of the agit-films build on a "sjužet", many of them were also strongly influenced by the private, pre-revolutionary films in that they were solid melodramas. This fact was not frowned upon or considered to hamper the propaganda value of the films at the time. On the contrary. In early 1919, the theatre department of Narkompros, announced on Gorkij's initiative a melodrama contest with the following prerequisites:

Так как мелодрама строится на психологическом примитивизме — на упрощении чувств и взаимоотношений действующих лиц, — желательно, чтобы авторы определенно и ясно подчеркивали свои симпатии или антипатии к тому или иному герою.

(Tamašin 1961, 271)

233

Notwithstanding the fact that they aimed at an agitational content reflecting the political reality of the time, many agit-films thrived on conventions developed in pre-revolutionary Russian films. True, several *agitki* had a strong documentary accent, especially when they described social milieu. Some, in fact, had newsreel footage of meetings, demonstrations and events from the fronts edited into the fictional material. Nevertheless, it is striking how often themes are conveyed by melodramatic formulas. Sometimes a love-story works only as a spin-off effect from the "sjužet", but it can also just as well supersede the revolutionary theme, reducing it to the function of a mere colourful setting.

In a film backing small scale private enterprise, made during NEP a couple of years later, we even find the bourgeois triangle love-drama fully restored again under the illuminating title "There is no Happiness on Earth" (Net sčast'ja na zemle) 1922.

Even Lunačarskij, in his article "Revolutionary Ideology and the Cinema" published in 1924, recommended the melodramatic form as being most suitable for the film medium. Of course, he added, some adaptation of it would be necessary in order to meet the demands of the new Soviet cinema. The melodrama was infinite, as it could encompass the history of mankind, the class-struggle, the revolutions of the world, all kinds of realistic, romantic, fantastic and satiric themes. Lunačarskij concluded:

Рядом с обработкой мелодраматической, выдвигающей на первый план индивидуальные, а также коллективные героические фигуры и группы, рисующие ярко-контрастными красками социальные противоположности, полные патетики и перипетий, чрезвычайно рекомендуется также и комедийная форма.

(Gak & Glagoleva 1965, 37)

Over the past three decades there has been a gradual reevaluation of the pre-revolutionary Russian cinema among Soviet film historians and critics. It is now generally recognized as being full of nuances and expressiveness. Some historians even assert that the present Soviet opinion of directors as Bauer and Protazanov are closer to views held among critics in 1917 than to those developed in film polemics during the 20s (Selezneva 1972, 25). Still, there is one more myth to disperse.

It is time that Soviet film historians broke the watertight bulkhead sealing off the films made by private firms *after* the October Revolution. Their influence must be recognized and taken into consideration by any attempt to explore the complexities of immediate post-revolutionary Russian society, when the cinema began to grope for new solutions appropriate to the new social reality.

Bibliography

Boltjanskij, G.
1959 "Velikaja oktjabr'skaja socialističeskaja revoljucija i roždenie sovetskogo kinoiskusstva", *Iz istorii kino*, sb., tom 2, Moskva.

Bratoljubov, S.
1976 *Na zare sovetskoj kinematografii*, Leningrad.

Brinton, M.
1975 *The Bolsheviks & Workers' Control (1917 to 1921) The State and Counter-revolution*, Detroit.

Brügmann, U.
1976 *De russiske fagforeninger i revolution og borgerkrig (1917–1919)*, Aarhus.

Drobašenko, S., Rizaev, S., Zak, M. et al. (eds.)
1969 *Istorija sovetskogo kino 1917–1931*, tom 1, Moskva.

Gak, A. & Glagoleva, N. (eds.)
1965 *Lunačarskij o kino*, Moskva.

Gorsen, P. & Knödler-Bunte, E. (eds.)
1974 *Proletkult 1–2*, Stuttgart–Bad Cannstatt.

Lebedev, N.
1956 *Očerk istorii kino CCCP, nemoe kino (1918–1934)*, Moskva.

Paech, J.
1974 *Das Theater der russischen Revolution*, Kronberg Ts.

Pankratova, A.
1976 *Fabrikräte in Russland*, Frankfurt am Main.

Rosolovskaja, V.
1937 "Obščestvennye i političeskie organizacii v kinematografii i ix bor'ba v 1917 g.", *Russkaja kinematografija v 1917 g.*, Moskva.

Selezneva, T.
1972 *Kinomysl' 1920-x godov*, Leningrad.

Tamašin, L.
1961 *Sovetskaja dramaturgija v gody graždanskoj vojny*, Moskva.

Taylor, R.
1979 *The Politics of the Soviet Cinema 1917–1929*, Cambridge.

Zorkaja, N.
1962 *Sovetskij istoriko-revoljucionnyj fil'm*, Moskva.

Works of reference:

1961 *Sovetskie xudožestvennye fil'my*. Annotirovannyj katalog, tom 1: Nemye fil'my (1918–1935), Moskva.

1961 tom 3: (added to the indices) "Katalog fil'mov častnogo proizvodstva 1917–1921", Moskva.

Richard Taylor

Agitation, Propaganda and the Cinema: the Search for New Solutions, 1917–21

Lenin said, "Of all the arts, for us the cinema is the most important" (Boltjanskij, 1925, 16–17). It was a functional, rather than an artistic judgement, as Lunačarskij, the People's Commissar for Education, underlined: "The fact that Lenin was prepared to concede pride of place to the cinema among the other arts shows that in art he valued above all else its colossal agitational and propagandist rôle" (Gak & Glagoleva, 68–9). But, before this rôle could be properly and effectively fulfilled, the Bolsheviks had first to gain control of the cinema, or what remained of it. Just as the normal administrative structure of the Soviet state had been disrupted by war and revolution, so the production and distribution system of the existing conventional cinema network in the R.S.F.S.R. had crumbled under the combined strain of political and economic pressures. It had thus become virtually impossible to realise the government's policy through the usual channels.

It was partly for this reason that the new government decided against the immediate and wholesale centralised nationalisation of the film industry, although in the chaotic conditions of the months following the October Revolution they had little alternative. Centralised organisations were established fairly rapidly but in the early stages their existence was largely confined to paper: Soviet power was not yet strong enough to realise its ambitions. For instance, on 9 November (Old Style), only two weeks after the Revolution, the Extra-Mural Section (Vneškol'nyj otdel) of Narkompros (the People's Commissariat for Education) was created (Boltjanskij, 1959, 85). It was eventually to play an important rôle in the development of the Soviet cinema, but at the end of 1917 there seemed no way of giving it power without frightening private enterprise into further spasms of flight and destruction. In December therefore the complete nationalisation of the cinema was considered and rejected, but even the mere consideration of the subject was enough to cause O.K.O. (the United Society of Film Producers or Ob"edinënnoe kinoizdatel'skoe obščestvo) to declare war on what it described as the "usurpers" (zaxvatčiki) (Boltjanskij, 1959, 79). At the same time some of the Moscow entrepreneurs had begun to spread alarmist rumours about the imminent confiscation of all cinema goods, (Aksel'rod, 26) while the journal *Mir Ėkrana*, which had become a mouthpiece for private enterprise, reported in highly emotive terms the alleged requisitioning of cinemas in a number of cities (MĖ, 26.4.18) and later carried stories of unruly hooliganism (MĖ, 19.5.18; see also Listov, 1969, 7).

Clearly the new authorities had to tread carefully. As a tentative first step a Cinema Subsection (Kinopodotdel) was established under this Extra-Mural Section, which was now headed by Nadežda Krupskaja. Instead of complete and outright nationalisation the Bolsheviks permitted, and at the local level encouraged, a somewhat random pattern of municipalisation by local soviets according to local circumstances in accordance with an N.K.V.D. decree published on 18 January 1918 (*Vestnik otdela mestnogo upravlenija komissariata vnutrennix del*, 1918: 3,1). But this measure provoked an immediate response from the private sector. *Mir Ėkrana* described the threat of nationalisation as the "sword of Damocles" that hung over the cinema (MĖ, 26.4.18, 1), but the journal *Proėktor* saw the problems facing the film industry as economic, rather than political (*Proėktor*, 1917: 17/18, 1; 1918: 1/2, 1). However, in an ominous and prophetic article entitled "An Attempt to Murder the Cinema" (Pokušenie na ubijstvo kinematografii), published late in 1917, a writer in *Vestnik kinematografii* (Cinema Herald) commented:

The thought of a cinema monopoly has recently arisen here. Apparently the talk is of creating a monopoly of both film production and the theatres themselves.

This is an extremely stupid idea.

In fact a monopoly can be created only in those branches of production where production takes place in accordance with a definite and known pattern: thus railways are monopolised because the transport of freight and passengers keeps to a certain pattern; the production and sale of salt may be monopolised, for here again quality does not play a major rôle. But already with the monopoly of tobacco production, for instance, doubts arise because there are many sorts of tobacco and a particular blend is required. What is more, the production of cinema films is an art, like painting, sculpture, music. Can a state monopoly be established in such a branch of production? Clearly this is madness ...

Cinema films cannot be produced according to a pattern. They must reflect the individuality of the artist, the director (VK, 1917: 123).

History was to demonstrate otherwise, for the considerations raised by this writer are the exact inverse of those informing later Soviet film production, although there can be little doubt that Lunačarskij, and probably Lenin as well, preferred a gradualist approach. However, as in the case of the decrees on land, peace and bread, the central authorities were not in complete control of events. In Moscow and Petrograd the local soviets had already established their own Cinema Commissions without reference to, or control by, Narkompros. Admittedly they did little more than sequestrate the odd cinema and order the compulsory registration of material stocks to avoid hoarding and speculation, but their very existence nonetheless provoked a hostile reaction (see Taylor, 1979, 45–46).

In May 1918 Narkompros assumed central control of the Film Section of the Moscow City Soviet, which had itself absorbed the wartime Skobelev Committee, and thus the control to be exercised by Krupskaja's Extra-Mural Section began to take shape. The government's overall control was strengthened by a number of indirect measures, the most important of which was the Sovnarkom decree of 22 April 1918 which made foreign trade in all spheres a state monopoly. This particular measure provoked another strongly worded outburst from *Mir Ėkrana*:

Our entire film industry, now standing so firmly on its feet, will inevitably collapse ... as the new decree makes it quite impossible to import from abroad the materials needed for a film studio ... The "nationalisation" of foreign trade will lead to the paralysis of the film trade, turning Russia into an isolated state and the film industry into a corpse (MĖ, 12.5.18).

But it would be wrong to assume that the nationalisation of foreign trade was solely a political manoeuvre. Although ideological consider-

239

ations and consequences certainly played their part, the prime motivation for such controls was sheer economic necessity.

Despite their precautions the Soviet authorities became the victims of crooked dealings. The most spectacular involved the Italian-born Jacques Cibrario who in July 1918 was given 220 000 gold roubles and commissioned by Preobraženskij, then head of the Moscow Cinema Committee, to purchase film equipment in the United States for export to Soviet Russia. Once in America, however, Cibrario used the money for his own purposes and the Soviet authorities never saw either their roubles or their equipment. In addition Bruce Lockhart is alleged to have attempted to smuggle out the master copies of the Tsar's family films, the so-called *Carskaja xronika*, to Great Britain. (See particularly: Boltjanskij, 1959, 81–2; Preobraženskij, 89 and note 1.)

Russia's dependence on foreign products also made her peculiarly vulnerable to disruptions in international trading patterns and some of the results of this dependence may be seen in the cinema. There had been a severe shortage of film stock and other basic materials as early as 1916 when the effects of war and the decisions by the British and Swedish governments to classify film stock as a non-exportable strategic material had drastically reduced the supply that could be imported into Russia (Ginzburg, 156). The confusion that reigned in the period of Revolution and Civil War made the situation more critical; a number of entrepreneurs, optimistically regarding the Bolsheviks as merely a passing irritation, buried their supply of films to prevent them from falling into the hands of government sympathisers (Preobraženskij, 88 & Forest'e, 98). Others, who realised that the Bolsheviks had come to stay, fled (if they had not fled already) to areas still controlled by the Whites, notably the Crimea, and from there they went on to Paris, Berlin or Hollywood. In these White areas producers concentrated on the traditional type of psychological melodrama that Soviet critics were later to denounce as either pre- or counter-revolutionary. In the Red areas private firms continued to exist, but they were largely engaged in fulfilling film contracts for state organisations (SXF: I, 5–26; see also Kate Betz's paper). In a sense this arrangement suited both sides: the government could be sure of a supply of films to order, without having as yet to take the ultimate step of nationalisation, whilst the producers could be sure, or at least less unsure, of both employment and a supply, albeit erratic, of materials.

Nevertheless the threat of complete nationalisation still hung over the industry and O.K.O. appealed both to its members and to the public at large to boycott cinemas that had been taken over by the government or its local organs, and encouraged audiences to prevent government films from being shown (*Kinogazeta*, 1918: 3; Lemberg, 1930, 15–16, Petrovič, 182). The attitude of the entrepreneurs to the authorities had been further soured by the constant and widespread power cuts which, it was felt, affected the cinema unfairly. The film press was full of complaints about these economy measures and there were periods when all the cinemas in Moscow were forced to close at the same time (Lebedev, 1965, 141). Matters came to a head in February when the electricity supply to cinemas in Moscow was cut off completely for a fortnight and only restored when Vserabis, the Union of Art Workers, pointed out that electricity consumption was in fact greater when people stayed at home (Listov, 1969, 14 & Višnevskij, 66–9; cf. *Proėktor*, 1917: 17/18, 1). The cinema, as well as occupying people's minds, also warmed their bodies. In a period of chronic fuel shortages this function could not be ignored, particularly if it proved to be more economical than the alternative. A foreign writer has described a typical visit to a Moscow cinema at this time:

I visited the "Mirror" kino in Tverskoi, another of Moscow's fashionable thoroughfares. As the name implies, the "Mirror" was once a hall of mirrors. When I saw it, it was the remains of mirrors, many of which got bent when the Reds and the antis were slaughtering each other. The decorated ceiling had been newly decorated by shot and shell, and had a special ventilation system introduced by the method of dropping eggs from aeroplanes. The windows were patched with odds and ends of timber, and the seats were in splints and looking unusually frowzy. Most of them were just plain wooden benches. Two dim lights made their appearance during the intervals, which were pretty frequent. An ancient screen, suffering from jaundice, and a worn-out projector, buried in an emergency structure and half hidden by a dirty curtain as though ashamed of itself, completed the fitments.

The film was a genuine antique of pre-war Russian manufacture. It was in rags, and the reel was so broken that the "curtain fell" every few minutes (Carter, 240).

In these circumstances it is perhaps hardly surprising that the summer of 1918 saw a further wave of emigration by film makers to the by now German-occupied southern Ukraine. Six months later Lunačarskij was to blame this movement for the "catastrophic" state of the Soviet cinema (Listov, 1969, 13). The government felt itself forced to take more stringent action to control the situation and it reacted by ordering the registration of all cinema equipment and forbidding its transfer without official permission (*Izvestija V.C.I.K.*, 19.8.18., cf. Aksel'rod, 33). The Moscow Cinema Committee was, however, one step ahead. Having introduced controls of this type in March, and tightened them early in June (Listov, 1969, 32), the local Soviet now further strengthened its hold by a decree introducing film censorship on 18 June 1918 (*Proėktor*, 1918: 1/2, although there is some evidence that censorship of sorts had been introduced in Moscow as early as March 1918 (*Izvestija Moskvy i Moskovskoj oblasti*, 1918: 40 (288)). The results of the censor's deliberations were to be published in *Kinobjulleten'*, but only one issue appeared—in the autumn of 1918. Another decree confirming registration was announced on 17 July 1918 (*Proėktor*, 1918: 1/2). But there was a constant danger that the more the Bolsheviks tightened their control over existing cinema institutions, the more their opponents would be inclined to flee, taking their much-needed equipment and personnel with them.

However, the acquisition of the Skobelev Committee's film studios by the Moscow and Petrograd Cinema Committees had finally enabled , the Soviet authorities to begin direct production of *agitki*, short agitational films which dealt with a particular topic in a strongly visual manner and with great simplicity. The production of *agitki* was hampered only by a chronic shortage of film stock. In September 1918 Leščenko, head of the Petrograd Cinema Committee, announced an agreement with the German Kodak firm for the immediate supply of film stock. This agreement would have alleviated the shortage but it was overruled by the government because it involved too many risks on the Soviet side, and because the authorities did not wish to be caught out again (Aksel'rod, 32–3). Some film stock was however being imported through Latvia and sold illegally on the black market to private firms, but it was not enough to meet the demand. In November 1918 the Cinema Committee signed an agreement with N. A. Minervin for the re-emulsification of already exposed film stock (Aksel'rod, 34). This method involved the replacement of the exposed layer of emulsion on the film with a new layer so that the stock could be used more than once, thus reducing the need for further imports. But this agreement too had little practical effect because Minervin was able to produce only small quantities of re-emulsified stock that were of both poor quality and low sensitivity. This was in itself a major achievement for a man who had to work, eat and sleep in a single room and whose lack of elementary technical equipment was such that the film itself had to be hung to dry on the branches of the trees in the dusty courtyard! (Kulešov & Xoxlova, 65). Despite their limited success, Minervin's experiments are an instructive ex ample of the desperate measures that were being employed.

The first *agitki* were shown both by the agit-trains and in the cities. Narkompros claimed that during this period its Film Section, despite the shortage of materials, produced six feature-length films, twenty-two *agitki* and forty-three newsreels, and that, "All the most important moments in the life of our Republic have been immortalised on film, even if only on a small scale" (NKP, 87). It is hardly surprising to learn that these films were very popular with children. Between July and December 1918, 112 035 children attended special film shows in Moscow alone (NP, 1919: 30), while reports from various agit-trains show a similar success in the villages. The *Lenin* train, for example, attracted an audience of 22 800 children in the period January–March 1919 (Listov, 1969, 6).

In December 1918 the Narkompros board convened a conference with members of the Moscow and Petrograd Cinema Committees. Delegates included Lunačarskij, Krupskaja, Leščenko, N. F. Preobraženskij (head of the Moscow Committee), Vsevolod Mejerxol'd, D. P. Šterenberg and Vladimir Tatlin (Listov, 1969, 14–15). The conference recommended the establishment of a centralised organisation under Narkompros that would control the local Cinema Committees, and suggested the opening of negotiations with Vesenxa, the Supreme Council of the National Economy) for the transfer of all cinema affairs to Narkompros (NP, 1918: 23/25). The resolution passed by this conference was considered by the Presidium of Vesenxa in January 1919. In March 1919 the 8th Party Congress adopted a resolution entitled "On Political Propaganda and Cultural-Educational Work in the Countryside" (O političeskoj propagande i kul'turno-prosvetitel'noj rabote v derevne), which urged that the cinema and

243

other forms of communication "must be used for communist propaganda" (R.K.P.(b)., 1959, 433).

By this time it had become apparent that the process of gradual nationalisation had reached its limits. Unless the government took a decisive step, either there would be little left to nationalise or the central authorities would be presented with a *fait accompli* by the actions of the local soviets, and either situation would be a recipe for continuing confusion. To forestall further wastage of meagre resources Lenin signed a decree nationalising all cinema enterprises on 27 August 1919 (*Izvestija V.C.I.K.*, 2.9.19). The All-Russian Cinema Committee was entrusted with overseeing the whole process of nationalisation.

Since the beginning of 1918, and particularly as the authority of the Bolshevik government had been extended beyond the confines of the large cities, the Moscow Cinema Committee had tried to extend its influence too. Hence, by August 1919, the Committee's activities were no longer confined to Moscow, and so it was re-named the All-Russian Cinema Committee. On 18 September a decree was published over the signature of Lunačarskij that transformed this Committee yet again into the All-Russian Photographic and Cinematographic Section of Narkompros (Vserossijskij fotokinematografičeskij otdel Narkomprosa), or V.F.K.O. for short. V.F.K.O. was to be headed by Leščenko, who also signed the document (*Izvestija V.C.I.K.*, 18.9.19) and had previously been chairman of the Petrograd Cinema Committee. Some sources maintain that the actual act of nationalisation was merely a recognition by the government of what had already been effected by the spontaneous activity of the masses (Boltjanskij, 1959, 95). However, Leščenko himself was a proponent of the gradualist approach and the fact that, as late as March 1920, Lenin had to send a telegram to local authorities which, amongst other things, asked for information about their progress in nationalising the cinema, would suggest that this is a misleading assertion (Gak, 1973, 52). Indeed it was only in November 1919 that the Moscow Cinema Committee was itself fully re-formed as an integral part of Narkompros, some of its lesser functions being assumed by the new Photographic and Cinematographic Section of the Moscow City Soviet (Fotokinosekcija pri Mossovete (Boltjanskij, 1959, 95)). This was the first of a network of such sections to be established by V.F.K.O.; the sections were subordinated to V.F.K.O. but also linked to the local soviet and they were intended to ensure that orders from the central authorities were in fact being carried out. But, even on paper, the administrative centralisation of the cinema was not yet complete. On 29 January 1920 the V.F.K.O. board acted to nationalise the remaining rental offices in Moscow and on 5 November 1920 the process was concluded with a decision to pay cinema workers from state funds (Boltjanskij, 1959, 95). Even this was in any case only the beginning of a centralised film industry for there was little equipment left for production, the distribution network had broken down, the cinemas were in a bad state of repair and, even worse from the point of view of communications, the majority of cinemas had closed because of the shortage of films, fuel and electricity.

The shortage of film stock meant that virtually no new feature-length films were being produced. Film production in the years 1918–20 was concentrated almost entirely on the more urgently required documentary and newsreel films and on the *agitki* (Lemberg, 1959, 126). Lenin, according to Lunačarskij, recognised the necessity for such concentration when he stated that "the production of new films, imbued with communist ideas and reflecting soviet reality, must begin with the newsreel" (Boltjanskij, 1925, 17–18). The nationalisation decree had, it is true, uncovered a new supply of films that had been hoarded by entrepreneurs in the anticipation of a Bolshevik defeat in the Civil War and a subsequent return to full-scale private enterprise. However, the majority of these films were of pre-revolutionary Russian origin, and the remainder had been imported: they consisted of so-called "psychological" or "salon" melodramas of the type that Hollywood thrived, and the Bolsheviks frowned, on. Films like this were considered ideologically unsuitable for a Soviet audience, but the shortage of new films was acute and the supply of acceptable old films worn and dwindling, so it was decided to show these films to the ccompaniment of a lecture on their weaknesses by a Party worker (Aksel'rod, 36). From the propaganda point of view this was a disaster, because the speaker was often ignored or even shouted down. The practice was therefore soon discontinued.

The Soviet cinema, as a result of the emigration already mentioned, was also quite clearly going to suffer from a shortage of skilled and trained personnel in all spheres for some time to come. There were, however, plenty of unskilled volunteers, usually young and infused with revolutionary ardour (see, for instance, Kosincev, 6); with the emigration of the entrepreneurs these new recruits could not be trained in the conventional manner through an apprenticeship in a well established studio. The only solution was to establish a film school to train these and other necessary technicians, actors, directors, etc. At the suggestion of the director Vladimir Gardin a State Film School (Gosudarstvennaja kinoškola) was established by V.F.K.O. in Moscow, with Gardin himself as its first director (Gardin; I, 167–70; Višnevskij, 71; SK, 1969: 41 (352); Kulešov & Xoxlova, 58–62). Lunačarskij remarked:

> We need cadres of workers who are free from the habits and strivings of the old bourgeois entrepreneurial hacks and are able to elevate the cinema to the heights of the artistic and socio-political tasks facing the proletariat, especially in the current period of intensified struggle (*Iskusstvo kino*, 1969: 10, 41).

Initially the Film School produced two *agitki*: *In the Days of Battle* (V dni bor'by), using film from the Polish front, and *Hammer and Sickle* (Serp i molot), a morality tale of life in the countryside. Both were directed by Gardin, with Tissè as cameraman and Pudovkin playing the leading role (IK, 1969: 10, 41). Thus, like the agit-trains, the Film School in some ways represented the Soviet cinema in embryo. When the supply of film stock had been exhausted Lev Kulešov and his Workshop of *naturščiki* (actors with no conventional training) occupied themselves by trying out their theories of film and movement in miming so-called "films without film" (fil'my bez plënki) (Kulešov & Xoxlova, 67–79). In 1920 Kulešov spent some time on an agit-train and produced his first film *At the Red Front* (Na krasnom fronte), which Lenin apparently saw and liked (Kulešov & Xoxlova, 63–6). But the full effects of the Film School did not become apparent until the Civil War had been won and a more permanent organisational structure for the Soviet cinema had been established. Thus, accumulated difficulties had largely crippled the existing conventional network of cinema production and distribution so that the Bolsheviks had to create their own structures and methods of control and communication.

The Soviet Union covers, in the words of Vertov's later film title, "A Sixth Part of the World". Such a vast country with a widely scattered population and a rapidly changing front required above all a mobile, flexible and reliable medium of communication between the centre and the regions, at least until the regions had become sufficiently stable to permit the establishment of more permanent and conventional organisations. The structure of the Soviet agitprop machine eventually developed to combine a network of stationary *agitpunkty* (from the Russian *agitacionnyj punkt*, an agitational point or centre), placed at strategic points like railway junctions or large settlements, with an increasing number of travelling agitational trains (*agitpoezda*). The trains were to serve as the standard-bearers of revolutionary agitation, moving wherever they were most urgently required, while the *agitpunkty* were to concentrate on propaganda saturation of the population in a given place. 140 *agitpunkty* were established in 1919, following a decree of 13 May (Astaf'eva, 16, 18) and a further 220 were set up in 1920. The first *agitpunkty* were located in railway termini or junctions, but this arrangement severely disrupted the normal workings of the railway network and so a standard design for purpose-built *politdoma* (from *političeskij dom*, literally "political house"), stationary centres for in-depth propaganda saturation of the local population, was evolved. It is not known how many of these were eventually constructed but it is worth noting that the design included a library, schoolroom, canteen, cinema and stage, with, for larger centres of population, the addition of Komsomol and Party rooms, a chess room and a music room. In many ways the *politdom* resembled the concept of a modern community centre with its amenities, although its purpose in the context of the Civil War was of course primarily and overtly political.

The function of the mobile agitational centres, usually trains, was however altogether more dramatic and, in the short term, more important. The concept of the agit-train was a logical historical development, mixing the artistic tradition of the strolling player (*gastrolër*) and his later counterpart in the early history of the cinema with some of the most modern technological capabilities. In the cinema the historical continuity of the concept was particularly noticeable, if only because the cinema had a more compressed and recent history. Before the construction of permanent cinema buildings, and the development of the regular distribution system associated with them, exhibitors had toured the country with a single projector and a selection of films, stopping in each town until their audience potential was exhausted, and then moving on (Mesguich; Xanžonkov, *passim*). The idea developed and there were several ambitious attempts to establish

247

mobile cinemas on barges in the early 1900s (e.g. Xanžonkov, 12), but none was successful and, with the construction of conventional permanent cinema buildings, the practice died out. During the First World War mobile projection equipment was again used, this time for morale-boosting and agitational activities at the front. After the October Revolution the Bolsheviks set aside a compartment in their troop trains that was reserved for the agitprop section of the Red Army. This section distributed leaflets, newspapers and posters. It was in fact in the Military Department of the Party publishing house that the concept of the agit-train was born (Burov, 5; Bibikova, 166). It represented both an amalgamation of previous techniques and a refinement of them, and it constituted the first attempt at establishing a direct link between the revolutionary centres of Moscow and Petrograd and the peripheral areas of the emergent Soviet state, the beleaguered fronts of the Civil War. The main fleet of agit-trains and the steamer "Red Star", as we shall see, were controlled from the centre but smaller operations, such as the seven agit-lorries used in Petrograd in 1919, were run by the local soviets (Marchand & Weinstein, 40). In difficult terrain agit-sledges were also used (*Iz istorii Graždanskoj vojny:* III, 686).

The first agit-train represented a direct experimental extension of the idea of the agitprop compartment to that of the full-length train. The V.I. Lenin Mobile Military Front Train (Voennopodvižnyj frontovoj poezd imeni V.I. Lenina), the first of several to carry the leader's name, was hurriedly prepared and painted with pictorial slogans in the Kursk railway works in Moscow, and it left the capital for a trial run to Kazan on 13 August 1918. The train varied in its composition from seven to nine coaches, equipped with a bookshop, library, office and living quarters. The "Lenin Front Train" and its crew spent two weeks distributing pamphlets and newspapers to units of the Red Army stationed along the track, and they returned to Moscow in early September (Burov, 6; cf. *Iskusstvo kino*, 1968: 10, 114–17). This experiment had been confined to agitational work among the military. It was felt to have been so successful that Trockij ordered five similar trains from the Moscow regional railway, but production difficulties delayed the delivery of the last of these until 1920 (Burov, 6).

On 31 January 1919 the Presidium of the Party's All-Russian Central Executive Committee (Vserossijskij central'nyj ispolnitel'nyj komitet, or V.C.I.K. for short) created a Special Commission to run its planned fleet of agit-trains and steamers and to study the problems of communication between the centre and the provinces that the project had exposed. The Commission officially had four members: Sosnovskij, Minin, Eremeev and Burov, but Burov later claimed that he and Eremeev had done all the work (Burov, 6). It is significant that the Commission was directly subordinated to V.C.I.K.: this was a further sign not only of the importance attached to the whole project but also an indication that the old machinery of government was being by-passed because of its inefficiency and unreliability. The Narkompros organisation, consisting of a thinly spread network of schools, "people's houses" (*narodnye doma*), libraries and bookshops, was inert and unwieldy. Agit-trains, on the other hand, were a fast, flexible, more direct and dynamic method of communication with the masses. They had other advantages as well: a train carried with it a skilled team of agitprop officials, some of whom specialised in particular fields appropriate to the areas they were visiting. A Narkompros official had, as was inevitable for an individual in such circumstances, to spread himself as broadly as possible, covering the whole range of subjects on which the central authorities might deem it fit to disseminate information. Similarly, his "people's house" lacked the dynamism and the psychological advantages of a train, because it was always there, even when inactive. Trains, because they came and went and were based on Moscow, were regarded by the population at large as "direct representatives of supreme power" (Karpinskij, 26), and became known as "V.C.I.K. on rails" (Burov, 7; cf. Voevodin, 73–4). It was because of the status bestowed upon them by their direct relationship with the centre that the agit-trains as a whole had to strike a balance between the twin tasks of agitation and in-depth propaganda. Had their activities been too closely concentrated on the superficial, "they would come, talk, and everything would remain unchanged" (Karpinskij, 26).

The second generation of agit-trains was more ambitious than the "Lenin Front Train": they were composed of fifteen to eighteen coaches and each train had a radio transmitter-receiver for communication with the home base in Moscow. From fifteen to eighteen political workers were employed and in addition, there were 80–85 technical assistants. The trains were divided into different working departments. The principal ones were the Political Department, which controlled instruction and agitational lectures, and the Information Department, which helped the Political Department to prepare the necessary propaganda material. There was also a complaints office which received petitions from the population and passed back information on the sources of political discontent both to its own Political Department and to the authorities in Moscow. Finally there was the ROSTA Department which was responsible for organising the publication of newspapers, leaflets, posters and appeals and for running the train's radio transmitter. In addition most trains had a film department, a book store, a shop and a space of exhibitions on various themes. The entire organisation of the train was supervised by a political commissar who was appointed directly by the V.C.I.K. Presidium: Kalinin was to hold this position on the "October Revolution" (Oktjabr'skaja revoljucija) train, and Molotov on the "Red Star" (Krasnaja zvezda) steamer. Such was the importance attached to the experiment.

The authorities paid considerable attention to the external appearance of the trains: when a peasant encountered the "direct representatives of supreme power" for the first time his first impressions could be all-important in determining his future attitude for or against the new régime. The early agitprop coaches had originally been covered with posters but these had not lasted long (Bibikova, 166) and the agit-trains themselves were carefully decorated with oil paints (Speranskaja, plates 113–30). In the first flush of revolutionary enthusiasm Symbolist and Futurist motifs were used in the paintings, but these were apparently either misunderstood by the peasantry, or quite simply mystified them. Dziga Vertov, who worked on the "Red Cossack" (Krasnyj kazak) train, collecting material for his newsreels, later recalled:

> Not only the painted-up Cossacks depicted on the sides of the trains were called "actors" by the peasants—so too were the horses, merely because they were wrongly shod in the drawing. The remoter the place, the less the peasants understood the overtly agitational meaning of the drawings. They examined every drawing carefully and every figure separately. Whenever I asked them if they like the drawings they would answer, "We don't know. We're ignorant, illiterate folk". But this does not prevent the peasants from laughing unequivocally at the horse-"actors" when they talk among themselves (Drobašenko, 89–90).

Vertov's recollection is confirmed by a contemporary newspaper report: "Around the carriage that was decorated with Cubist posters there was laughter and joking. The new movement in painting amused the crowd of elderly peasants" (quoted in Bibikova, 169). Kalinin, who was put in charge of the "October Revolution" train, told V.C.I.K. in October 1919 that he

> reallsed that such a train would be most effective in influencing the masses. Everywhere we stopped it produced a tremendous impression and attracted an enormous number of people. People walked round it, picked out a picture, argued amongst themselves (whether they were literate or not) as to what a particular drawing depicted. We heard constant arguments round this or that carriage. In a word these trains immediately brought the local population closer to us (Karpinskij, 61).

The "October Revolution" was in fact decorated by an artistic collective headed by the well-known poster artist Dmitrij Moor, who painted one of the carriages himself (Bibikova, 172). Writing in 1920 Burov claimed of the agit-trains in general that:

> The early paintings were extraordinarily unsuccessful. The carriage sides were covered with Futurist and Symbolist paintings depicting enormous monsters denouncing the Revolution. The majority of these illustrations were unintelligible and often bewildered the local population. The organisers had no experience in this field and the artists were given almost complete freedom of action.
>
> Now the sides of the trains (and steamers) are decorated with pictures having a *realistic content*, and Futurism has been completely routed (Burov, 9).

Realistic tendencies began to dominate the painting of the agit-trains from the autumn of 1919, for instance in the work carried out by a group of artists headed by V. M. Vinogradov. Their first job in October 1919, was to paint the "Ja. Sverdlov" train, that was to be based in Ekaterinburg but about which we know little else. Their task was to decorate twelve carriages in four weeks, and for this they produced 24 sketches (Bibikova, 174.) Having achieved this feat Vinogradov and his team went on to paint the "Red East" (Krasnyj vostok), which travelled to Turkestan in January 1920, with predominantly oriental motifs (Bibikova, 175; Burov, 14; cf. Speranskaja, plates 120–1). Most of the decorative work was however executed by another artistic collective led by I. Nivinskij, head of the artistic sub-section of the V.C.I.K. Commission. They painted the "Red Cossack" (Krasnyj Kazak) when it was formed from the carriages of the "Lenin No. 1" (see below), choosing the motifs in consultation with the Cossack Section of V.C.I.K. (Bibikova, 176–7). (It was of course, these "realistic" motifs that Vertov's peasants found so amusing.) In August 1920 the train was further transformed into the "Ukrainian Lenin Agit-Train" (Ukrainskij agitpoezd im. Lenina) and a commis-sion of local party representatives and the artistic collective examined the carriages with a view to "ukrainicising" the decorations. In partic-ular they gave specific instructions for the necessary alterations to an illustration of "A Meeting of Cossack-Women":

> The clothes must be altered to correspond with reality. (The collar should be concealed, with a narrow strip of embroidery on the collar and the bodice and on the sleeves starting below the shoulder. There should be a necklace. The hair should be plaited. The girls should wear combs in their hair. The married women should have their heads covered with scarves. The skirts should be short. An embroidered dress should peep out from beneath the skirt. The feet may be bare.) (Bibikova, 182).

Such meticulous attention to minutiae confirms the importance at-tached at the highest level to the decoration of the trains. Bibikova has found in the archives the record of a meeting of the V.C.I.K. Depart-ment of Agit-Trains and Steamers (until January 1920 the Commis-sion) thought to have been held in April 1920, at which Burov declared that "designs of a Futurist character would not be accepted" and that "if the artists do not appreciate the concept of editorial control [their ideas] will be rejected" (Bibikova, 183). Art had proved to be too important politically to be left to the artists themselves.

The cinema played an important part in the success of the agit-trains. Most peasants had never seen a moving picture before (cf. Lenin's remark, quoted in Gak, 1973, 42, that efforts should be concentrated "in the villages and in the East where (cinemas) are novelties and where, for this reason, our propaganda will be especially successful"). The Bolsheviks were able to capitalise on the novelty value of the film in two principal ways: first of all, they could associate themselves in the public mind with technology, modernisation and progress and, second, they could utilise the medium to bring pictures of the new Soviet leaders to the population at large. To the peasantry Lenin might appear as the new tsar, as an almost God-like figure and indeed, following his attempted assassination in 1918, he was shown in a widely distributed newsreel walking in the Kremlin courtyard with Bonč-Bruevič. This sequence was filmed and used quite deliberately to scotch rumours that Lenin had been killed (Gak, 1972: II, 28 et seq.).

While the supply of film stock permitted, the duty of the film workers on the trains was twofold: first, the demonstration in the provinces of agit-films produced at the centre (the Lenin newsreel sequence mentioned above would be included in this category) and, second, the supply of newsreel and documentary material from the provinces back to the centre where it was edited by Lev Kulešov, Dziga Vertov, Esfir' Šub and others who were later to play a leading rôle in the development of the Soviet cinema. Their experience at this time did much to shape the theories of the cinema that they developed separately later. Kulešov used some of the footage he had shot himself in the film *At the Red Front* that I have already mentioned, and much of the material brought back by the trains was incorporated into Dziga Vertov's series of newsreels, *Kinonedelja* (Cine-Week) and later into his documentary feature films *The Anniversary of the Revolution* (Godovščina revoljucii) and *The History of the Civil War* (Istorija graždanskoj vojny) (Drobašenko, 317). Eduard Tissė, who later became the cameraman on some of Ėjzenštejn's major films, was also involved in this work. The needs of the moment gave rise to two new genres of film: the agitational film-poster (*agitacionnyj kinoplakat*) and the *agitka* proper. The former was quite simply what it claimed to be, a filmed version of a poster theme and in essence the cinema's equivalent of Majakovskij's poster poems. The *agitka* proper was also short and explicit, conveying a simple message on a single subject with directness and economy. Of the 92 films produced by Soviet film organisations in the three years 1918–20, 63 were in this category and most of them were less than 600 metres in length, or less than thirty minutes when projected (based on information in SXF: I, 5–26). The *agitka* genre had a decisive influence on the stylistic development of the Soviet film: the essence of economy and dynamism in the visual presentation of material was developed in the principles of editing or, as Ėjzenštejn was later to call it, "dynamic montage".

The *agitka* had to convey its message entirely by simple, visual means. It had to attract and hold the attention of its audience and leave them with an impression of dynamism and strength. These principles were embodied in different ways in the theoretical teachings of Lev Kulešov and his Workshop at the Film School, in the documentaries and manifestos of Dziga Vertov's Cine-Eye (Kinoglaz) group, in the films of Šub, Ėjzenštejn, Pudovkin and others.

Sometimes the *agitka* was devoted to a topic of general interest, and sometimes to a more specialised problem. One of the most celebrated was *Hydro-Peat* (Gidrotorf), personally approved by Lenin, which explained the advantages of lifting peat by the use of hydraulic power (Gak, 1968, 12; Boltjanskij, 1925, 27–32; Drabkina, 25–7). Made in 1920, *Hydro-Peat* reflects a move away from the rather simplistic visual agitation of the first films towards an adaptation of the medium to encourage economic improvements. Of course this move also underlines the transformation of the Bolsheviks' position from that of a state of siege to the point where they could assume that they would maintain their control over the levers of power and therefore begin to concentrate on the details of government. In November 1920 Lenin said that "Propaganda of the old type describes and illustrates what communism is. This kind of propaganda is now useless, for we have to show in practice how socialism is to be built. All our propaganda must be based on the political experience of economic development. That is our principal task" (CW: XXXI, 371). But, although the number of agitational and propaganda films that were intended to improve the efficiency of the Soviet economy was increasing, the majority of these films were still overtly political, depicting the trials of the Whites, the perils of counter-revolution, intervention and restoration, and the horrors inflicted on the toiling masses during the tsarist era. It was this latter type of film that was shown to the peasantry in large numbers. For agitational purposes it was often sufficiently effective, for an audience that had never previously watched a film, to show a newsreel of the Bolshevik leaders, thus establishing a new kind of quasi-direct rapport between the rulers and the ruled: hence the Lenin newsreel already mentioned. The trains themselves were also the subject of films. In 1919 the cameraman A. Lemberg made a film of the activities of the agit-steamer "Red Star" (Krasnaja zvezda) and in 1922 he followed this with a film entitled "*The First 'Comrade Lenin' Agro-Train*" (Pervyj

254

agropoezd imeni tovarišča Lenina) (Lemberg, 1959, 127–9). Dziga
Vertov wrote a script for a documentary film to be shot from the
agit-train "Soviet Caucasus" (Sovetskij Kavkaz), but it was never
made (Listov, 1970, 31). The shortage of materials and the resulting
emphasis on newsreels and other films of more immediate political
value meant that other, more ambitious, plans had to be shelved as well,
so that a series of films on the history of Russian and world culture,
planned by a group that included Gor'kij, Blok, Brjusov, Aleksej
Tolstoj and A. Serafimovič was never started (Lebedev, 1968, 85).

The *agitki* were shown above all in areas where the need for active,
and visual, agitprop work was perceived to be most urgent. The
second train to bear Lenin's name, confusingly called the "Literary-
Instructional Lenin Train No. 1" (Literaturno-instruktorskij poezd
im. Lenina No. 1), was sent through the parts of the North-Western
province recently evacuated by the Germans on a six-week journey
that ended in mid-March 1919. The train, headed by Sosnovskij, a
member of the V.C.I.K. Commission established the previous January,
visited Pskov, Riga, Vitebsk, Vil'na, Minsk, Xar'kov and Kursk, thus
eventually covering the whole of the former front against the Germans,
and entering what were still in some cases disputed territories. After
a three-month wait in Moscow, which produced accusations of time-
wasting, the "Lenin" returned to the Ukrainian front where the Red
Army was now fighting Denikin's troops. From October till the end
of 1919 the train travelled through Siberia, visiting Samara, Omsk
and Ekaterinburg. The aim was to improve the flow of grain to
the cities and alleviate the worsening food situation there caused by
Denikin's advance to Tula. In this respect agitation was intended to
have an immediate and tangible result. When the "Lenin No. 1"
returned in January 1920 it was repainted and re-named the "Red
Cossack" (Krasnyj Kazak).

The "Red East", equipped with a special section to deal with
Moslem affairs, spent the first half of 1920 in Turkestan. The "Soviet
Caucasus" spent the three summer months in the malaria-infested
regions of the Caucasus, while the "Red Cossack" toured the Don
area shortly after Denikin's defeat. However the two most important
components of the operation were the train "October Revolution"
and the steamer "Red Star", both of which were in differing ways
atypical of the operation as a whole but illustrate the basic aim of
taking a communications medium out into the field.

255

On 23 October 1919 Kalinin, who was acting as political commissar on the "October Revolution", delivered a report on the train's activities to the Presidium of V.C.I.K. (see above). The train's function was that of standard-bearer to the agit-train fleet, concentrating on political demonstration and only superficial instruction. Even more than the average agit-train, it symbolised the presence of the central Bolshevik government in the remoter areas of the R.S.F.S.R. Between April 1919 and December 1920 the train made twelve forays into the countryside, all headed by Kalinin and each averaging three weeks in length, with a ten to twelve hour stop in each settlement. The other trains took up to three months for an average exercise and usually stopped for up to two days at a time in any one place. During its travels the "October Revolution" ranged as far as Minsk and Irkutsk, Petrograd and the Don Basin. In the course of 1919 the "October Revolution", "Lenin" and "Red Star" between them organised a total of 753 public meetings attended by 1 300 000 people (Maksakova, 11). By the end of 1920 the "October Revolution" alone had provided over 430 film shows which drew an audience in excess of 620 000 people (Maksakova, 27–33). Apart from the films mentioned above, the trains showed films specifically aimed at an audience of children in the daytime, such as *The Fisherman and the Little Fish* (O rybake i rybke), *The Festival of Communist Youth* (Prazdnik Kommunističeskoj molodëži), *For the Red Flag* (Za krasnoe znamja), and at an audience of adults in the evenings, for example, *Saviours of the Homeland* (Spasiteli rodiny), *For a New World* (Za novyj mir), *The Victory of May* (Pobeda maja), *Eyes Were Opened* (Glaza otkrylis'), and the anti-religious *The Exposure of the Relics of Tixon of Zadonsk* (Otkrytie moščej Tixona Zadonskogo). These films were frequently accompanied by lectures from agitators, sent by the Party's Central Committee, or instructors sent by the various People's Commissariats (Sergeev, 99).

The presence of cinema facilities on board fulfilled an additional function as a magnet (Sergeev, 122); people who came initially and solely to watch films frequently became involved in other activities as well, ranging from purely political agitational work to the campaigns for the eradication of illiteracy and for increased economic efficiency. There is however no evidence that at this stage film was used at anything more than a superficial level in the literacy campaigns; the cinema brought the message that illiteracy was undesirable but the medium itself was not widely employed as a teaching aid, probably because the shortage of appropriate facilities precluded the economies of scale that would have made the idea financially viable. In addition the agit-train workers were preoccupied with the more immediate problems facing the leadership: at one time, for example, the interval between film showings was used for appeals to the peasantry to send grain to the towns to alleviate the bread shortage there (Maksakova, 62).

Kalinin had defined his task on the "October Revolution" as "to listen to the voice of life itself" and he maintained that "the very contact with the representatives of the central workers' and peasants' power should raise popular morale and dispel the doubts sown by Kolchak's *agents-provocateurs*" (*Izvestija*, 1.5.19). The speeches he made during the train's journeys amply confirm his attempts to realise these intentions. The threat posed by the train was tacitly admitted by the White forces when one of their aircraft strafed and bombed it in June 1919 (Sergeev, 122–3). *Izvestija* reported that, "The train's journey is marked by the excitement and enthusiasm of the masses. After talking to Comrade Kalinin old men in the countryside declare, 'we shall drive our sons into the Red Army'" (*Izvestija*, 22.6.19). Apart from recruitment the agit-train had other immediate practical results: in July 1919 Kalinin was able to organise the gathering of the harvest in Atkarsk and avert a bread shortage (Sergeev, 133), and in September he was able to inform the leadership in Moscow of shortages of vital materials in Syzran, and of essential instructors in Samara (Sergeev, 144). Such contact was an important short-term task of the agit-trains in a period when the conventional administrative structures had disintegrated.

The activities of the steamer "Red Star" are also well documented. On 31 May 1919 Molotov was appointed political commissar, and one month later Lenin gave him the following letter of introduction:

> The bearer of this, Comrade *Molotov*, is personally known to me as an old party worker and has been appointed plenipotentiary representative of V.C.I.K. on the literary-instructional steamer "Red Star". I ask all authorities and organisations to afford him *every* assistance and, in order not to delay military information, to provide him with a direct (telephone) link (*Istoričeskij žurnal*, 1940: 3, 32).

Nadežda Krupskaja was appointed as the Narkompros representative on the steamer and she was therefore in charge of the film section

(Gofman, 64). She later recalled that "Il'ič himself wanted to go but could not leave his work for a minute" (Krupskaja, 1957, 423–4). The account that Krupskaja wrote of her journey shortly afterwards (Krupskaja, 1960) conveys a vivid impression of the way in which the fabric of a modern society, especially when it is not rooted in that society's historical and national traditions, can easily be fragmented by the pressures of revolution and civil war. The reception that awaited the crew of the "Red Star" in Nižnij Novgorod, where it was to start its voyage down the Volga, was symptomatic of the generally chaotic conditions prevailing at that time and of the difficulties facing the government in its attempts to communicate with the provinces:

> The Red Army soldiers would not let us through even with passes from V.C.I.K.: they were not even aware of its existence (Krupskaja, 1960, 115).

And this was eighteen months after the Revolution! Local Party workers complained to the crew of "apathy in the ranks of Party workers" and "alienation from the masses". In Čistopol' Krupskaja considered that the efforts of the Bolsheviks were being carefully undermined in the schools:

> Scripture is not taught but the icons have been left in the schools, so as "not to disturb the population"; there is one teacher for extra-mural education and he considers that politics should not be mixed with cultural work. Nowhere have I seen such systematic sabotage of the measures of the Soviet authorities in the field of popular education (Krupskaja, 1960, 122).

Shortly afterwards Krupskaja wrote to Z. P. Kržižanovskaja, her deputy at Narkompros, asking for further supplies of "wholesome" films, pamphlets of Lenin's speeches and writings and other similar forms of literature for distribution to the local population (Krupskaja, 1963: XI, 191). Both Krupskaja's letters of this period and the diary that she kept are valuable sources of information on the practical aspects of the steamer's journey and the problems encountered. They also confirm that Lenin himself was aware of the difficulties confronting Bolshevik agitators and propagandists in the field.

The "Red Star" was equipped with a printing press, bookshop and radio transmitter-receiver; this enabled the crew to maintain direct contact with Moscow, to produce a newspaper and to distribute it in towns and villages that had had no communication with the outside world for many months (Gofman, 65–6). There was again a space for a travelling exhibition, the theme of which was changed according to the needs of the area visited: subjects ranged from the electrification of the countryside to advice for mothers on hygiene and the care of children. In addition the steamer towed a barge which served in effect as a floating cinema accommodating about a thousand people, and the presence of this was vital to the success of the whole enterprise. In sailing along the Volga and Kama rivers the crew were attempting to propagandise a population that was not only overwhelmingly illiterate but also multinational and, perhaps more importantly, multilingual. The distribution of printed matter soon proved pointless and, as the agit-workers sent from Moscow were Russian-speaking, agitation through the spoken word was also fraught with difficulties. In these circumstances the cinema performed its unique function as a universal medium of communication: assuming that the films survived the process of projection, the same *agitka* could be shown to Čuvaš, Baškir, Tatar and other audiences, all of whom would stand an even chance of grasping the point that was being made to them. At the time Nariman Narimanov, the Azerbajdžani writer and a leading Party activist, remarked:

In the East, where people have grown accustomed to thinking primarily in images, the cinema is the sole possible means of propaganda because it does not require the preliminary, gradual preparation of the masses. The Eastern peasant accepts everything he sees on the screen as the most fundamental and genuine reality (Kubelikov, 9).

In addition, the cinema, being a completely new experience for the peasant, performed in itself a powerful propaganda function for the new régime. In the course of its three-month voyage the "Red Star" organised 196 film shows attended by a total of 225 000 people (Maksakova, 11). Like the agit-trains, the steamer played an essential rôle in establishing the film as an effective medium for agitation and propaganda and in the longer term in spreading the cinema as a leading form of entertainment for the masses outside the cities, and the eminence of many of the people involved bore witness to the significance attached to the project by the central authorities.

Of course the whole scheme met with countless difficulties. Lack of a coherent overall plan and a decision instead to respond pragmatically to immediate conditions meant that the trains remained idle in Moscow when the need for their presence elsewhere was considered less than urgent. This policy was dictated by circumstance: the number of reliable and effective agit-workers was limited in the initial stages before any training scheme had been started, equipment was in very short supply and communications were erratic. Hence the efforts of the V.C.I.K. Commission responsible had to be concentrated on areas where they would achieve maximum political impact, and these were mainly those regions that until recently had been occupied by the various counter-revolutionary forces and in which there lingered a residue of the anti-Bolshevik agitation and propaganda to which the population had apparently been subjected. Despite their limitations, however, the agit-trains were deemed sufficiently successful to be continued on a larger scale and on a more permanent basis throughout the 1920s. Although there is evidence to suggest that they continued to be used into the 1930s (cf. Medvedkin, 32–56) (and that they are still used, albeit on a limited scale, in Siberia in the 1970s) the significance of their rôle has diminished as the network of conventional cinemas has spread to the remoter areas and as the film has yielded its position as the foremost medium of information and propaganda to the radio, which, despite its lack of any form of visual communication, and of the opportunity for mass experience, has the overwhelming advantages of immediacy and directness. Now, of course, radio itself is yielding pride of place to television.

In 1920 the central controls over the trains were reorganised. In January Lenin issued a series of instructions designed to increase their effectiveness (Krupskaja, 1932, 175–6; Gak, 1973, 22–3). The existing V.C.I.K. Commission was demoted to a Department of Agit-Trains and Steamers (Otdel agitparpoezdov V.C.I.K.) which was concerned only with the more mundane administrative aspects of the project. Its overall policy functions were transferred to a special commission immediately under Sovnarkom which was specifically given the right to turn to Lenin directly if the normal channels of communication through the governmental apparatus proved ineffective. Lenin also urged more detailed changes in the operation of the actual trains. He stressed the importance of increasing the supply of both literature and films on specific matters from anti-religious propaganda to methods of improving agricultural and industrial efficiency. Agit-workers were instructed to examine more scientifically the effectiveness of individual films and to report their findings back to V.F.K.O. so that a systematic programme of effective propaganda films could be produced. Litvinov was personally ordered to survey the foreign film scene with a view to the importation of suitable material. Finally, the range of the trains was to be made more flexible by providing them with fleets of bicycles, motorcycles and other locally available means of transport to improve the distribution of leaflets and other printed propaganda. Such methods had in fact already been given a trial run on the "October Revolution" (*Izvestija*, 1.5.19).

In March 1920 the Ninth Party Congress recommended that increased resources should be made available for propaganda work among the peasantry (R.K.P.(b), 1960, 405), and in April the new department in charge of the agit-trains defined the areas within which the programme could most usefully be developed (Maksakova, 13). The aim was to increase and improve contact between the centre and the regions, thereby encouraging a more coherent and consistent implementation of policy overall. Once an adequate degree of overall control had been established and an effective governmental structure re-created, the task of everyday agitation and propaganda could safely be entrusted to the local representatives of Soviet power. This did not imply any relaxation of centralised control but was merely a reversion to the conventional hierarchical channels of the governmental process. Gradually the trains and their functions were replaced by an improved and vastly expanded network of *agitpunkty* and the type of workers' and peasants' clubs that survive to this day. The agit-trains had represented a spontaneous, but essentially temporary, response to the emergency that had faced the Bolsheviks after they had assumed power. Their exact rôle in gaining support for the new government is debateable: important perhaps, but probably not pivotal. Their real significance lies elsewhere: the agit-trains represented one of the first attempts to create and manipulate a mass medium (in this case, the cinema) for political ends. In the history of the trains, their organisation and their methods, we can thus see in embryonic form the history of political communication in our century: where public opinion counts, so too does propaganda.

References

I am grateful to the editors of *Soviet Studies* and to the Syndics of the Cambridge University Press for permission to use some of the materials first developed in my article "A medium for the masses: agitation in the Soviet Civil War", Vol. XXII (1971), 562–74, and my book *The politics of the Soviet cinema, 1917–1929* (Cambridge, 1979).

Aksel'rod, L., "Dokumenty po istorii nacionalizacii russkoj kinematografii", *Iz istorii kino*, No. 1 (1958), 25–37

Astaf'eva, M., "Dekret, pročitannyj arxitektorom", *Iskusstvo kino*, March 1969, 16–19

Bibikova, I., "Rospis' agitpoezdov i agitparoxodov", in: Speranskaja, 166–98

Boltjanskij, G. M. (ed.), *Lenin i kino* (Moscow, 1925)

Boltjanskij, G. M., "Velikaja Oktjabr'skaja socialističeskaja revoljucija i roždenie sovetskogo kinoiskusstva", *Iz istorii kino*, No. 2 (1959), 63–116

Burov, Ja., "Vozniknovenie, apparat i rabota agitparpoezdov V.C.U.K.", in: Karpinskij, 5–17

CW: see: Lenin

Carter, H., *The new theatre and cinema of Soviet Russia* (London, 1924)

Drabkina, E., "Arxivažnejšee delo", *Iskusstvo kino*, January 1965, 25–7

Drobašenko, S. (ed.), *Dziga Vertov. Stat'i. Dnevniki. Zamysli* (Moscow, 1966)

Forest'e, L., "Velikij nemoj", *Vospominanija kinooperatora* (Moscow 1945).

Gak, A. M., "Lenin i kino. Poiski novyx dokumentov", *Iz istorii kino*, No. 7 (1968), 7–20

Gak, A. M. (ed.), *Lenin. Sobranie fotografij i kinokadrov* (2 vols., Moscow, 1970–2)

Gak, A. M. (ed.), *Samoe važnoe iz vsex iskusstv. Lenin o kino* (2nd edn, Moscow, 1973)

Gak, A. M., and Glagoleva, N. A. (eds.), *Lunačarskij o kino* (Moscow, 1965)

Gardin, V. R., *Vospominanija* (2 vols., Moscow, 1949–52)

Ginzburg, S. S., *Kinematografija dorevoljucionnoj Rossii* (Moscow, 1963)

Gofman, C., "K istorii pervogo agitparoxoda V.C.I.K. 'Krasnaja zvezda'", *Voprosy istorii*, 1948, No. 9, 63–70

Iskusstvo kino: "Vysšaja kinoškola strany. Beseda s A. N. Groševym", *Iskusstvo kino*, October 1969, 41–4

Iz istorii Graždanskoj vojny v S.S.S.R. Sbornik dokumentov (3 vols., Moscow, 1961)

Karpinskij, V. (ed.), *Agitparpoezda V.C.I.K. Ix istorija, apparat, metody i formy raboty. Sbornik statej* (Moscow, 1920)

Kozincev, G. M., *Glubokij ėkran* (Moscow, 1971)

Krupskaja, N. K., *Politprosvetrabota* (Moscow, 1932)

Krupskaja, N. K., *Vospominanija o Lenine* (Moscow, 1957)

Krupskaja, N. K., "Po gradam i vesjam sovetskoj respubliki", *Novyj mir*, November 1960, 113–30

Krupskaja, N. K., *Pedagogičeskie sočinenija*, Vol. 11 (Moscow, 1963)

Kubelikov, E., *Kinoiskusstvo Azerbajdžana* (Baku, 1960)

Kulešov, L. V. and Xoxlova, A. S., *50 let v kino* (Moscow, 1975)

Lebedev, N. A., "Boevye dvadcatye gody", *Iskusstvo kino*, December 1968, 85–99

Lebedev, N. A., *Očerk istorii kino S.S.S.R.* (Moscow, 1965)

Lemberg, A. G., "Iz vospominanij starogo operatora", *Iz istorii kino*, No. 2 (1959), 117–31

Lemberg, E. G., *Kinopromyšlennost' S.S.S.R. Ėkonomika sovetskoj kinematografii* (Moscow, 1930)

Lenin, V. I., *Collected works* (CW) (45 vols., Moscow, 1960–70)

Listov, V., "U istokov sovetskogo kino", *Iskusstvo kino*, March 1969, 2–15

Listov, V., "Načalo Zametki o stanovlenii socialističeskogo kino na sovetskom Vostoke", *Iskusstvo kino*, August 1970, 28–36

Maksakova, L. V., *Agitpoezd "Oktjabr'skaja revoljucija" (1919–1920)* (Moscow, 1956)

Marchand, R. and Weinstein, P., *L'Art dans la Russie nouvelle: le cinéma* (Paris, 1927)

Medvedkin, A., "294 dnja na kolesax", *Iz istorii kino* No. 10 (1977), 32–56

Mesguich, F., *Tours de manivelle: souvenirs d'un chasseur d'images* (Paris, 1933)

NKP: *Narodnyj komissariat po prosveščeniju. 1917–Oktjabr'–1920. Kratkij otčët* (Moscow, 1920)

Petrovič, A., "Russkaja periodičeskaja kinopečat' pervyx poslerevoljucionnyx let (1917–1924)", *Iz istorii kino*, No. 6 (1965), 175–203

Preobraženskij, N. F., "Vospominanija o rabote V.F.K.O.", *Iz istorii kino*, No. 1 (1958), 85–91

R.K.P.(b)., *Vos'moj s"ezd R.K.P.(b). Mart 1919 goda. Protokoly* (Moscow, 1959)

R.K.P.(b)., *Devjatyj s"ezd R.K.P.(b). Mart–aprel' 1920 goda. Protokoly* (Moscow, 1960)

SK: "V.G.I.K.—50. Cifry i fakty", *Sovetskoe kino*, 1969, No. 41 (352)

SXF: *Sovetskie xudožestvennye fil'my. Annotirovannyj katalog. Tom I: Nemye fil'my (1918–1935)* (Moscow, 1961)

Sergeev, B., "Agitpoezdki M. I. Kalinina v gody graždanskoj vojny", *Krasnyj arxiv*, 1938, No. 1 (86), 93–168

Speranskaja, E. A. (ed.), *Agitacionno-massovoe iskusstvo pervyx let Oktjabrja. Materialy i issledovanija* (Moscow, 1971)

Taylor, R., "A medium for the masses: agitation in the Soviet Civil War", *Soviet Studies*, Vol. XXII (1971), 562–74

Taylor, R., *The politics of the Soviet cinema, 1917–1929* (Cambridge, 1979)

Vertova-Svilova, E. I. and Vinogradova, A. L. (eds.), *Dziga Vertov v vospominanijax sovremennikov* (Moscow, 1976)

Višnevskij, V., "Fakty i daty iz istorii otečestvennoj kinematografii (mart 1917–dekabr' 1920), *Iz istorii kino*, No. 1 (1958), 38–81

Voevodin, P., "Agitpoezd 'Oktjabr'skaja revoljucija'", *Partijnaja žizn'*, 1957, No. 5, 73–4

Xanžonkov, A. A., *Pervye gody russkoj kinematografii. Vospominanija* (Moscow, 1937)

Newspapers and Periodicals
Referred to in the Volume

Anarxija, Pg. 1917–1918, M. 1918
ARK = Kino-žurnal ARK, M. 1925–1926
Beseda, Berlin 1923–1925
Birjuč Petrogradskich gosudarstvennyx teatrov, Pg. 1918–1921
BV = Birževye vedomosti, Pg. 1914–1918
CF = Cine-Fono, M. 1907–1918
DN = Delo naroda, Pg. 1917–1918
Èpopeja, Berlin 1922–1923
Èpoxa, Pg. 1918
Figaro, M. 1918
Gazeta Futuristov, M. 1918
Grjaduščee, Pg. 1918–1921
IK = Iskusstvo kommuny, Pg. 1918–1919
IT = Iskusstvo i trud, M. 1921–1923
Izvestija, Pg. 1917–1918, M. 1918–
KB = Kinobjulleten', M. 1918
KF = Kino-Fot, M. 1922–1923
KG = Kinogazeta, M. 1918
KT = Kinoteatr, M. 1918–1919
KU = Knižnyj ugol, Pg.-M. 1918–1922
MÈ = Mir èkrana, M. 1918
Mysl' (gaz.), M. 1917–1918
Mysl' (lit. žurnal), P. 1918
ND = Novosti dnja, M. 1918
NP = Narodnoe prosveščenie, Pg. 1918–1920
NR = Naša rodina, M. 1918
NRK = Novaja russkaja kniga, Berlin 1922–1923
NS = Narodnoe slovo, Pg. 1917–1918
NV = Naš vek, Pg. 1906–1918
NVČ = Novyj večernij čas, Pg. 1917–1918
NŽ = Novaja žizn', Pg. 1917–1918, M. 1918
OT = Obozrenie teatrov, Pg. 1906–1918

PÈ = Petrogradskoe èxo, Pg. 1918
PiR = Pečat' i revoljucija, M. 1921–1930
PK = Proletkino, M. 1923–1924
Plamja, Pg. 1918–1920
PP = Petrogradskaja pravda, Pg. 1918–1924
Pravda, Pg. 1917–1918, M. 1918–
Proèktor, M. 1915–1918
Rodina, M. 1918
RS = Russkoe slovo, M. 1918
RT = Revoljucionnoe tvorčestvo, M. 1918
RU = Rannee utro, M. 1907–1918
RV = Russkie vedomosti, M. 1863–1918
Skify I, II. Pg. 1917, 1918.
Slovo, M. 1918
SS = Sovremennoe slovo, Pg. 1907–1918
La Trahison, Pg. 1918
UR = Utro Rossii, M. 1917–1918
Večernjaja žizn', M. 1918
VI = Večernie izvestija, M. 1918–1920
VK = Vestnik kinomatografii, M. 1910–1918
VL = Vestnik literatury, Pg. 1919–1922
VNP = Vestnik narodnogo prosveščenija sojuza kommun severnoj oblasti, Pg. 1918–1919
VO = Večernie ogni, Pg. 1918
VT = Vestnik teatra, M. 1919–1921
VZ = Večernjaja zvezda, Pg. 1918
VŽ = Vestnik žizni, M. 1918–1919
Znamja, M. 1919–1922
ZB = Znamja bor'by, Pg. 1918
ZM = Zapiski mečtatelej, Pg. 1919–1922
ZT = Znamja truda, Pg. 1917–1918, M. 1918
ZTV = Znamja truda. Vremennik [...]. M. 1918
ŽI = Žizn' iskusstva, Pg. 1918–1922

Index of names

269

Études de philologie slave

publiées par l'Institut Russe de l'Université de Stockholm

1. *Jacobsson, G.*, Le nom de temps *lěto* dans les langues slaves (Étude sémantique et étymologique). Uppsala 1947. Epuisé.

2. *Thörnqvist, C.*, Studien über die nordischen Lehnwörter im Russischen. Uppsala et Stockholm 1949.

3. *Nilsson, N. Å.*, Die Apollonius-Erzählung en den slawischen Literaturen. Uppsala et Stockholm 1949. Epuisé.

4. *Nilsson, N. Å.*, Gogol et Pétersbourg. Recherches sur les antécédents des Contes Pétersbourgeois. Uppsala et Stockholm 1954.

5. *Wallmén, O.*, Alte tschechische Pflanzennamen und Rezepte im Botanicon Dorstens. Eine kulturgeschichtliche und sprachliche Untersuchung. Uppsala 1954.

Études de philologie slave

publiées par l'Université de Stockholm
Rédigées par Peeter Arumaa

6. *Birnbaum, H.*, Untersuchungen zu den Zukunftsumschreibungen mit dem Infinitiv im Altkirchenslawischen. Ein Beitrag zur historischen Verbalsyntax des Slavischen. Stockholm 1958. 327 p.

7. *Nilsson N. Å.*, Ibsen in Russland. Stockholm 1958. 254 p.

8. *Rūķe-Draviņa, V.*, Diminutive im Lettischen. Lund 1959. 408 p.

9. *Bæcklund, A.*, Personal Names in Medieval Velikij Novgorod. I. Common Names. Stockholm 1959. 196 p.

10. *Nilsson, N. Å.*, Russian Heraldic Virši from the 17th Century. Stockholm 1964. 93 p.

11. *Sjöberg, A.*, Synonymous Use of Synthetical and Analytical Rection in Old Church Slavonic Verbs. Stockholm 1964. 136 p.

12. *Eriksson, G.*, Le nid *prav-* dans son champ sémantique. Recherches sur le vocabulaire slave. Stockholm 1967. 244 p.